THE HARM IN ASKING

THE HARM IN ASKING

My Clumsy Encounters with the Human Race

SARA BARRON

THREE RIVERS PRESS • NEW YORK

Library of Congress Cataloging-in-Publication Data
is available upon request.

ISBN 978-0-307-72070-2
eBook ISBN 978-0-307-72071-9

PRINTED IN THE UNITED STATES OF AMERICA

Book design by Jaclyn Reyes
Cover design by Dan Rembert
Cover photograph: Getty Images
Author photograph: Shervin Lainez

1 3 5 7 9 10 8 6 4 2

First Edition

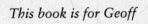

This book is for Geoff

Contents

PART IV: Survivor

THE HARM IN ASKING

Part I

Homebody

1

Scrub Toilet Super-Super (A Tale in Twelve Parts)

1. INTRODUCTION

Every week, I scrub the floors of my apartment. The way I go about the chore, personally, is I rip green abrasive tops off kitchen sponges, dampen them with soap and water, and glue them to the bottoms of my socks. Then I start gliding. It all looks a bit like cross-country skiing, which is effective for cleaning, but also exhausting. Once I'm done, I feel I deserve a treat. More often than not the treat comes in the form of a medical miracle show on TLC. This week's episode was about a legless dancer and recent Juilliard graduate. Asked about her personal triumph over adversity, she stared squarely into the camera.

"Here's what you do," she said. "You dream. You believe. You achieve."

"No, *you* achieve," I corrected. "*I* do not achieve. Juilliard won't let *me* spin on stumps instead of pointe shoes."

For years, I've been jealous of the ailing and deformed: quadriplegics, human mermaids. A girl with organs on the outside. I don't crave the impairment, really, I just think the attention seems nice. And this puts me in the minority. Murmur, "That looks *fun*," at the sight of conjoined twins, and learn, ironically, what it means to feel alone.

2. MY SON HAS ASTHMA

Allow me to defend my position by explaining how I got here. You'll like me more that way.

When I was ten years old, my six-year-old brother, Sam, was diagnosed with asthma. This diagnosis was the stone that built the fountain, and it was from this fountain that a neediness would spring. It wasn't hope that sprang eternal. It was an aspiration for attention, the desire to feel special and unique.

Sam's diagnosis wasn't good news per se, but neither was it without its benefits. For it would gift unto my mother the eventual guiltless employment of a maid. And also a motto:

My Son Has Asthma.

Like most ineffective plans for coping, it emerged the day of diagnosis. I'd gone to visit my brother in his hospital room, where he lay ensconced amid festive pillows and Mylar balloons. My mother sat perched at his bedside massaging his scalp. The attending nurse breezed through. She fluffed Sam's pillows and saw me sitting in the corner.

"Wow!" she said. "In that polo shirt, you look *just* like Jerry O'Connell!"

It was 1989. Jerry O'Connell was not yet the strapping, chiseled husband of Rebecca Romijn, but rather the rotund child star.

The nurse departed. I said, "Mom. That nurse said I look like a boy, and that I am fat," and my mother, still massaging, turned impatiently toward me.

"Not now, Sara, please," she said. "Your brother Sam has asthma."

Sam was already buoyed by a virtual raft of gifts. He was getting a massage! He was going to be *fine*. This whole asthma situation looked awfully good from my vantage point and a moment or two devoted to my own problems was, I thought, a fair thing to ask.

I considered throwing a tantrum. However, my mother preempted my tantrum by suggesting a stroll down the hallway.

Sam and I agreed. Sam had energy to burn from all the ice cream he was getting. As for me, I hoped to run into a boyishly handsome nurse who would say, "Sorry to bother you, but I simply *had* to ask: Are you Tina Yothers? You two look exactly alike."

Sadly, the only person we ran into in the hallway was a sickly old man. He was balanced against a wall so he could let go of his cane and eat a Danish. He was blocking our path, and the fact of this had pissed my mother off.

"Look *out*!" she yelled. "*Please:* My son has asthma!"

The phrase became a generic exclamation, an *oy vey* stand-in employed to express varying emotions: Exhaustion, fear, surprise. Disappointment, foreboding, resolve.

Here, a sampling of occasions and the uses they'd inspire:

A hot day: "The humidity! My son has asthma!"

A long line: "This wait! My son has asthma!"

A casual dinner with friends: "Carol, pass the antipasto platter, please! I have a son with asthma!"

MY BROTHER RETURNED home after three days in the hospital. In an effort to keep his asthma in check, my mother fed him hyperactivity-inducing steroids chased with hysterical advice, including but not limited to, "You'll *die* if you smoke a cigarette" and/or "You'll *die* if you stand *near* a lit cigarette." The other order of business was to ensure a dust- and allergen-free home, and it was for this reason that my mother, for the first time in her life, decided to hire a maid. She'd dreamed of doing so for ages. We all had, as a matter of fact, since being near my mom when she cleaned guaranteed that you, whoever you were, would get to push her martyr button. You'd be minding your own business, for example, braiding your arm hair, when suddenly she'd have you by the wrist to coax you back behind a toilet.

"What do you see back there?" she'd ask.

"It's very clean," you'd answer. "So . . . nothing?"

"Nothing *but* . . . ?"

"Nothing but . . . evidence of how hard you work?"

"I slave."

"Nothing but evidence of how hard you slave?"

"Exactly."

The guilt my mother associated with hiring a maid floated away on Sam's first grating wheeze.

"I wish I didn't *have* to have one," she'd say about a person, like a person was an enema. "But I do, of course. I have a son with asthma."

3. *WITAM IS POLISH FOR "HELLO"*

The following Monday a van pulled into our driveway. A woman climbed out and walked toward our front door.

This woman was truly enormous. I never did measure her for fear she'd slap my hand off, but my guess is that she measured in at a healthy six-foot-one. She entered the house, and it was only then that I noticed the smell. It was as though she'd smeared herself in salmon, then thought, *That* was stupid, and then smeared herself in Pine-Sol.

"Al-oh," she'd said, in what I'd soon learn was a Polish accent. "I am Wanda."

"*Witam*, Wanda," said my mother. "I am Lynn. Lynn the missus and the mommy. *Witam, witam.*"

4. FOREIGNERS APPRECIATE THE EFFORT

My mother spent a portion of 1968 on a kibbutz in the company of an Israeli boyfriend named Yoni with whom she spoke Hebrew. The experience left her with the impression that she had a knack for language, and now, with a chance to test the theory, she'd spent the afternoon prior to Wanda's arrival riding her stationary bike, poring over a Polish-English dictionary.

"It's my way of reaching out," she said. "Foreigners appreciate the effort. I know these things. I traveled before I had you, you know. And before I had a son with asthma."

5. WANDA GO MUNCH-MUNCH

A house tour commenced between my mother and Wanda. With nothing better to do I trailed along behind. I listened as my mother used the occasional bit of Polish. There was *da* (yes) and *nie* (no), as well as the more complex *nie spóźnij* (do not be late) and *nie ukrywam moje pieniądze w moim domu* (I do not hide my money in my house).

As for the bulk of their communication, it was a language of their mutual invention. Watching it unfold was not unlike watching a lovers' waltz, the coming together of two halves of a whole. You can't put a price on chemistry, see, and these two shared a wavelength. Call it kismet. Then tell me this is easy to decipher:

"Go here for a vroom-vroom, yes? BSHHHHHHHH? Dusty dirty go gone!"

That's what my mother said to Wanda. And presume what you will, but Wanda did *not* respond, "Missus! Stop! *You* embarrassing *you*!"

No. She rather nodded like, *Thank you, Lynn, for showing me the vacuum in the closet.*

"BSHHHHHHHHH!" Wanda shouted. "Dirty go gone!"

"*Da!*" said my mother, and nudged Wanda toward the kitchen, where a plate of Triscuits sat on the counter alongside a hunk of cheddar cheese. My mother pointed at the cheese and crackers, and then at Wanda's stomach. "It goes GRRR? Wanda go munch-munch." She mimed feeding herself. "Okay, okay?"

Wanda nodded. "Yes. Okay."

They proceeded upstairs to the bathroom.

"One toilet?" asked Wanda. "One for the mister and the missus and the babies?"

"One bathroom, yes," said my mother. "Lynn no a fancy lady, Lynn house no so fancy. See the toilet?"

"*Da*. I see you toilet."

"Okay. Toilet yucky-yucky. So you scrub toilet *super,* Wanda. You scrub it *super*-super."

Wanda launched her sternum toward the toilet to pantomime aggressive scrubbing. "*Super*-super missus, yes?" she asked.

"Oh, *yes*," my mother answered. "This missus tells you: *Yes*."

The house tour concluded with a conversation on the subject of Sam's asthma. My mother called to Sam in his bedroom, and out he came, trotting along. She positioned him such that his back was to her and his face was to Wanda.

"Wanda," said my mother, "here is Baby Sam. If home is dusty dirty, Sam go, 'Hack, hack.' Dusty dirty bad for Sam. You no scrub super-super *all* the home, Baby Sam is . . ." She performed wheezing. She made a woo-woo noise like a siren. "Baby Sam to doctor. BABY SAM AT DOCTOR BAD!"

Wanda gave a solemn nod. She pointed a sizable finger at my mother. "You a mommy," she said.

"Yes," said my mother.

Wanda pointed back at herself. "I a mommy."

"Yes," said my mother.

"*I* a mommy. So *I* know: Mommies suffer for the babies. MISSUS SUFFER FOR THE BABY SAM!"

Indulgence, as a quality, is too winning to let go. By the time Wanda left later that afternoon, my mother had already booked her services for all forthcoming Mondays.

6. THE PUBE PROB (OR "THE PUBERTY PROBLEM")

After a month of Wanda's weekly visits, I developed a habit of locking myself in the bathroom.

My actions were prompted by Wanda's cleaning style, which was aggressive to the point of feeling competitive. The verbs "attack" and "stampede" jump to mind; she would *attack* one room and *stampede* into the next. Broadly speaking, the seriousness with which Wanda took her professional duties was to her credit. But as a ten-year-old on the cusp of an early-onset puberty, I found her diligence annoying. Eventually, I found *her* annoying, for I was in a life phase that included quite a bit of pelvic thrusting. Pelvic thrusting of varying, well, pelvises: my pelvis, the pelvises of my dolls. And it was as though Wanda had some sort of motion sensor planted somewhere in that strapping frame of hers, and any pelvic motion set her off. Consistently, she'd stampede into my bedroom to find me mounted atop . . . well, just go ahead and pick your poison: throw pillows, beach balls, felt hats. The list is long. So it was that a door with a lock became a top priority. I holed up in the bathroom because it was the only room that had one. And, thankfully, because Wanda was finished with it by the time I returned home from school. It may have been small and it may have lacked a television set. Nonetheless, it was private and available. My pelvic activities being what they were, these aspects were important.

7. THE PRIVE PROB (OR "THE PRIVACY PROBLEM")

Over time, a weird thing happened. Locked in the bathroom, I invented imaginary friends to keep me company. And if you're thinking, That's not weird. It's what kids do! I'll point out that I had no fewer than three, and that each one of these three was accessible to me only after I'd taken a shit.

It started out as a Monday-only thing. It became the entirety of my prepubescent life.

There's a percentage of my adulthood I frankly should've spent wising up on politics that's rather been devoted to unearthing the rationale behind all this. As an adult, I put a therapist on the job, and she stroked the old gal's ego by suggesting it was the byproduct of my intuitiveness. As in: a conversation with a nonexistent person works best if it's in private. Smartly I sensed this, and so grouped it in my head with another equally private activity. *I was VERY AWARE as a child*. You see the self-flattery there? It's way far up my alley. As such, I thought I ought to roll with it.

MY MONDAY ACTIVITY schedule, Age Ten:

> 3:30 p.m.: Arrive home, fetch granola bar, head to bathroom.

3:35 p.m.: Arrive in bathroom. Lock door. Eat granola bar.

3:40 p.m.: Random activity of choice, e.g. inspect mole, lie in empty bathtub pretending it's a sun-bed.

4:00 p.m.: Shit.

4:01 p.m.: Chat with imaginary friends.

5:00 p.m.: Listen for Wanda's departure.

5:01 p.m.: Confirm Wanda's departure.

5:02 p.m.: Wipe ass. Flush toilet.

5:03 p.m.: Unlock door. Depart bathroom.

I named my imaginary friends Nancy, Jenny, and Kelly. They were all orphaned teen models, and I'd been put in charge of caring for them after having been deemed a prodigy in the field of adolescent education. We all lived together in a pretty Victorian mansion. It was an imagined compilation of both (a) a Barbie Dream House, and (b) something I'd seen on a family vacation to Newport, Rhode Island.

It had a front porch, too, our mansion, that I'd extracted from a Country Time Lemonade commercial.

I was doted on and greatly admired by my orphaned teen models. They craved my advice on everything from boys to needlepoint to who among them had won a game of gin rummy. They were exhausting but rewarding, and in exchange for my wisdom, spent a large portion of their free time showering me with attention. They discussed my exceptionality in the areas of intelligence, acting, singing, dancing, flexibility, and improv. They told me I, too, could be a teen model.

"Really?" I'd ask. "Modeling? You think?" and Jenny would answer, "With a bod like yours? Oh *yes*. Just give it time."

The personalities and circumstances surrounding Nancy,

Jenny, and Kelly suggest a sharp eye for twenty-first-century television. I intuited the basic constructs for both *Sex and the City* and myriad reality shows before either even existed. À la Miranda, Samantha, and Charlotte, my imaginary friends were divergent in both their interests and dimensionless personalities. Nancy was passionate about good manners and landscape painting. Jenny enjoyed male chest hair, sex, and makeup. Kelly liked kickball and swearing. Additionally— and in the vein of reality shows from *America's Next Top Model* to the old Diddy classic *Making the Band*—Nancy, Jenny, and Kelly passed the time in an expensively decorated home engaged in inane conversations, waiting to hear from the God-Figure (e.g., Diddy, Tyra Banks, me) about their next scheduled outing.

Confine the idiots, goes this philosophy of entertainment. *And wait for disaster to strike.*

8. ENTER GOLDSCHMIDT

I was in a bad mood after a particularly draining Monday. A fourth-grade peer by the name of Becca Goldschmidt had tugged at the ill-fitting underpants I'd had on. To be fair, they *had* been bunched visibly beneath my stretch pants so as to resemble an untended dump, and very much begged for the plucking. So Becca Goldschmidt plucked. Fine. What I took issue with was that then she went the extra length of shouting to no one in particular, "SARA BARRON'S BUTT IS DISGUSTING! SARA BARRON'S BUTT IS DISGUSTING!"

"So *what*?" I yelled back. At which point Becca Goldschmidt shouted, "Oh my God! She *knows* her butt is disgusting!"

And then I said, "No I don't."

And then *she* said, "She doesn't even know how disgusting her butt is!"

It was not to my taste, this sort of negative attention. True, I could get into a negative *reason for* the attention— see: a severe case of childhood asthma—but the attention itself I liked to be supportive and adoring. I did not respond well if it was otherwise. Becca Goldschmidt spoke negatively about my butt, and I responded, "You are mean and I hope that you die." And as justice does not always reign supreme, *I* was the one who then got sent to the principal's office. I had to spend my lunch period in there with this genuine delinquent by the name of Benjy Jacobs. Benjy and I sat side by side as I ate a cheese sandwich and he drank four cans of Mountain Dew. Benjy and I sat side by side as Benjy then vomited the four cans of Mountain Dew into the wastebasket between us.

I was exhausted by the time I got home, eager to sequester myself in my Victorian mansion. I craved the attention and affections of my orphans/models. I dashed to the kitchen for my granola bar, then up to the bathroom. I ate the granola bar. I sang "Uptown Girl" into the removable showerhead. I shat. I started talking.

"Attention, everyone!" I began. "Who needs to go to the mall?"

"I do!" said Jenny. "I need new tights and bras!"

"Tights and bras, yes. I shall add them to my list. Anyone else?"

Nancy had been working on a landscape painting of our Newport–Barbie doll–Country Time Victorian mansion and wanted my advice on how best to improve it. Kelly cared to dish on Becca Goldschmidt.

As a prodigy in adolescent education, I was able to balance their various needs. First, I told Nancy that in order to improve her painting, she needed to paint a centaur on our mansion's front lawn.

Jenny tapped her toe impatiently.

"Ms. Barron!" she shouted. "I need tights and bras *now*. My date with Leonardo is *tonight*!"

I answered, "I'm coming, my dear," and turned quickly back to Nancy. "My point—and then we simply must get going—is that this guy should have big muscles and blond hair on top, but then be a horse on the bottom."

I was ten, and so the statement's bawdy implication didn't strike me. All I'd had in mind was that part in Disney's *Fantasia* where all the strapping, erotic centaurs charge about to the beat of Tchaikovsky's *Pastoral Symphony*.

Kelly asked, "A man *and* a horse?! That's fucking awesome!"

"Watch your mouth, Kelly. Please."

Nancy continued. "It *is* awesome, Ms. Barron. Thank you so much for the helpful advice."

"My pleasure, Nancy."

"Also, I wanted to say I think your butt and underwear look beautiful today."

"You do?"

"Oh, *yes*. You look like you are in a beautiful bikini."

"That's sweet of you to say."

"Sweet of *her*," Kelly clarified. "Not like Becca Goldschmidt, the cunt."

"Kelly! We don't use that word in this mansion."

"Sorry, Ms. Barron. I thought, well, maybe I could. Maybe *just* for Becca Goldschmidt."

I thought for a moment. I told her okay.

"Hey, Ms. Barron!" called Jenny. "Can I French-braid your hair?"

"You *may* French-braid my hair. But only once I'm driving. Right now, I want everyone into the car."

I reached for a handheld mirror that was stationed atop the toilet tank. I used it as a steering wheel. Then I looked to Jenny.

"You *may* French-braid my hair . . . *now,*" I said.

"Your hair is *so* silky," she responded. "You are *so* going to be a teen model."

"Thank you," I said, and rotated the mirror to signal steering into the mall parking lot. "Oh, now look: here we are at the mall. Let's go to a store with some bras."

We arrived at the store with some bras.

"Oh-la-la! Look at all those fucking bras," said Kelly.

"Let's try some on!" squealed Jenny.

"Yes, let's," I agreed.

I removed my shirt. I did not *imagine* removing it. I *actually* removed it. Then I *actually* grabbed two fresh rolls of toilet paper and, having imagined them to be the world's most fashionable bra cups, I *actually* pressed them to my chest.

"What do you think?" I asked. "Are you like, 'Wow! You look like Tina Yothers'?"

"Yes," said Jenny. "That's exactly what I'm like."

9. THE GARTH ALGAR TRIANGLE SHAPE

I felt feminine and reenergized in my toilet-paper bra. Still, though, I had the issue of my hair to contend with. It was positioned in what I like to call "The Garth Algar Triangle Shape."

The position meant that I now faced competing needs.

On the one hand: I needed to get up, to get a comb, to fix the Garth Algar Triangle Shape. But on the other: I *had* just taken a shit. I knew the proper course of action was tending to my ass before my hair. But in this particular instance, the pull of the hair was too strong to be ignored.

With my stretch pants still around my ankles, I stood up. I hobbled to the medicine cabinet, set down my toilet-roll brassiere, and took out the comb. My ass—exposed, unclean—now faced the bathroom door. I took the time I needed with my hair, pressing and prodding until it was more Tina Yothers up-do than Garth Algar Triangle Shape.

"You look beautiful," said Nancy.

I nodded to myself, about myself.

"I do," I said. "I *really* do."

10. ANGELINA IS ASTUTE

I believe it was Angelina Jolie in her title role as Mrs. Smith who said, "A happy story is only one that hasn't finished yet."

It was on this particular day that I forgot to lock the bathroom door. The attack on my butt, the injustice of how it was dealt with. The principal's office. The vomit. It had all been too much. And I had lost my bearings. And forgot.

So it was that while teasing my hair into the requisite up-do the bathroom door swung open.

Wanda stood behind me.

"Wanda!" I yelled, and promptly dropped the brush so that I might cover my chest and crotch. "I'm *in* here!"

Wanda spotted the hand-mirror-cum-steering-wheel sitting on the bathtub ledge. She noticed the toilet paper rolls-cum-bra lying on the floor. She studied me. You'd think a person might turn her head out of pity, at the very least, but no. Wanda just stood there, calm. Unflustered. She pointed to the brush.

"You drop you brush," she said.

"Duh!" I said. "I *know*!"

Wanda shrugged.

"Okey-dokey, baby. Listen," she said, and pointed at the various items, at the occupied toilet bowl. "You go 'La la' to you friends. You have nice times, fun times. But I scrub bathroom super already before. So you be clean. *Keep* clean. Okay okay?"

"Yes," I huffed. "*Okay.*"

Wanda left and I locked the bathroom door. I looked at the clock. It was 4:45 p.m. I sat still for a moment. I listened to hear if Wanda would tell my mother what had happened. Was that even her style? And if it was her style, what exactly would she say?

"Missus, you baby is crazy. The big one. Look out!"?

The situation felt terribly unfair. I'd been so nervous Wanda would find me pelvic-thrusting at any number of objects, and I'd worked to avoid this, and for what? So she could find me while filthy *and* primping? I was in the market for attention always and forever, but why must it come to me like this? *Why* part and parcel with *such* profound embarrassment? I wanted to be coddled! Special! Unique! And that's a different thing from being caught when you are filthy. Filthy and primping like some attractive orphaned teen.

11. THE FUTURE'S SO BRIGHT I GOTTA WEAR SHADES

Wanda had seen me for what I was. And what I was was filthy. After the reveal—after *my* reveal—I felt consistently, upsettingly exposed whenever Wanda was around. This did nothing to satiate my need for attention. It rather stoked the flames. The cruel elements of an unfair world had *made* me forget to lock the bathroom door, and I craved compensation. I had suffered *An Offense*! I now deserved *A Treat*! I wasn't picky, either. Anything would do provided it presented me in an attention-worthy light:

1. Sam's asthma could go away in the same week I contracted a temporary but nonetheless frightening disease from a sewing needle.
2. Sam could get so fat from his steroid medication that my parents would stop loving him.

3. I could be asked to do a modeling shoot: "Excuse me, but would you like to do a modeling shoot? We need someone to sit naked in a bathtub eating peanut-butter cups."

But months passed by and no such dreams came true. I held out hope that one day maybe they would, and told myself that in the meantime I should do as I had always done. I should turn to my imaginary models.

"Excuse me, Ms. Barron?"

"Yes, Nancy?"

"I did some new paintings I thought you'd like to see. Since, well, you are very good at painting judging."

"Why, yes, Nancy. Thank you."

"Here is one of Sam. You will see that he is fat and also crying."

"Why, yes. I *do* see. But *why* is he crying?"

"Because he lives with foster parents now who tell him that he's boring."

"And also that he's fat?"

"Yes. And also that he's fat."

The shame I felt at having been caught in the throes of these conversations had been jarring enough to make me conscious of my volume, and to prompt an unfailing diligence where the bathroom door lock was concerned. However, it had not been enough to curb the impulse to have the conversations in the first place. Bathroom socializing was just who I was now. It gave me the energy to persevere: at school and at home. In the face of Sam's asthma. Until my modeling career took off.

I do not know if I was ever again overheard, but I was never again confronted. I figured that Wanda never wound up mentioning my antics to my mother simply because my mother never mentioned them to me. As time went on, as I realized with increasing surety that Wanda had kept my secret to herself, I felt increasingly grateful to her, more trusting and impressed. I was, if not attached, then comfortable. If not adoring, then admiring.

In short, I was a fan.

12. STOMACH, YES

One year into Wanda's employment, she broke the news that she was going back to Poland. She told us over breakfast.

We were all together in the kitchen, Wanda, my mother, and me. My mother was eating a bag of homemade trail mix, I was eating Eggo waffles, and Wanda was fiddling with a tiny hunk of cheddar cheese. Eventually Wanda said, "Missus, hear me. Please. Father in Poland is bad sick."

My mother turned to face her.

"Bad sick?" she asked. "Wanda: He is cancer sick?"

Wanda nodded yes. My mother started pointing to various body parts. "Cancer sick where, Wanda? Brain?"

"No."

"Lungs?"

"No."

"Stomach?"

"Yes."

"Oh, *Wanda*." My mother placed a hand on Wanda's shoulder. "Missus super sorry. Missus let you go."

I could tell from my mother's tone, and Wanda's too, that stomach cancer was serious business. I felt a flash of jealousy, but only a flash. For while stomach cancer would trump Sam's asthma, it would also maybe kill me. And if it killed me, then Sam would get my room.

ONE WEEK LATER, Wanda left. The van dropped her off for one last time. And for one last time, it picked her up again. She waved good-bye and I waved back. I was sad to see her go. My mother was too, of course. I could hear the strain in her voice as she talked on the phone to her friends.

"What? No! I'm great. *We're* great. I mean, I *have* been working full-time. And running the house. What? No: My cleaning woman left. Her dad's got cancer. What? No: Stomach. I *know*. And, of course . . . yes, exactly. My little one has asthma."

I'd listen in for a while, then go for a shit in the bathroom. I'd occupy myself in the usual ways: I'd look at a portrait Nancy had painted. I'd listen as Jenny explained how although Sam *was* the one with asthma, *I* was the one with a future as a model. Although she wouldn't say it in those words exactly. It was more like, "You're awesome, Ms. Barron. One day, you're gonna look good in some bras."

I'd nod in agreement, all the while fingering a swollen gland I'd started hoping was a tumor.

And Kelly would smile. She'd give a thumbs-up.

"Show that bullshit to your mom," she'd say.

"I will," I'd say, and wipe myself, unlock the door, and hurry down to dinner.

2

Bonjour, Delphine

The Buddhist word *"samsara"* refers to life's daily suffer-
ings. The adolescent dynamic between my brother and me
suggests my parents had this in mind when selecting our
names.

Our childhood dynamic was, if not stellar, then acceptable. I resented the skill with which Sam usurped attention. I tried and failed to compete. But these resentments
were never an active dislike. They were just a desire to be
rid of him. A kind of "No *personal* offense, but my parents
find you *too* compelling. I would like for you to leave."

Our adult dynamic is even better. Sam makes a depend-
able companion in the slow march toward our parents' inevitable deaths. It is therefore important that I am around
when he needs me. Or rather, it is important that *he's*

around when *I* need *him*. So I pursue him via voice- and e-mail. I leave messages in which I say: "Hi there. It's me. What if *Mom* dies first? That'd be weird, right? Okay, bye. Call me back."

So we get along now and fared okay as children.

Adolescence, however, was war. Adolescence was *samsara*.

THE PROBLEM STARTED my freshman year of high school. I had been encouraged by my parents to join an extracurricular club. I was trying to decide between the Student Coalition for Animal Rights and the Student Coalition for Awareness. I eventually decided on the Student Coalition for Awareness after realizing I was too passionate about bacon to do much in the way of animal rights.

The purpose of the Student Coalition for Awareness was to allow its members a sense of superiority to all nonmembers. Beyond that, we worked to raise awareness around the issue of modern-day sexism. Our mission statement read, "Feminism Forever, Sexism for Never." We'd attend weekly lectures on female oppression at nearby universities. To keep myself from falling asleep during these lectures, I'd imagine that I was the one delivering them.

Other activities included choral performances at battered women's shelters. These I saw as an opportunity to channel my desire for attention into my individual choral performance. We would sing rousing standards like "Freedom Is Coming" or Bette Midler's "The Rose." Song choice depending, I would sing either very high or very low to ensure the battered women could hear my voice above those of my fellow club members.

By the end of one semester, I'd been inspired to replace the word "women" with "womyn." I'd advise friends and family, strangers and enemies, to do the same.

"So I ran into this woman I knew from . . ."

"I'm sorry. But are you spelling that 'whoa-MAN' with an *a* or 'whoa-MIN' with a *y*?"

"What? Um, oh. I guess, well, I'm spelling it like . . . you do. Like . . . with an *a*."

"Right. Well, you might want to *not*. Unless, of course, you think *womyn*—WITH A *Y*—are undervalued slaves in a patriarchal society."

"But I . . ."

"What's that? *Right*. I didn't think you did."

AROUND THIS TIME, Sam turned eleven. He was enjoying the slow burn through puberty, and while normally an older sister wouldn't have to clock such horrors, I did, and that was thanks to Sam's problematic lack of self-consciousness coupled with his poor taste in home decor. Somehow, somewhere, he'd scored five life-size posters of Carmen Electra, and used them to wallpaper his bedroom. In each and every one, Carmen's tanned and glistening body had been dressed in a bikini and posed on all fours like a dog.

Sam's behavior conflicted with my burgeoning feminist tendencies, and a civil war erupted. It began with frequent, high-pitched screams.

"You're an asshole! You hate womyn! You hate *me*!"

Or perhaps: "You degrade us! You exploit us!"

Sam's favorite joke—owing to a recent social studies lesson on the Navajo tribe—was to respond to me with various Navajo-inspired nicknames.

"Shut-up, Yelling-Stupid-Whore-on-Couch."

"DON'T CALL ME THAT, YOU SEXIST PIG!"

"Fuck you, Dumb-Slut-Red-Hair."

In the early stages, our parents' method for handling an argument was to refuse to get involved. My mother would tell us to be quiet or to go outside. So we would go outside. But then a neighbor would inevitably complain about having to hear us. There'd be the eventual knock at the door.

> **Neighbor:** Lynn, listen. I'm sorry to bother you, but your kids are out there right now and they are *screaming*. About . . . my *God*, I don't even *know* what. Sam just said something about a "fat bitch pig with a cowlick"—is that a thing?—and then Sara said Sam was a "fat fucking Jew who should die." And anyway, listen: You know I love you. You know I love *them*. But I've got my own kids at home. I can't have them hear that sort of thing.

MY MOTHER WAS a reasonable woman when spoken to reasonably. If a neighbor complained, she would apologize to the neighbor and come outside to get us, to bring us back inside. At that point, we'd be forbidden from watching TV, and so at that point, we'd try to behave.

But not for long.

Eventually, inevitably, Sam would peek his head into my bedroom and say, "Carmen Electra has big hot boobs and Sara Barron is a big dumb bitch." Or I would peek my head into Sam's bedroom and say, "I'm hiding your inhaler, by the way. And if you have an asthma attack, I will *like* to watch you die," and it would all start all over again.

Sam and I stayed stuck in this cycle for ages and then instead of getting better, it got worse. The anger I felt toward my brother was compounded over time by my parents, who condoned his sexist posters by permitting him to keep them up.

My dad defended his position.

"Sara," he said, "listen to me. Please. Your brother's having a hard time. He's going through puberty. He's puffed up on steroid medication. Your mother tells *me* that the teachers tell *her* that he gets teased all the time, and I'm sorry—Sara, I genuinely am—but if he comes home and wants to look at girls, well, I just don't have the strength to tell him no."

"'*Girls,*' Dad? Did you just call them '*girls*'?"

"Sweetheart, I'm sorry. I should have called them womyn. With a *y*. You are absolutely right."

I threw my hands up in exasperation.

"Oh, like *that's* gonna help! Your antisocial sexist son handles his *hatred* of womyn—WITH A Y!—by staring at *objectified* womyn? And you *let him*? I mean, my God. MY GOD! Way to go and raise a rapist! I hate you all! I'm so ashamed!"

It seemed that my parents had gone from Maintaining a Neutral Position to Maintaining Sam's Position. This upped the ante of my attack on Sam. I went from verbal sparring to property destruction. I snuck into his bedroom one afternoon and, with indelible marker in hand, defiled Carmen Electra. I bestowed unto her a bowler hat made of penises, and handfuls of wiry pubic hair.

The ante? It was upped.

In response, Sam destroyed my prized possession, a framed, autographed photo of Tyne Daly. He swiped it during my Student Coalition for Awareness meeting, and used my mother's garlic press to break the frame. On the actual photo he wrote, "I AM A BITCH. I AM A DUDE."

Ante upped again.

I showered his pillowcase in the oily detritus found in an empty sardine tin. He bit my sizable calf muscle to the point of bleeding. He punched my face. I punched his face. He snuck into my bedroom, dismantled a cardboard box, and drew a bull's-eye upon it. Sam then took a shit on the bull's eye.

Ante upped again.

I cried when I saw the shit on the bull's-eye. Sam cried too, in an effort to drown me out, and our combined volume hit such a high level that a neighbor finally called the cops. The cops' arrival felt dramatic enough to make Sam and me shut up. As it turned out, though, one of the guys was a friend of my mother's from high school, so she, my mom, was able to smooth it all out.

"Howard? Mehlman? Lynn Barron! Or, well, I should say Lynn Handelman! Highland Park High School class of 1965!"

My mother apologized on behalf of her children. She was pitch-perfectly contrite, and Officer Mehlman was charmed and sympathetic. In truth, the whole thing hadn't been that big of a deal. Nonetheless, my parents were exhausted and embarrassed, and to punish my brother and me, they insisted we sit beside Sam's bowel movement for the remainder of the day.

Which we did. We had to wait eight hours to be *allowed* to clean it up.

THE ARRIVAL OF Officer Mehlman served as a climax in my adolescent war with my brother and led my parents to the unsurprising conclusion that they had to get rid of one of us. Only temporarily, of course. Only for the summer. Seeing as how Sam was the younger and more likable of their two children, I knew I'd be the one to go.

I took the situation in my stride. In fact, I was really excited about it.

All previous summers I'd been forced to attend local park district camps, hellish bogs at which underwashed counselors initiated moronic activities. They'd hand out Popsicle sticks and be like, "Make your mommy a jewelry box!" They'd demand I sing songs that asked not nearly enough of me: "Hey Sara / Someone's calling my name /

Hey Sara / I think I hear it again . . ." *Such* consistent insults to my vocal talents. I figured even minimum-wage employment would be a step up, and the previous summer I had accepted a position assistant-teaching geriatric water-aerobics. The students were all hard of hearing, so for an hour every weekday, I'd stand on the side of a pool opposite the teacher repeating her instructions. She'd say something like "Okay, ladies!!! Ballet legs!!! Starting on your left. One!!! Two!!!!" and I'd stand across the pool and shout, "She said, 'Ballet legs on your left. One. Two.' "

I pretty much just acted as a human microphone.

I was not a child who loved summer. But that could change with parents desperate to be rid of me.

I suggested overnight camp as an option, for I imagined that, unlike park district camp, the whole thing would be a sort of fairy wonderland of floral garlands and canopy beds. My mother laughed the whole thing off, though, once she learned eight weeks of overnight camp would cost in the neighborhood of five thousand dollars.

"It's too ridiculous for me even to be angry!" she said. "It's *beyond* making me angry! It's just making me laugh! Ha! Ha, ha, ha, ha, HA!"

There was another, cheaper option: a Jewish overnight camp run by a modern conservative sect. Their pamphlet promised, "Your Chalutzim camper will return and tell you, 'Ema! Aba! I *want* to go on Ta'am Yisrael! I *loved* my Chalutzim Hebrew immersion!' She'll return a young woman who's cultivated her *own* interest in Jewish themes and culture!"

"Sounds disgusting," said my mother. "I mean: The phrase 'Chalutzim camper'? I want a shower just *saying* it. You?"

I did think my mother had a point. And I did want her to shower after saying the word "Chalutzim." At the same time, though, I didn't know what else to do. I couldn't think of any other options.

IT WAS APRIL of the same year the first time I heard the phrase "exchange program."

I'd been in my fourth-period French class when my teacher, Madame Cohen, explained the situation: We Highland Park High School students of the French language had been presented with the chance to travel to Cluses, France, a mountainous town near the country's Swiss border. If we chose to participate, we would be assigned a Clusien host *famille* whom we would stay with for three weeks in July. At the end of those three weeks, we'd return home with our exchange students in tow. They would then enjoy the Midwestern United States for an additional three weeks.

Madame Cohen laid out these circumstances, and asked who among us thought we might be interested.

I pictured my brother's feces and my demolished photo of Tyne Daly.

I raised my hand.

"*Moi*," I said. "I am interested. *Très*."

I WENT HOME that afternoon and shared the idea with my parents.

They were initially intrigued but also concerned about cost and spot availability.

"It sounds okay . . . in theory," said my mother, "but do not get your hopes up. I can't imagine France will work out cheaper than Wisconsin. Furthermore, do you have to apply? Is it in any way selective?"

I *did* have to apply. But it was *not* in any way selective. And that was because so few of my classmates wanted to go. Most of them had already locked down their plans for overnight camp. This fact was a large part of the appeal. I loved the idea that I would wind up in what I thought of as a fashionable minority, that my summer activity would make me unique. I'd return to school the following fall, and as my peers rambled on about another campfire circle, I would recount my Alpine meanders. I would speak on the subject, and my peers would be intrigued. In fact, they would be *so* intrigued that it would start to overwhelm me.

"Calm down!" I would tell them. "I *know* you all have questions, but you will *have* to wait your turn."

As for the cost of the program, my parents agreed to keep an open mind and later that week joined me at the informational meeting. Midway through, Madame Cohen addressed the cost issue head-on. The program, she said, would be ". . . cheap as you're gonna get for France." And she really wasn't kidding. She wrote a number on the chalkboard. It was very, *very* low.

France, impossibly, was a cheaper option than Wisconsin.

France, impossibly, my parents could afford.

I watched them absorb the good news. They hugged each other and hugged me. They stuffed a deposit check into Madame Cohen's clipboard.

"*Please* don't lose that," said my mother. "Sara's *got* to go."

Madame Cohen assured my mother that she would not lose the deposit check, and true to her word she did not: one week later, my spot on the trip was confirmed.

To celebrate, my parents treated me to the immediate purchase of compression stockings for long-distance air travel, as well as a vest with inner pockets to make me less susceptible to pickpocketing. The week after that, I was assigned to my Clusien hosts, La Famille Raffal. They were four, *la Madame et le Monsieur, et* their children, Guy *et* Lucille. Lucille, the younger, was the one with whom I'd be eventually exchanged, and Guy was her eighteen-year-old brother.

I thought it was the ideal host familial setup. Lucille and I, having been denied the bond of sisterhood thus far, would take to each other like *le beurre* on brioche. We'd spend our days lounging in nearby meadows, weaving floral accessories.

"*Pour toi,*" she'd say, handing me the belt she'd made of daisies. "But . . . oh la la! Eet eez too grande! Too beeg! Because toi, you are . . . how you say?"

"Too skinny."

"*Oui!* Too skinny for zee day-zee belt I make!"

No matter, we'd just use it as a jump rope, laughing all the while. "Ha!" we'd laugh. "Ha, ha!"

Evenings I'd reserve for Guy so that he and I might nuzzle in front of *la famille*'s grandfather clock. In a pre-departure lesson on Cluses city history, Madame Cohen had explained that Cluses was famous for its clock production. I interpreted this to mean that the Raffal *famille* would own a grandfather clock, and that its forceful, repetitive bong would signal to Guy that it was time to caress my hair. He'd do so staying all the while thoughtfully aware of the floral tiara I had on. Then he'd whisper my name desirously.

"Delphine . . ."

I'd decided that alongside my compression stockings and vest with inner pockets, I'd need a French name for French travel, and decided, finally, on Delphine. I was going for exoticism, some clear indicator that while my peers had spent their summers at their Wisconsin overnight camps, *I* had mingled with the Europeans. *En* France, *les hommes* would be magnetized by the winning combination of my French name and American vivaciousness. Back home, I'd present the situation as one forced upon me.

"*Je m'appelle* . . . Forgive me. My English just keeps

slipping. I'm *Delphine* now. It's what my host family called me. It just sort of stuck."

I LEFT FOR France in early July with fifteen of my fellow classmates. I was thrilled by exactly none of them. Do excuse me while I generalize, but my feeling is that early teens enthused about international travel are real assholes in the making, kids with grating personalities. I include myself in this, of course. Our group was divided into three distinct subgroups: socially incompetent brainiacs, self-satisfied horizon expanders, and rebellious types with behavioral problems whose parents, like mine, needed a break from their kids.

As I was neither cool enough for the rebel sect nor bright enough for the brainiacs, I settled comfortably in with the self-delighted horizon expanders. Specifically, a second-generation Indian named Sidd. Once at the airport, he and I had shared a laugh at the expense of Madame Cohen after she'd asked a black gentleman if he could help us with our luggage. The gentleman stared at Madame Cohen, leaving room for an uncomfortable pause.

"I don't work here," he said finally. "Find someone who does."

Madame Cohen turned back toward us.

"Honest mistake," she said.

"For a racist," Sidd whispered, and we laughed and struck up a conversation on religion—"It's for the weak"—as well as our impressively high maturity levels— "I'm just, like, different from the other kids my age. I want to see the world!"

Sidd and I never discussed Sidd's sexual orientation. But I figured he was gay. Effeminate male feminists will tend to force that assumption.

MY CLASSMATES AND I boarded the airplane and clumped across four rows at the back. Midway through the flight, Danny Carter, a member of the rebel sect, caused a ruckus by forcing his needle-thin legs through the elastic bands of his sleeping mask so as to give the visual impression that he was wearing a sanitary pad.

"I'm in a bad mood!" he screeched, running knock-kneed down the aisles. "Boo-hoo-hoo! I'm bleeding! I'm crying! I'm bleeding! I'm crying!"

I might've done one of those fist-in-the-air, power-to-the-people hand gestures and been all like, "Feminism forever, motherfucker. Sexism for never," except for the fact that one of the rules driving my *personal* feminist style was to avoid peddling my views to boys I thought were cute. And Danny was cute. Empirically cute. I therefore kept my opinions to myself, and this didn't matter much anyway, seeing as how the extent of Madame Cohen's disciplinary action was to tell the other students to ignore him.

So you see, my blind eye turned to the mockery of the menstruating wasn't spineless so much as it was respectful.

WE ARRIVED AT Charles de Gaulle Airport and hopped a train to Cluses. I exited alongside my classmates onto the train platform where a cluster of people stood waiting to greet us. They were the host mothers, mostly, women who fulfilled American stereotypes of effortless French attractiveness: They all had well-groomed hair and well-shaped eyebrows. The cowl necks of their respective sweaters were all positioned so as *not* to mimic one's emergence from an impossibly enormous foreskin, which is how I, personally, always look when I wear one.

Among these women stood a lone man. He was possessed of a decidedly less French-ish fashion aesthetic. It's one I refer to these days as "the Pedophile." "Look over there," one might say. "He's sporting the Pedophile."

In pursuit of said look, one combines any number of the following statement pieces:

- Large-framed glasses
- Tucked-in shirt
- Wispy mustache
- High-waisted pants

I spotted this man in the crowd and I knew. I knew the way a mother knows her babe from smell alone: This man was mine. *Mine.* He was my fate, he was my father: He was Monsieur Raffal.

Sidd saw me see Monsieur Raffal.

"Yikes. Sorry," he said, and then was swept lovingly away by a woman who looked exactly like Madeline Kahn.

IT SEEMED SO unfair to Delphine. Why, as her class-mates had *their* hair affectionately tousled, *their* opinions solicited on sweet versus savory pastry, why was Delphine asked only, "Sara? Barron?" then led wordlessly on to a lair of unspeakable depression known as an apartment? My actual parents' house was nothing noteworthy in the size department, but still: There were windows. There were, to be fair, windows *chez* Raffal, but these were few and far between and the consequent lack of natural light had been compensated for with beige walls and a singular unframed poster of a tiger.

Delphine's pedophiliac-looking papa explained to Delphine that her French siblings were not at home and that Delphine would therefore be eating dinner alone with her *papa* and *maman*.

I see, said Delphine. *So what are we going to eat?*

We are going to eat a rabbit, said her papa. *Maman has cooked for us a rabbit.*

Delphine, though, did not want to eat a rabbit. She was

afraid to eat a rabbit. But she was also *more* afraid to tell her papa, "No. I will not eat a rabbit." So Delphine ate a rabbit. She chewed a rabbit. She tried not to cry.

Then she thought: This rabbit tastes like chicken.

And then she thought: Okay. So I will tell myself it's chicken. It's chicken, it's chicken, it's chicken.

Delphine repeated her mantra. She did so without interruption since her *papa* and *maman* said nothing to each other through the dinner. They did not speak to each other, and they did not speak to Delphine. They just stared at their plates of rabbit/chicken. Delphine could hear them chew their rabbit/chicken.

Delphine finished her own plate of rabbit/chicken. When she did, her papa stood up. He opened a cabinet door and took out a coloring book. Delphine's papa gave it to Delphine, who, to remind you, was fifteen years old at the time.

"Here," said her papa. "Eet ees a toy for you."

Then he walked her to her bedroom. He told Delphine to sleep.

But Delphine didn't sleep. She *couldn't* sleep. All she could do was collapse in hysterics on the carpeted floor for an uncountable number of hours. When eventually she hoisted herself up and brushed her hand against her cheek, she discovered it speckled in filth: hairs, unidentifiable pellets, profuse amounts of dust to which she'd lost her immunity thanks to the immaculate home her real parents kept so as to soothe the asthma of her nemesis.

Delphine endured. And then thought, *God,* I'm fucked. Par-*don.* I mean, *Mon dieu. Je suis foutue.*

THE FOLLOWING DAY started with a bit of *famille*-bonding as a precursor to an all-exchange-group tour of the Evian factory. I emerged from my bedroom with bloodshot eyes and strolled into the kitchen. I feared I'd be confronted with a rabbit omelet care of Madame Raffal, but the only sign of life was the young woman seated at the kitchen table.

"Sara?" she asked.

"Yes. *Oui*," I said. "Lucille?"

"Yes. *Oui*," she said.

She, Lucille, was eating a sandwich of mayonnaise and rabbit. "Sand-weesh?" she asked. "You want?"

"No, *merci*," I said. Lucille shrugged like, *Suit yourself.* We sat for a moment.

"And your brother, Guy?" I asked. "He is home now too?"

"*Non,*" said Lucille. "He go to zee house."

"Zee house?" I repeated. "What house?"

Lucille furrowed her brow. She thought how to say it in English. Seconds went by. Five. Ten. Twenty. Finally, she said, "Zee house for zee pee-pull . . ."

She trailed off. I tried to help.

"A house for the people?" I asked. "What kind of people?"

"Zee house for zee pee-pull . . . *comme ça*," Lucille said, and then she wound her index finger near her head in the universal sign for nut job.

I thought for a moment. Seconds went by. Five. Ten. Twenty. Finally, I said, "A mental hospital? For Guy?"

"*Oui!*" said Lucille. "*Exactement.* Guy, he ees having many problems all zee time."

This was surprising information. It was not every day I heard of someone going to a mental hospital. It was also depressing information. I'd had high hopes for Guy and me. Perhaps, then, I should have been either surprised or depressed. Or surprised *and* depressed. Perhaps I should have been even the littlest bit curious as to the circumstance that had landed Guy in a mental hospital in the first place. But I was not.

On the contrary, I thought I understood.

I considered the tan walls and the tiny window. The *maman* and the *papa* and the unvacuumed floors. I considered the rabbit—the sound of someone *chewing* rabbit— and then I considered Lucille. I looked her up and down.

If my sister looked like that, I thought, *I think I'd go crazy too.*

First off, let me say how impressive it was that Lucille was able to sit upright in light of how much metal she'd voluntarily inserted in her face. And when I say "face," I do mean "face." Her ears had been reserved for spacers, those dime- to quarter-sized horrors one puts in one's earlobes so as to free them of any speck of natural elasticity; her hair, for jet black dye. I may lack a knack for deductive reasoning, but even *I* know an aesthetic like this means a lady does not care to flower-weave.

Lucille invited me into her bedroom. It was similar to my brother's bedroom insofar as she had covered it in posters. However, Lucille's posters were of the death-metal variety, and their method for objectification was to present womyn bound, gagged, and raped by mythic demons. These visuals were used as a backdrop upon which to scrawl band names like Cannibal Corpse and Grave and Suffocation.

It became clear to me on this, our first morning together, that Lucille's idea of a good time was having me translate English-sung death-metal lyrics she'd read in the liner notes of various CDs. We'd cover impressive ground over the course of three weeks, studying useful English phrases like "meat hook" and "open wound," "skull scorch" and "embedded in my cortex."

These translations became my little morning pick-me-up.

Because it picks one up, considering how best to mime a phrase like "At one with my sixth sense, I feel free to kill."

MY AMERICAN SCHOOL had chosen to do its exchange program with a French school on a year-round schedule. As such, my mornings with Lucille were followed either by field trips with our French and American cohorts, or by hours in class spent studying alongside her. I'd never heard of a year-round schedule before, and while it sounded like an okay place to be enrolled—to miss out on summer if it meant you made it up elsewhere in the year—it was *not* an okay place to be exchanged. If that was the case, then you, the exchanged student, wound up spending your summer in school. It meant you wound up missing your vacation.

The fact of this put most of my fellow Americans in a mood to misbehave.

We all took a language class together each week, and while the horizon expanders feigned interest in what the teacher was saying, the brainiacs would sleep. The rebels, for their part, would work to make the teacher's life a living hell. The worst of those rebels was Danny Carter, he of the midflight makeshift sanitary pad. He was always raising his hand and asking the teacher: *"Voulez-vous couchez avec moi ce soir?"* The teacher would ignore him or whatever rebel companion he'd inspired to behave similarly. She would turn promptly back to the rest of us for help translating a word like "locker," for example, or "napkin."

But the rebels were not to be deterred.

They'd shout over whoever tried to answer, phrases ranging from "fat dick" to "big dick."

"American friends: Please tell zee word for *casier. Oui?* Sara?"

"Ca veut dire—"

"FAT DICK!"

"*Non,* Danny. 'Locker.' *Maintenant*: Who know zee word for *serviette*? Oui? Sidd?"

"*Ca veut dire—*"

"BIG DICK!"

"*Non,* Danny. 'Napkin.'"

This sort of rabble-rousing happened all the time. I found it only mildly annoying, however, and that is because every moment spent away from Lucille's death-metal posters felt like a momentary reprieve from a terrible headache. Sidd didn't seem to mind much either, and I attributed this to the fact that he was as attracted as I was to Danny.

Danny.

His grotesque personality was juxtaposed by a dumpling of an ass and the pillowy lips of a young Macaulay Culkin. I make this particular comparison, as I think Macaulay evokes just the right sort of sexual appeal. And just in case this makes me *sound* as pedophiliac as Monsieur Raffal *looked,* I'll say again that I was fifteen at the time, and Macaulay, one year younger.

Sidd and I would sit beside each other, and as Danny yelled "fat dick" umpteen times or asked some nearby French girl if she was "having a boner"—the word *bonheur* sounds dangerously like "boner" and translates roughly to "good time"—we'd glare at him and say what an asshole he was. But we were stern in content only. There was saliva dripping from our mouths and it set a different tone.

Neither Sidd nor I discussed our true feelings toward Danny, and that is because it is embarrassing to crave someone so rudely disgusting. It is also a natural part of life. But we were fifteen at the time, not yet hardened to the sad reality that men who act the part of douchebag(uette) don't make you go, "Eww," really. They make you go, "Let me up on it, boy. Let's grind." Additionally, Sidd was in a life phase wherein he was writing his overall effeminacy off as general charisma rather than definitive homosexuality, so being, like, "Look at Danny's ass, Sidd! JUST LOOK AT DANNY'S ASS!" would not have helped his cause.

I, too, had reason to keep my mouth shut. The last young lady to express interest in Danny had paid a pretty penny for it. Julie was her name, and she was one of our fellow exchange students. Rumor had it that following our Cluses arrival, Julie had written Danny a note suggesting a late-night rendezvous, and that Danny, in response, had written "SLUTTY BITCHES RULE!" *on* Julie's note, which he'd then taped to a tree in the French schoolyard.

Attractiveness-wise, I was the "Before" to Julie's "After," the Gary Busey to her Nick Nolte, the Jan to her Marsha. I therefore shuddered to think what would befall me if *I* made a move, passed a note, snaked an arm around a waist, and so on. Instinct told me that regardless of other particulars, stained underpants *would* be involved.

Like Sidd, I kept my hands to myself, my attitude seemingly disdainful.

SIDE NOTE: JULIE did not wind up a stripper or unkempt agoraphobe or whatever else can result from grade-A humiliations in one's formative years. My ten-year high school reunion revealed her to have maintained a slender waistline and scored a decent job. I can't recall what exactly, other than it made me feel bad about myself. As for Danny, he was but a less noble Dexter, a less accomplished Keyser Söze. For he was not justly punished for his crimes. He'd remained empirically attractive, and this, I thought, was a real heap of bullshit, since when are schoolyard bullies *ever* rightly punished? Everyone I know has got a story on the subject, yet no adults will admit to having played the starring role.

An annoying social blight. I thought I'd do my own small part to solve it.

1. Danny's full name is Daniel James Carter.
2. Daniel James Carter spent large portions of his adolescence getting aphrodisiac highs from the mistreatment of his fellow humans.
3. If you know Daniel James Carter—if you see him on the street—point a finger at him. Tell him, "I know what you are." If he claims to be reformed, tell him, "You don't *look* reformed, so much as you look headed to a strip club. A nice one, but still," since—if my high school reunion is to serve as any indication—you'll have found him in a rigidly starched button-down shirt he's paired with jeans of a wide leg and flamboyant back pocket. So it is your judgment shall be just and true.

ON OUR WEEKDAYS off from French schooling, my classmates and I went on field trips to towns like Sochaux to visit the Peugeot headquarters or to Albertville to see the out-of-use exhibition halls from the '92 winter Olympics. These tours didn't feel informative so much as they did boring to the point of physical discomfort: like being given a sedative, then forbidden from sleep. Worse still were our euphemistically titled "scenic hikes" in which we were forced to meander around a hill, then graze on a picnic lunch of butter and mayonnaise sandwiches.

I understand it's not the best way to score likability points, bitching about your teen tour *en France,* about *la pauvre petite toi* wandering amid Alpine foothills. In my own defense, I would therefore like to say that I've done so only so that I might demonstrate how deeply I hate nature walks. I *hated* them. I *hate* them. I can just about struggle through a city walk where there's at least the option of a subway, but where walks through nature are concerned, my baseline mood is one of real misery. I become obsessed with the repetitive quality of the scenery. Oh, that's a nice mountain, I'll think. And then three hours later when I'm inevitably staring at the same mountain, Oh, what a nice mountain. Honestly, though, what I wouldn't do for a hammer to the vaginal canal. Anything, really, to save me from the boredom.

As for the weekends, I would spend them *chez* Raffal. They were nothing more than a test, really, to see how much snot my shirtsleeve could absorb. It needed a good wringing out by the time they were over, and that's owed to the crying jags that, in turn, were owed to the homesickness.

If a month earlier you had told me that I would get to France and *cry* because I *wanted* my *family*, I would have showed you my brother's bowel movement and told you that you were less intelligent than the bowel movement itself.

But that was then. This was now. This was weekends spent alone with Papa, Maman, and Lucille.

In the otherwise sparse living room, both Papa and Maman had their own La-Z-Boy chairs. They would spend the weekends in those chairs, in the lack of natural light. They didn't talk a lot, or at all. They would mostly watch TV. Sometimes Maman would go to the bathroom and come back with a tube of unidentifiable cream, which she would then rub *on* her knees and *in* her armpits. Sometimes she would get out of the La-Z-Boy chair to go make rabbit and mayonnaise sandwiches for Papa,

Lucille, and me. You'd think that by this point I might've put my foot down about the whole rabbit situation, but honestly, whatever animal I was eating by this stage was *way* beside the point. For while Maman was nice enough to make the sandwiches, she was not nice enough to wash her hands before she made the sandwiches. I would watch Maman squeeze the unidentifiable cream onto her hand and into her armpit, and then I would watch her compile those sandwiches and I would think, I am *eating* her armpit! I am *eating* the cream! I resented Papa for leaving the domestic duties entirely to Maman, although this had less to do with my burgeoning feminist tendencies and more to do with Maman's cream-application situation. In Papa's defense, however, he did give me four more coloring books during the course of my stay.

I had no choice but to interact mostly with Lucille. She spent large portions of our weekends together chasing not only my explanations of death-metal lyrics, but also proof of my own affection for the genre.

"Good, yes?" she'd ask while adjusting her dog collar. "You like?"

Was there a question? I mean, please. There I was in my breathable travel shirt and the compression stockings I'd taken to wearing as everyday socks. I'd been reared on musical theater. I believed a musician's primary responsibility was evoking joy and/or lyrical dance. The clearest sense I had of "dark" and "rebellion" was Paula Abdul's "Cold-Hearted Snake" music video, and suffice it to say that *Do you think he really thinks about you when he's out / He's a cold-hearted snake, girl!* sung while jazz-handing in a high-rise thong is quite the far cry from *Let's flagellate the sluts with their serpentine wings,* for example, or *Blood spills on the sluts grinding the staff of the priests.* Still, though, I told Lucille I liked her music very much, and that is because it's simply the right thing to do when dealing with a human in a dog collar.

Confronted with this style of individual, an instinct flares within.

Agree or you'll be harmed, it says. *Or, worse yet, prolong the interaction.*

AT THE END of three weeks, we, the Americans, left Cluses with our French counterparts in tow. Little fanfare surrounded our departure, save for a party at our temporary French school at which there were doughnuts and a game of Danny's devising called Pin the Tail on the Fag. It involved chasing Sidd around and slapping Sidd's ass. Then you'd shout, "TAG, FAG! YOU'RE IT!"

Sidd tried to defend himself by standing with his ass against the wall and, when that didn't work, by hiding in the womyn's bathroom. I went in there to pee and found him locked in the handicapped stall.

"Are you okay?" I asked.

"No!" he answered. "*Why* does he think I'm a fag? Honestly! Like, *why*?!"

I did not answer back, "Because you are, Sidd. You *are.*" And that is because I, Sara Barron of the Student Coalition for Awareness, would never use a word like "fag." All I did say to Sidd was that Danny was an asshole, and that, clearly, Sidd was not a fag. But then I went back to the party. I felt bad for Sidd, yes, but I did not feel bad *enough* to start showering him with affection. Sidd's gorgeous French *maman* had come to our going-away party, and after everything I'd been through, the sight of her laughing, engaging, trying to protect him from his various aggressors, it was all a bit much. It made me jealous of Sidd. It felt like, "Yeah, well, I'm sorry about this whole fag situation. But at least you didn't eat your weight in skin-cream sandwiches this month."

Misery is supposed to love company. But I've always felt like *my* misery prefers someone who's doing okay. Someone with enough energy to keep the attention on me.

THE THREE WEEKS I spent in France were the first three weeks I'd ever spent away from home. My parents came to greet me at the airport. When I saw them for the first time it was inexplicably bizarre to feel an emotion other than annoyance. Something had shifted in the time I'd been away, and for the first time in a long time they looked to me like allies. For they spoke in fluent English. They could operate a vacuum. Their faces were un-pierced.

My parents hugged me hello and introduced themselves to Lucille. But Lucille acted cold. Reserved. My parents wrote this off as a simple case of shyness. They waited until we were all together in our car—my parents in the front seats, Lucille and me in the back—to try to coax her into conversation.

"So Lucille," said my dad. "Did you have a nice flight? Did you get any sleep?"

Lucille, still, said nothing. I decided I should answer for her.

"Dad," I said, "we don't want to talk right now, okay? We're back from *France,* for God's sake. Hello? France? Do you even *know* how jet-lagged we feel?"

It was a faux snap. A love nip. That I wasn't afraid of my father, that he was there to knock about, it made him so much less annoying than he'd ever been before.

My mother piped in.

"If you think France is bad," she said, "try Israel. It's *eight* hours ahead. I was there, you know. In 1968."

My mother paused. She turned around to face us.

"So Lucille," she said, "are you excited for Chicago? It is home to deep-dish pizza and many good museums."

Lucille shrugged but did not speak. She put on her headphones and turned on her music.

My mother, father, and I all listened to Lucille's music *through* Lucille's headphones.

"Is that . . . music?" asked my mom.

"Yes," I answered.

"I see," she said. A pause. Then: "How good is her English?"

"What?" I asked.

"How. Good," my mother repeated. "Is. Lucille's. English?"

"Oh," I said. "It's good."

"I see," she said. "And can she hear me through the headphones?"

I looked at Lucille, who was looking out the window.

"Lucille?" I called, but she did not turn around.

"No," I said. "She can't."

"Then tell me," said my mother, "what the *fuck* are in her ears?"

"Lynn!" cried my dad.

"What?" asked my mom.

"They're called spacers," I said.

"They're *disgusting*," she said.

"I know," I said. "But you'll get used to them after a while."

MY MOTHER WAS lucky insofar as she didn't have to spend a lot of time around Lucille's earlobes. In Chicago, as in Cluses, the schools had worked to coordinate various weekday field trips to keep the students busy. Lucille had a lot of free time too, but rather than spend it at our house, she liked to spend it at the local mall.

My dad had to ferry her there and back whenever she wanted to go, but he said it was worth it if it kept my mother calm.

"She hates those ear things, your mother. And as for the drive, it's not really that bad. Lucille puts on her headphones, and I put on my Cole Porter CD, and it's kind of like being alone."

Ours was a three-bedroom house, and this meant shifting the sleeping arrangements so as to accommodate three kids instead of two. My mother asked if I wanted to sleep in my room, in my bed, near Lucille, or in Sam's room, on his bunk bed, near Sam and Carmen Electra.

There was no question to this question. I knew what I wanted to do.

I ENTERED SAM'S room humbly, with metaphoric cap in hand. Literally what I was carrying was a magnet from the Evian factory that I'd intended to keep for myself.

I found my brother Scotch-taping his nose to his forehead. His chin was flecked with spit he looked too bored to wipe away.

"Hi," I said, and handed him the magnet. "Here's a magnet."

"Thanks," he said.

"You're welcome," I said. I pointed at his face. "I like what you're doing there with the tape. Your nostrils look . . . long."

"Thanks," he said.

"You're welcome," I said. "Also, I was thinking I might sleep on your top bunk. Instead of in my room with Lucille."

"Sure," he said. "No problem."

There was a pause during which we both looked to the wall separating us from what had been my bedroom but was now Lucille's unkempt lair.

"Her earlobes *are* awful," Sam said.

"I know," I said. "It's like someone yanked them off her head and used them as a teething ring . . ."

"And then sewed them back on," he said. "I know exactly what you mean."

As we learn to accept that we'll one day find ourselves attracted to douchebag(uette)s for the simple reason that they've got butts like Chinese dumplings, so must we learn to devise strategic methods for the self-serving laying of blame. Don't hate your brother, hate Carmen Electra. Don't hate your sister, hate how she spells "womyn." Aim low, ignore, endure. It sounds bleak, I know. But it's worth it, I think, if you wind up less alone.

3

The Stupids Step Out

When I was a child, my parents upheld the tradition of taking Sam and me on summer vacations. They were generally tight-fisted with money, but vacations they viewed as a worthwhile luxury. My mother in particular, who felt she was broadening her children's horizons. Miami Beach, the Grand Canyon, Manhattan's Upper West Side. Glance upon these diverse sections of the vast nation, cultivate an open mind.

"It'll shock you," she'd told me en route to San Diego, "how changed you'll feel by the time we get back. Changed *how*, it's hard to say. But you'll be . . . different. You'll have seen . . . the world."

But then in the summer of 1990, our excursions came to a halt when my father lost his job. He had spent fifteen years

employed by a company at which he wrote dictionary definitions. Until, that is, he showed up one morning and was
called into an office and they said the word "downsize."

And that was pretty much that.

My parents responded to the news in different ways. My
father, having arrived home in the middle of the day with no
clear sense of when or why he'd have to leave again, sat sobbing on the couch, whereas my mother scrambled around
searching for any and all returnable items. She found a
handful of sweaters and a pack of frozen shrimp. She called
her travel agent to cancel our forthcoming trip to Boston.

I was personally saddened by my father's job loss. It
wasn't pleasant seeing him wedged in the fetal position,
sobbing. More to the point, I had been looking forward
to authentic chowder. I now planned to pass the afternoon
shut in my bedroom feeling sorry for myself. But I did not
manage this successfully. Not once I heard my mother yelling from downstairs.

"EVERYONE INTO THE DEN!" she yelled. "I CALL
A MEETING OF THE FAMILY!"

This meeting had no precedent, and unfolded rather
like how I'd seen family meetings of the mafia portrayed
on-screen. Except that we had women. And inhalers.

"There's family business to address," she said. "New
arrangements must be made."

She told us all to get a pen and paper and write down
two cost-free activities that we each found personally
enjoyable. Having done so, we'd read them aloud and
construct what, in twenty-first-century parlance, is most
commonly called a staycation. Everyone did as instructed,
and we wound up with the following.

1. Family walk; family picnic
2. Reading books; family walk

3. Wash the car; sit on a float
4. Doughnut

Sam was the one who wrote "doughnut." I was the one who brought up car washes and float-sitting. As I am accountable only for myself, I can explain only my own choices:

Waving at subservient masses from atop one's colorful, motorized throne *is* an empirically pleasant leisure activity.

As for car washes, they'd been a venerable obsession for years. I'd seen the activity portrayed on-screen numerous times, always as a precursor to some bit of alluring body contact between those doing the washing. The lady character would get doused in sudsy water, desired, and pursued. The overused scenario had left me with the impression that if only I stood with my family in our driveway lathering up the Ford Escort station wagon, one of my male contemporaries might roll by on a skateboard for a look at soapy, eroticized me. I'd be sun-kissed, and possessing of the additional glow one gets embracing life.

"Join us," I'd urge the passerby. "It's, like, *so* the more the merrier."

And then: My family evaporates into thin air! The male contemporary tackles me nonviolently to the ground! I lie beneath him giggling and breathless, and he's overcome with what he calls my ". . . natural beauty. Wow. Do you know Cynthia Rhodes?"

"I don't," I say. "Whosoever is Cynthia Rhodes?"

"She plays Penny in *Dirty Dancing*," he says, "and you look exactly like her. Or, I guess, she looks like you."

ALL SUGGESTED ACTIVITIES were approved, save for my float-sitting, which my mother claimed involved excessive sun exposure. But the others were honored with their own special day: Barron Family Walking Day. Barron Family Reading Day. Barron Family Make-a-Doughnut Day. The lack of float-sitting was replaced with Barron Family Pool Day. We followed through with Barron Family Car Wash Day, but no male contemporary swung by on a skateboard. This disappointment was compensated for when my mother and brother—the latter in a wet T-shirt, plumped decidedly up by asthma medication—shared an amusing exchange:

Sam: I am fat.
Mom: Congratulations.
Sam: I am fat. Look. (Pointing at his chest.) Boobs.
Mom: Those aren't boobs, Sam. They're nipples.
Sam: Nipples *are* boobs, when you're fat.
Mom: (Looking at the nipples.) Huh. I guess you're right.

My parents, high on resourcefulness, acted atypically relaxed. Their money-saving feathers couldn't ruffle, not even if Sam or I misbehaved. And Sam and I misbehaved. During Barron Family Pool Day, Sam purposefully shat while sitting on the pool deck. He was seven. This story, euphemistically titled "Sam at the Pool," is key in my family's anecdotal canon. For this particular retelling, I called my brother and left a voice mail in which I asked, in effect, what he'd been thinking at the time. The voice mail he left in response has here been directly transcribed:

I used to have a very hard time moving my bowels. I hated to do it, especially in a strange bathroom. So I'd be really hesitant to go use the bathroom. So it was just like, "Oh. There's no way I'm getting up to go to the bathroom. I'm having fun in a pool and don't want to do that . . ." And so I was all like that, until I had to go. I was sitting poolside, and . . . I don't know. Mom and Dad were right there, so I didn't think I'd get away with it secretly or anything. It wasn't like, "Ooooh. I'm gonna get in trouble." I wasn't even ashamed. It was more like, "Well, whatever . . . Dad'll clean it up."

Sam intuited correctly. He shat on a pool deck, and my father's course of disciplinary action was to reach for his towel so he could clean it up himself.

"Ah, well," he said to no one in particular. "Parenthood, right? All in a day's work."

I wasn't much better, shoplifting Purdue packaged ham on Barron Family Make-a-Doughnut Day. We'd gone to the grocery store to buy vanilla extract and I wandered off to the cold-cuts department. That's where I saw the ham, and stuffed it down my underpants. When inevitably my mother found the ham—I'd tucked it *under* the fitted sheet that went *over* my single mattress—I decided to admit the theft rather than lie about having spent her money.

My mother ruffled my hair in response.

"Well," she said. "It *is* a special week."

These Barron Family Activity Days occurred most often in public, and this meant we earned a positive reputation for spending so much quality time together. In the latter half of Barron Family Pool Day, we had gone to *shmy* at a local art fair.

"*Shmy*" is a Yiddish term for "stroll, wander, or window-shop," and the subtext of the word, at least in my experience, suggests that one's superior for having done so—that is, for having looked but not bought. If one says, "I'm *shmying*," one's also said, "I'm not so self-indulgent as to *buy*, of course. I've merely looked."

So we'd gone to *shmy*, and while *shmying*, we'd run into one of my mother's friends.

"You Barrons!" said the friend. "Just yesterday I was driving around and saw you all out together walking! Now here you are again, all out together buying art!"

"We're not buying art," said my mother. "We're *shmying* art."

"Well, it's lovely, whatever it is. It'd be great if *my* kids did a little more walking or *shyming*. Just a little more willing participation, you know?"

"Can't say I do," said my mom. "My kids are up for anything. I'm very lucky."

"Anything" may have meant a walk or a *shmy*, but it also meant public shitting and shoplifting. However, my mother didn't want to share the full picture of her experience, and who could blame her? She had admirers now. She had an image to maintain.

The week was labeled a success. My parents had enjoyed the frugality, and as for me, I loved the faint hints of encouragement. I loved the sense that we were up to something special. Might I have *preferred* a situation wherein the glory was mine and mine alone? Of course. My ideal would have been to spend the whole of our staycation sitting by myself on the float of my dreams in the center of town. But something is better than nothing. A *little* attention at an art fair is better than *no* attention at some chowder hut in Boston. And as for Sam? Well, Sam was so mellow he'd shat on a pool deck. Sam was happy. Sam was fine.

These joys and satisfactions snowballed into an ambrosial cocktail that convinced my parents to forsake family vacations entirely. Instead, we reserved a week every August for Barron Family Activity Days. We did it from that first year in 1990, when my father lost his job, to 1997, when I left to go to college.

August 1993 was noteworthy in that we spent the whole of the week at a nearby nature preserve. Which is not to say we camped, as the budget-conscious Barrons would sooner max out credit cards than we would attempt to pitch a tent. We rather drove there and back every day to attend a series of free classes. We flower-pressed, fire-started, and bird-identified. It was during one such bird-identification class that my father won the contest for "Best Ruffed Grouse Drumming" under the tutelage of a woman named Leona. Leona was a burly instructor, and she rewarded my dad with a bandanna that said, YOU BELONG TO THE EARTH.

"How's about a round of applause for Mr. Barron!" she yelled, and handed over the bandanna.

As instructed, the seven of us clapped: my mother, my brother, me. A retired couple. A child with muscular dystrophy. Her father, who'd come to push her in her wheelchair.

The gang of us clapped for my dad.

"Thank you," he said.

"You're welcome!" said Leona. She paused. She said, "Well? Aren't you gonna put it on?"

I struggle to adequately explain how bizarre it would be to see my dad in a bandanna. In a feeble try, though, a short list of things that'd be more normal:

1. If I grew myself a penis.
2. If I found out my mother and father were brother and sister.

Nevertheless, my father wanted to be gracious to Leona and not at all dismissive of her gift. So he bit the bullet and tried it on. The resulting visual made my mother laugh so hard, she pissed herself. I know because she told me.

"I've laughed so hard I've pissed myself!" she said. "Are we having fun here, *or what*?!"

IN THE MIDDLE 1990s, Barron Family Activity Days expanded to include seasonal variations. Each new season brought a fresh bounty of opportunity. In fall, there was

Barron Family Raking Day and Barron Family Pumpkin Carving Day. We enjoyed Barron Family Biking Day, exploiting the chill in the air all twenty miles to the Harold Washington Library in downtown Chicago. Once there, we would bounce in unison to a free Klezmer band concert. In winter, there was Barron Family Sledding Day and Barron Family View-a-Manger Day. This last one involved ordering Chinese takeout, and eating in the car. As we ate, my father would drive us around nearby gentile suburbs like Highwood and Lake Forest, so we could point and laugh at the plastic or ceramic mangers. In 1994, there was a not-to-be-repeated Barron Family Caroling Day. The problem here was that we'd gone to a concert known for its audience participation, but then my manner of audience participation embarrassed my parents. I'd been standing directly in front of them bellowing along to "Good King Wenceslas," when I overheard my mother tell my father, "She is *screaming*. Just *screaming*. Are you going to handle this, or should I?"

I have a long history of giving myself over to the music, of getting brought back to reality when other people's words and/or facial expressions suggest I've embarrassed myself. Perhaps the '94 caroling attempt was the first time this happened. I can't quite recall. Regardless, I was not yet ready to be humbled into silence, to accept my singing voice as that of a rangeless Ethel Merman. My parents, lacking the heart to interrupt me, put the kibosh on all future family caroling events. This ensured that if I cared to carol in the future, at least they wouldn't be around to hear it.

BACK WHEN BARRON Family Activity Days were in their nascent stages, I enjoyed them by virtue of the flickers of praise they could provide. But as late adolescence approached, the experience redefined itself as one of deep humiliation. Throughout high school, my spring break activities were but a guidebook for extraditing oneself from an already shaky social circle. My peers would go to Cancún, and I would stay with my family in Chicago. My peers would return cornrowed and tanned, and I would return having seen *Dead Man Walking* or *The Birdcage*. I knew a mean little thing named Avital Goldfarb. Her locker was next to mine, and I was nice to her out of fear, mostly, but also because in the case of spring break, I wanted to know how the other half lived.

"Hi, Avital. So how was Cancún?"

"Oh my God. BEYOND," she said. "It was, like, totally beyond."

"Oh, wow," I said. "What happened?"

"Well," she said, "David Weinberg and me fucked on a swim-up bar and then went to a bubble party after."

At the age of sixteen, I was not yet aware that a bubble party was a rave-like experience at which suds were poured on partygoers, who, more often than not, were outfitted in lingerie. I thought a bubble party was what happens when you and a chosen companion stomp around on bubble wrap to pop the bubbles.

"I love bubble parties!" I said. "My brother Sam and I had one at home!"

"Just the two of you?"

"Yes."

"In your house?"

"Yes. Since we couldn't get down to the 'Cún."

"That's really weird. I mean, like . . . wait: Did you just say 'the 'Cún'?"

Winter break was not much better. At the end of 1995, my mother finagled a deal on one-size-fits-all snow pants. The purchase facilitated the first of the Barron Family

Sledding Days, in which my parents, brother, and I all wound up in matching snow pants. Because it was sunny this day, and all of us were nauseatingly pale *and* steered through life by my mother's hypochondria, we were also all face-painted with zinc oxide.

I enjoyed a half hour of good clean fun before a Jeep Cherokee's worth of my classmates arrived outfitted in Oakley-brand everything. They carried a thermos each, and moved amidst a swell of smoke that smelled of marijuana.

This brings me to the problem inherent to adequate sledding terrain: There's never anywhere to hide. Interactions are inevitable. I wound up having mine with Jason Zellman.

"Oh, hey," he said.

"Hey," I said.

"Nice snow pants," he said.

"Thanks," I said. "What's in your thermos?"

"Vodka," he said. "What's on your face?"

"Zinc oxide," I said. "It makes me less susceptible to melanoma."

The exchange was unpleasant enough and it was made even worse by the history I shared with Jason Zellman. Three years prior, he'd overheard me in the junior high school cafeteria tell a friend, "You know what's the worst thing? Butter on ham," and then—and for reasons unknown—he made a beeline for me so as to slap a slice of butter-logged white bread on my cheek.

What a boy named Jason Zellman was doing with so much butter on white bread, I'll never know. But that's beside the point. What I'm trying to convey is that the experience was remarkably disgusting, and that under even the best circumstance, in Jason Zellman's presence I now felt vulnerable. As I also felt vulnerable when I was in a pair of snow pants to match my parents' snow pants, the above conversation was a real one-two punch in the adolescent misery department. Physically painful, almost. Like pouring vodka down my snow pants. Like *feeling* vodka soak my nonabsorbent jeans.

AN ODD THING happens in one's early twenties, and that's how associations shift regarding nerdish adolescence. Once a liability, the experience morphs suddenly and without warning into a fashionable bit of personal history. I believe this to be a first-world affliction. I can't say for sure, as I don't get out much to those third or second worlds—I am too afraid of food poisoning and/or slipping into an unsolvable depression—but here in the first world, we like to dish on what we've been through. We hit our twenties and find we crave a little color to our pasts.

I was on the Internet the other day, stalking the wife of a current enemy. This proved an easy task, as she maintained a comprehensive blog. She'd stocked it with information like what restaurant she went to for dinner and how much she loves her second husband.

Included in the margin was a *15 Things About Me* list, and number 13 read as follows:

"I have suffered. A lot."

I mention the excerpt, as it perfectly illustrates my point: We believe that to Suffer As a Child secures us our status as a Winningly Complex Adult.

It is a popular trend but it is also misguided. For it prompts even the most stupidly, thoroughly, symmetrically attractive to swear they've done just that. They were nerds! Dorks! Tomboys! So thin that someone teased them!

I was such a dork growing up, but it was worth it! It's what made me who I am today.

Of course, there's an unstated presumption at work,

and that's that who they are today is something other than mind-numbingly mundane. The whole thing's a reach at seeming humble and complex, a bit of self-delightedness sold as self-effacement.

The behavior is annoying, to be sure, but it is not without its upshots. Namely, that when I entered my early twenties, Barron Family Activity Days morphed yet again. This time into something I was proud of. Suddenly Barron Family Pedal-Boating Day wasn't embarrassing so much as it was adorable. Adorable and hilarious! A contributing factor to the unique piece of sass I'd become! Tell a person post-collegiately, "Sorry I can't make it to your party. It conflicts with family pedal-boating," and prepare to bask in public praise.

"Did you say 'family pedal-boating'? OMG. How cute are you?"

"Whatever. We're, like, total nerds."

"Whatever! You're awesome!"

Praise is what's awesome, and seeing as how my twenties were otherwise a revolving door of waiter shifts and unbiblical sex, any meager boost to my self-esteem was welcome. In 2004 I had a boyfriend I both scored and maintained owing almost entirely, I think, to Barron Family Activity Days. On our third date, he invited me to a party, and I declined the invitation citing a conflicting visit home. I said, "I really would love to, but the thing is, my parents schedule these, like, Family Activity Days." I leaned coquettishly in on my elbow. "And they're simply not to be missed. It's *so* super-nerdy. Oh my God. I'm such a dork!"

It's really effective, seeming all at once unavailable *and* family oriented, and this guy slipped into the palm of my hand like it was greased and hanging on a better-looking woman. Someone more authentically aloof. Things between us fell apart eventually, of course, once my neediness and lack of generosity shined through. But just because victory isn't yours forever, well, that doesn't mean it wasn't yours for once.

THIS BRINGS US to today: Sam and I are both in our thirties. My mom is sixty-five. My dad is sixty-nine. The four of us do still indulge in Barron Family Activity Days, but my feelings surrounding these activities have shifted for what I think might be the final time.

They *had* been enjoyable, and then embarrassing, and then exciting to exploit.

They *have,* however, gotten sad.

The time we now spend together sledding, say, or communally wading in lakes, looks less "cute" than it does deranged, and the problem (from what I can gather) boils down to lack of grandkids.

Let me here state that if you care to feel the active withering of your own, *personal* womb, you ought to try burying your arthritic mother in the sand in lieu of the toddler you've failed to produce.

The subtext of most of what my parents say these days smacks of "*We* don't need grandkids! *We're* thrilled to be here, just us four!"

It's pretty depressing, and it's made even more depressing by the fact that they know they're not getting one anytime soon. Sam makes just above minimum wage as a line cook, and I lack any vague interest in putting someone else's needs before my own. So my parents get depressed. They try to act like they're not, but they are. If you ask them their opinion on the matter, my father, teary-eyed, will tell you, "Oh, you know. It's fine." But my mother, more defensively, will say, "*My* kids are creative, *okay?* They're artists. You have grandkids, I have artists. Sam and Sara are creative artists, and artists take longer when it comes to having kids."

If by "artist" she means that Sam peels carrots for a living or that I've done a stand-up act in sweatpants, fine. Whatever gets you through.

What gets *me* through, of course, is knowing that I've suffered. Oops. Sorry. I mean, ". . . is knowing that I've Suffered." It's knowing it's been hard but it's been worth it. It's knowing I am one Winningly Complex Adult.

4

Seven Ages of a Magical Lesbian

The Infancy

In December of my eighth year I received various Salon Selectives hair-care products from off my Hanukkah wish list. This was undeniably thrilling. However, the problem with the gift was that I didn't understand its limits, and so got *quite* upset when they failed to make me look as though I'd just stepped out of a salon. I smelled pretty good—like papayas and Vaseline—but my hair, as usual, maintained its Garth Algar Triangle Shape.

Well, I was devastated. Just *devastated*. I'd been saving my gift for first use before an exciting holiday party thrown by my mom's friend Alison. Alison lived with another woman named Emily. This circumstance struck me as compelling by virtue of being unique. Something all their own. I peppered the car ride to their party with questions on the subject. These served as interstitials to my attention-seeking sobs.

"Are they friends?" I asked, and wiped at my nose.

"They *are* friends," said my mother, "but also, they're in love. Like mommies and daddies. But instead of a daddy, there are two mommies."

The most interesting part of this conversation was not that someone could have two mommies, but rather that mommies and daddies were supposed to be in love. I thought love was something reserved for people much younger and more fetching than my parents. I hadn't ever thought about *how* they met or what they would've been like *when* they met. Had I invested the time, I think I would have pictured them meeting for the first time on the street.

My mom: Hello. I agree to make the dinners, and I like to have my back scratched.

My dad: Okay. Then I agree to make the lunches, and I like when you leave me alone.

It was difficult to make the connection between, for example, Marty and Jennifer in *Back to the Future,* and my mom and dad in what, at this time, would have been their seventeenth year of marriage. I had to work to understand that although the versions were different, the model was the same.

Like small dogs and big dogs, I thought. Or salad and ham.

Minutes passed, and I chewed on the idea and sobbed a little more about my hair. It was only as we approached the parking garage to Alison and Emily's Lake Shore Drive apartment that the issue of the Two Mommies could register. Could even *start* to register.

"*Two* mommies," I repeated.

"Yes," said my mom. "They're called lesbians. They're lesbians, and that's fine. Repeat what I just said."

" 'They're lesbians, and that's fine.' "

"Good. Now let's go to a party."

We took the elevator up to the penthouse apartment, and it, the elevator, opened *into* the penthouse apartment. My mood lifted instantly at the sight of it all: textured floral wallpaper and an adopted Asian toddler. A footstool embroidered with a picture of a clown. A porcelain panda whose head had been stylishly flattened to serve as a tray. The whole thing was very *Charlie and the Chocolate Factory,* but minus the psychedelic influence and any vague sense of impending molestation.

My mood had improved, as I said; however, I still continued crying. Just for the sake of it, really. Just because I've always liked when people ask me how I'm doing.

"Oh my goodness!" said Alison in greeting. "What is it, my darling? What's wrong?"

"We're having an . . . issue," said my mother. "*Someone* thought her new shampoo would solve her . . . problem."

"But *that's* no problem," said Alison, and, with no further words exchanged, put a hand on my back and nudged me toward her rose-scented bathroom, where she did a number on me with a flatiron. When I emerged, I looked *awfully* adorable. "Like I just stepped out of a salon" was still a stretch, but it was nonetheless the singular moment of my life in which the adjective "polished" could be justifiably attached to me.

The party rolled on and I feasted on sprinkled doughnut holes served atop the head-tray of the porcelain panda. I played hide-and-seek with Alison and Emily's daughter, a pudgy Asian two-year-old named Lily. Christmas music played, and was interspersed with the musical soundtracks

I myself would have chosen: *Annie, A Chorus Line,* and *Cats.*

The party was an altogether transformative experience, for it led me to the belief that lesbians were but magical confections that brought joy to all the land. They were regal, special, and festive. They were like beautiful unicorns, those lesbians, for you had to search to find them. Oh, yes. You had to dig around. I had a gone a full eight years without knowing they were out there, hidden away in luxurious penthouse apartments. But *now* I knew, and on the car ride home gazed out the window at Lake Shore Drive and all its gorgeous aspirational housing where the lesbians were, where the lives were happy.

I'm going to be one, I thought. I'm going to try.

The only hitch in my plan was that I didn't grasp its linchpin. I did not understand that in order to be a lesbian I must be physically attracted to women. I had observed Alison and Emily throughout their party and they had displayed nothing in the way of physical affection. They'd exchanged a few exasperated looks about the placement of the hors d'oeuvres. They'd laughed together at an anecdote about the pitfalls of business travel. That had been the extent of it, however, and while at eight years old I did understand Alison and Emily were, as my mother said, "in love"— that their relationship model was Mommy/Daddy and not Friend/Friend—I could not make the leap from "in love" to the specific physical logistics that being in love would entail. My sexual understanding started and ended with French kissing, and in much the same way I did not imagine my parents French kissing, I did not imagine Alison and Emily French kissing. More to the point, I did not understand that Alison and Emily *wanting* to French kiss each other was a large part of what made them lesbians in the first place.

That piece would take me more time.

AGE 2

The Schoolgirl

In March of my eleventh year, I attended Diana Bloomberg's twelfth birthday party sleepover. Diana Bloomberg was a young woman with tremendous breasts and an older sister named Amy. Amy also had tremendous breasts, as well as a belly-button ring. The Bloombergs were wilder than the rest of us by virtue, I think, of their breasts and their piercings. We all played a game of Truth or Dare in which I was forced to describe the last time I'd seen my brother's penis. It was a traumatic truth, to be sure, but my dare had been to let Diana measure both my labia with a ruler, and then report back to the group on which one was longer.

So I chose to think about my brother's penis. When I did, Amy inquired on why.

"*Why* wouldn't you let Diana measure your labia?" she asked. "What, are you afraid you'll get turned on?" A pause. "Oh my God. You *are*. YOU *ARE*! You like girls! You're a lesbo! SARA BARRON IS A LESBO!"

"No I'm not," I said. "My labia are weird and different lengths. I don't want *anyone* to see them."

I stated that I was not a lesbian *not* because I was mortified to be one, but rather because I could hear an aggressiveness in Amy's voice, and on instinct—and without considering any of the relevant specifics—I thought to myself, *Shut it down.*

My attempt was successful. My admission that my labia were, in fact, "weird" and "different lengths" stole focus and got the group of us off the subject of lesbianism and onto the subject of labial length.

Minutes passed. We then moved from the subject of labial length onto the subject of my brother's penis and, from there, onto the subject of whether any of us had ever done anything sexual with a cousin. It turned out that one of the other girls, Jamie, *had* once cupped a cousin's scrotum. So we focused on that for a while.

It was only with the focus off me and on Jamie and the scrotum that I had the necessary mental space to consider the specifics of what Amy Bloomberg had said:

"You like girls. You're a lesbo."

IN THE YEARS between this accusation and my initial meeting of Alison and Emily, there had been moments—flashes of knowledge I could not identify for you now—in which some hint of understanding would flutter through me. Something about lesbians, about how maybe their magical unicorn ways were not defined by a lavish apartment and good taste in wallpaper. But these thoughts were fleeting and left me, still, without a full grasp of the idea. *Still,* I had only a vague sense that maybe—just maybe—there was something I was missing.

But what could it possibly be?

The path to understanding was not like flicking on a light switch. It wasn't off, then on. It was running up a mountain, working hard to reach the top. It was earning, as reward, a clear perspective. The lay of the land. My brain had made its slow, subconscious effort for years—climbing . . . climbing . . . sloooooowly climbing—until Amy Bloomberg, good coach that she was, jumped in and pushed me to the top.

I stood there now, seeing it. *Getting* it.

A lesbian is a woman who has sex with other women. She kisses these women. She wants to touch their breasts.

I was now in a position to understand physical attraction because I myself was now in the full-on throes of puberty. Contrary to what Amy Bloomberg had announced to my fellow partygoers, I was not wrangling with lesbianism so much as I was dealing with an obsessive interest in the penis. I liked, for example, to ogle my pediatrician's. I saw him frequently thanks to my ongoing hope that any of my various symptoms might blossom into something bigger. And this pediatrician had an affinity for a particular pair of tan slacks that showcased his central crotch with the efficiency of a spotlight. Powerless against the urge to stare, I'd run a script in my head whenever I saw him, a monologue directed at his penis: "Hello there, you. What's that? Shake *hands*? I'd love to, really I would, but my mother's right there going on about my brother's asthma. Another time perhaps."

The supermarket was the other hotbed of heterosexual attraction. I loved phallic vegetables, and so would stay stationed in the produce department while my mother shopped elsewhere in the store. I'd tickle my cheek with a cucumber or an elongated heirloom tomato. I'd carry out all the conversations that I couldn't with my doctor's crotch.

"Whatcha doing later?" I'd ask. "How's about you and I get to know each other better?"

If a lesbian was stirred by Jessica Rabbit (let's say) in the same way I was when I saw a nice long heirloom tomato, then no. Being a lesbian was not a realistic option. It would require too much work.

I ARRIVED BACK at my parents' house the Sunday after the sleepover, and went straight upstairs so that I might carry out my usual weekend routine: I would grab a tube of VO5 hot oil from the bathroom, and bring it with me into my bedroom. I would close my bedroom door and rub the oil on my Ken doll, and I would consider the truth. I would consider *my* truth:

I was not, at present, a lesbian.

The larger question, then, was whether or not I could become one over time. I did *want* to become one. I liked the two lesbians I knew. I'd invested serious time in envying their lifestyle, and now, with a clear sense of the backbone of that lifestyle, I could tell it was suitably attention-getting and unique. When my family was out with Alison and Emily's family, the latter group would steal focus. They would get all the attention. And as theirs was a liberal neighborhood, this was some positive attention.

Well, aren't you all interesting to look at!

Or: *Well, isn't that lovely. So nice to see you out!*

Everything about my parents' lifestyle seemed dull and average by comparison. It seemed so much more fabulous to live in the city, to fall out of your front door into a throng of *fans,* ostensibly, who viewed you as exciting.

It *is* my perfect fit, I thought. Perhaps the urge will come.

But then at age fifteen I landed myself in that Student Coalition for Awareness. I attended this one LBGT seminar at National Louis University and learned that, sadly, it would not. Lesbianism was not something I'd grow into. Why? Because: Sexism for Never and Gay Is Not a Choice. In 1993, I did actually own a T-shirt that read GAY IS NOT A CHOICE. Alison and Emily's holiday party had become a family tradition by this stage, and in December of 1993 I made a point of going to their party in my GAY IS NOT A CHOICE T-shirt. I wore it over a turtleneck. For warmth. And marched proudly around. For attention.

AGE 3

The Lover

The summer of my seventeenth year, I worked at a bookstore in a strip mall. The bookstore was called Crown Books, and it was a poor man's Barnes & Noble.

"If You Paid Full Price, You Didn't Buy It at Crown Books."

This was the Crown Books slogan.

I think it's lovely in theory, a bookstore geared toward the spendthrifts, but in practice it meant the store was frequented mostly by the mentally retarded. They had a home/center nearby, and they'd come in droves on the weekend to browse the magazine rack and sleep in the armchairs. Most of the visitors were male and at some point during their visit a large percentage of these gentlemen would take porno magazines with them into the bathroom. We were an all-female staff, and we'd take turns at the end of the shift removing the abused paraphernalia from the stalls.

It was not *not* depressing, cleaning up these magazines and/or watching the gentlemen clutch them to their chests. To lighten the mood, I'd spend my days off going to the movie theater that was also in the strip mall. I saw pretty much everything that summer, most notably a film called *Female Perversions*. I knew nothing about *Female Perversions* prior to seeing it. I just went because the show time worked with my Crown Books schedule.

Female Perversions starred Tilda Swinton as Eve Stephens, an ambitious lawyer by day who, by night, performed masterful oral sex on other women.

I am eternally grateful to this film, for it provided me with four years' worth of masturbation material. I saw the movie *once*, and it got me through *four years*. Androgynous Tilda descending into her myriad Sapphic entanglements beat out (as it were) all the other visuals I'd previously employed: John Stamos. A greased-up Ken doll. My pediatrician reimagined with the body of a greased-up Ken doll.

I am additionally grateful to *Female Perversions* because in more recent years, it has offered a compelling conversational entrée into certain social situations. Let's say that I am at a cocktail party—this doesn't happen much, but let's just *say*—and I have run out of things to talk about. I will then turn to the woman who is closest to me, and I will ask a question on the subject of teen heartthrobs.

Mind you, I'm never that interested in her answer. It's just that I want the question asked of me.

"So," I will ask, "who was your favorite teen heartthrob?"

And she will answer Luke Perry, Kirk Cameron, or some other similar type.

And then *I'll* answer, "Oh, really? That's nice. For me, though, it was always Tilda Swinton. What? Yes. Her. I know, *right*? It's like, 'Why am I so weird?'!"

TEN MONTHS LATER, what had been my Crown Books summer job was now my Crown Books weekend job. I worked all Saturdays and Sundays, and this included the Saturday of my senior prom. I had not been asked, and was therefore available to work from noon to nine p.m.

The situation had put me in a bad mood. To snap myself out of it, I decided to treat myself to a new CD. I would use my 10 percent company discount. I would peruse the Crown Books CD section. I would pick myself out something nice.

So there I was perusing. I'd been leaning toward "Tails" by Lisa Loeb when, for the first time in my life, I saw a k.d. lang CD. Its title was *Drag,* and k.d. lang appeared on its cover in a pinstripe suit jacket, silk cravat, and pinky ring.

Is that a *man* . . . a *wo*-man? I thought.

Indeed she was, and I found her incredibly attractive.

I was wildly excited to be, well, wildly excited.

After all this time, Tilda Swinton had some company. Finally, she did.

K.D. LANG AND Tilda Swinton served the same overall purpose, but my mind approached them both in different ways. I would masturbate to Tilda Swinton, but only in the context of *Female Perversions.* I would recall my favorite scenes, and those alone would do the job.

With k.d. lang, however, I would picture her and me together. No longer the voyeur, I was now a leading lady.

My k.d. lang fantasies would always take place in a so-phisticated bar. The conversation would always start with k.d. lang asking me if I was thirsty.

"As a matter of fact, I am," I'd say.

Then our environment would shift to an altogether different room that, for one reason or another, was decorated in an African safari theme. Once there, k.d. lang and I would begin aggressively humping as a precursor to compassionate, unintimidating oral sex.

Now, a lady simply does *not* masturbate to Tilda Swinton and k.d. lang without starting to wonder if perhaps there isn't a bit of the lesbian about her after all. The fact of it felt significant. However, it also felt significant that I wasn't attracted to any women I actually knew. Or met. Not ever. I had a particular taste for a particular type of dapper-butch lady and these types were not out wandering the streets of my Midwestern suburb. The lesbians I knew were Alison and Emily, who, while admirable in the aforementioned ways, were not to my physical taste. So too were there gentlewomen at my high school who I thought might be of a similar persuasion. But they were too . . . "granola" (I think is the word) for my liking. Where real life was concerned, I remained attracted exclusively to men. I'd outgrown my interest in the phallic vegetable, but a well-articulated male crotch was still the thing to turn my head.

The situation was perplexing.

AGE 4

The Soldier

In September of my eighteenth year, I moved to New York City for my freshman year of college. I brought with me a desire to dominate the Broadway stage, as well as a more latent interest in some real-life lesbian encounters. I hoped the city's bustling streets and homosexual-friendly acting classes would present me with a bevy of dapper-butch options. A Tilda or k.d. doppelgänger. Someone equally manly. But not, you know, a man. I hoped to meet a woman of this description and to make of her a ladylove. For to begin my lesbian exploits while I was in *college*? While I was in *New York*?

I could think of nothing more unique.

The one hint of potential came from Leah, a young lady in my Level 1 Emotional Arcs class. She looked like a tiny Tony Danza, and the first time I saw her I thought, How 'bout you and I head to Meow Mix for a round of Shirley Temples? How 'bout we go figure out what's what?

The sad thing, though, was that in reality, I could not follow through.

At the root of my k.d. lang fantasies was this idea that *she'd* come on to *me*. Ideally, in a sophisticated bar. I had no real interest or ability in initiating flirtation myself, be it in an acting class or dormitory cafeteria. So it was that Leah and I fell into the standard friendship of all college freshmen in New York: we discussed how the city had changed us.

"The other day, I walked down *Fifth Avenue*, Leah. At *night*," I might say. "That sort of thing changes a person."

Leah and I would sit together and talk at lunch, and then at night, or rather, once every few nights, I would masturbate to the idea of her in a pinstripe suit, seducing me.

Where once were two, there were now three: Tilda. k.d. Leah.

I SPENT THOSE first few months of college wondering if somehow, some way, something might actually happen between Leah and me. She was not a likely possibility, but she was at least a *more* likely possibility than either Tilda or k.d. I wanted to measure an actual lesbian experience against my various heterosexual carryings-on. For I did carry on, as it were, heterosexually. There weren't a lot of opportunities, but there were some. I met a guy to whom I eventually lost my virginity. However, he had a penis so big, I feared I would die, and this, in turn, prompted me to limit all future hetero experiences to bases one through three. Not forever, of course. But for a while.

On the subject of these experiences, I'd like to say that each one felt correct. That's talking in terms of biology. However, they also felt mostly underwhelming, and this, too, fueled my lesbian curiosity. I'd held out hope that Leah might be the woman to help me work through these various issues, but then one afternoon she and I ran into each other on the street and hugged hello, and I felt the wider-than-a-mile straps of her brassiere beneath her shirt. And I thought, NOPE. I CANNOT DO THIS. I CAN'T BE TAKING OFF ANOTHER WOMAN'S BRA.

It was all so confusing! If a woman masturbates to Tilda Swinton and company, isn't she surely a lesbian? And yet, if she's repelled by reminders of the breasts with which she'd engage, isn't she most surely *not*?

I decided to ask someone about it. I had a new friend, Glen, who, like Leah, I'd met in my Level 1 Emotional Arcs class. He too was homosexual, and thinking he might offer me some insight, I took him out for pizza.

"I think I might be gay," I said.

Glen looked up.

"You're not," he said. "You're in New York; you *wish* you were gay. But you're straight. Like, *straight*. I mean, if I saw a vagina, and then I saw a penis go *into* that vagina, that is your level of straightness."

"But I masturbate to Tilda Swinton," I said.

"I masturbated once to Diane Lane. And what am I?

Not gay?" Glen raised his hands to draw attention to this pair of vintage day gloves he had on. "No. I *am* gay. I'm a gay man who, for one reason or another, decided to try something new."

"But I mean, like, a lot," I said.

Glen thought for a moment. "So it's not that you *have* masturbated to Tilda Swinton, it's that you *masturbate*. Presently."

"Yes."

"Exclusively to Tilda Swinton?"

"Three times out of ten."

"And what about the other seven?"

"It alternates between Leah from Level 1 Emotional Arcs, k.d. lang, and Tilda."

"And no men? Not ever?"

"Not really. Maybe like once every few months John Stamos pops in. Or an anonymous set of broad shoulders."

"But have you ever munched box?" he asked.

"No," I said.

"Kissed another woman?" he asked.

"No," I said.

"And so, do you, like, want to?" he asked. "Do you genuinely want to?"

I thought for a moment. I said, "I guess it's more that I, like, *want* to want to."

Glen nodded.

"Right," he said. "You're straight. As for the masturbation business, I think it's just that you're, like, connecting with female arousal. So it's sort of like, you don't *want* the box so much as you're identifying *with* the box."

"That sounds . . . right," I said.

"Because it is," he said.

My conversation with Glen left me feeling disappointed. I would've liked to have had my lesbian streak confirmed as lesbian-*ism*. Or, better yet, to have been deemed that rarest, most magical of unicorns: the True and Genuine Bisexual. Alas. Now I had the sense that I was neither.

TIME PASSED, AND I accepted the reality. I had infrequent, exclusively hetero engagements. I made a point of having full-on intercourse again. This second time and second partner made the experience, as a whole, seem less traumatic. It led to more times with more partners, each one of whom fell along a spectrum: from *good-to-the-point-of-obsession-worthy* to *just-do-it-so-they'll-go-away* grotesque. Despite where along the spectrum each occasion fell, they did all feel . . . right. And that, again, is talking in terms of biology. It was not my dream scenario, but there wasn't much that I could do about it. I rarely met a woman in person to whom I was genuinely attracted, and on the biennial occasions when it actually happened, the lady in question wouldn't pay me any mind.

Such was my real-life situation. As for my fantasy-life situation, Tilda, k.d., and Leah had, by this stage, all started feeling out of date. Ineffective. Stale. I let them drift further and further away until they reached the hinterlands, the Island of the Misfit Masturbation Fantasies, that sad but special place where out-of-use erotic dreams go to pass their final days. I replaced the old standbys with visuals and/or other fantasies that felt more current: Matt Damon as Jason Bourne. Some random stuff I'd seen on HBO's *Real Sex*. The *Real Sex* stuff did involve women sometimes, but by now I knew better than to attach much significance to that. I had grieved the loss of my potential lesbianism, lowered my standards, and hoped for something new. Something less: *one* evening's worth of experimentation at *any* point before I died. The prospect of lesbian experimentation was not as exciting to me as true, authentic lesbianism, for I was older now and out of college. I had absorbed the information that experimentation would never prove as attention-getting as lesbianism itself.

A painful truth, yes, but not insurmountable. One just adjusts her expectations: If you cannot have the whole hog, well, then you take what you can get of her vagina. If only just once. If only for the night.

AGE 5

The Justice

By the fall of my twenty-fourth year, I had graduated college and was in the midst of a three-month stint as a glorified busboy at an upscale restaurant. I wore a bow tie while employed, and shouldered the primary responsibility of serving rolls to customers. This sounds easy enough, but in the spirit of upscale service, I was expected to serve these rolls with fork and spoon, and the challenge this posed to my physical dexterity was on par with serving a tray of tennis balls with a pair of chopsticks. In any given shift, I'd catapult two to three into the heads of paying customers.

I was always being glared at by my coworkers, who seemed to think I'd been set down on this Earth for the sole purpose of cramping their fine-dining style.

There was, however, one exception to this rule. The exception's name was Janet.

Janet was the pastry sous-chef. She ate cakes and tarts all day, and yet was tiny like a Kewpie doll: big features on a big head, atop a shapely but minuscule body.

Janet and I were different insofar as Janet enjoyed a decent level of at-work popularity. She was not only tiny like a Kewpie doll, but also sexy like a kewpie doll; if you were into that doe-eyed, small-waisted sort of thing, then yes, you would have thought Janet was sexy. In addition to her winning physical appearance, Janet gave away scraps from her pastry department—misshapen cookies and so on—whenever her fellow staff was hungry.

These factors made Janet a popular lady. She had no real reason to be sympathetic toward me. Nonetheless, the first time she saw me mishandling the dinner rolls, she said, "You need tongs for that, right? It looks really hard!"

And I replied, "Yes! Thank you! It *is* really hard!"

Janet was herself heterosexual, and she'd recently been broken up with by a guy who liked to skateboard. What Janet liked about me, I think, was that I was willing to listen as she obsessed about her breakup.

So I would listen.

And listen.

And listen.

In a different situation I might've had less patience, but as the incompetent roll-chucking busboy, I didn't have much choice. I was desperate for a friend.

Janet and I would go out for drinks after work, and I'd sit and listen as she discussed various self-help platitudes: how it's good to take the road less traveled, how everything happens for a reason.

My mood and energy level depending, I might try to get Janet off the subject of the guy who liked to skateboard, and onto the subject of how likable I was if only you took the time to get to know me. While I was occasionally successful, mostly I was not. Mostly, she'd ignore my attempts and stay on her own favored topics: how times of pain are times of growth, how it's good to stay positive and be brave.

Janet and I drank mostly at dive bars. One night we were at a spot of such description when she chose to read aloud a poem.

"It's called 'Warning,' " she said, and unfolded the piece of paper onto which the poem had been transcribed. Then she started reading:

"When I am an old woman, I shall wear purple."

The poem continued on in this vein, describing all the while the joie de vivre the author would embrace when she was older. The twist at the end was the valuable realization that maybe she, the author, could stand to implement some of that joie de vivre into her *current* life. *Now.* Do you get it? Before it was too late.

The poem had the overall effect of forcing me to consider how I, too, might be entitled to just a bit of joie de vivre, to just little bit more fun.

You are *entitled,* I thought. *Sara Barron: You DE-SERVE it.*

That subtle pat to my own back felt really good, and prompted me to think I liked the poem.

"Wow," I said. "Thank you. That was . . . great."

"It *was,* right?"

"It *really* was."

"I love how it teaches you to just, like, grab life by the balls, you know? I mean, here I am, young and single. It's a wonderful adventure, in its way."

I'd spent plenty of time young and single, and while there *were* occasional fireworks unique to the experience—flushing once a day; un-judged excessive scratching—I'd found it mostly dull. The thing was, though, Janet had just read aloud a poem in a dive bar. A conversation in which I mentioned phrases like "sad reality" or "fundamental solitude" didn't strike me as wise or worthwhile.

"Being single *is* awesome," I told her. "You're going to love it. You're going to grow."

"Totally!" she said. "I feel so, like, hungry for new experience."

I nodded along, mostly in rhythm to Dolly Parton's "9 to 5," which, for one reason or another, was blaring through the bar speakers.

And that's when it happened.

Janet leaned in to kiss me.

I flatter myself to think this part of the story could titillate. On the off chance it does, though, I'd like to point out that, prior to this kiss, I'd eaten a gyro sandwich that caused bloating to the extreme, and that my zipper had therefore created a breath-stopping indentation in the flesh between my navel and pubic bone. Let me also point out that my general vicinity stank of seasoned meat.

Nonetheless, Janet told me I smelled "tasty."

"You smell *tasty*," she'd said.

"Really?" I said. "It's that gyro sandwich, I guess. From Mamoun's."

In terms of the actual kiss, the fulfillment of this long-standing dream, all I can say, really, is that it was . . . pleasant. I'm sorry! I *am* sorry and I *do* wish I could provide a more exciting version of events. But that's just as it was. Pleasant. The all-white chicken of the kissing world. More interesting than viscerally satisfying, I guess, and rather plagued by the problem of high expectations. But I committed nonetheless, and that was thanks largely to our fellow bar-goers. If you yourself are a young woman, and you plan, at some stage, to allow another young woman to have at your bottom lip like it's a pacifier, allow me to recommend doing so in a male-dominated dive bar. The gents in attendance *will* encourage you to carry on.

"Oh, yeah," they'll say. "OOOOOOOOH, YEEEEE-AAAAAAH."

Never before had I been made to feel so alluring, so attractive. Granted, these guys focused mostly on Janet— "Look at the little one! Dude! *Look at the little one!*"—but in a scenario like this, one's desirability has a spillover effect, and that was fine by me. I'm always of a mind to take what I can get.

SEVERAL WEEKS PASSED during which Janet and I hung out and made out, mostly in dive bars. We were scared, I think, to test the true mettle of our physical attraction, to face what would be asked of us in private. Lady-wise—and despite Janet's obvious attractiveness to the average, heterosexual male—I, personally, was not all that attracted to her. I certainly wasn't repulsed. I wasn't even *uninterested*. It's just that I wasn't *compelled*. How I felt about the actual, physical business with Janet, I've thought long and hard about how best to describe it, and the thing to say, I think, is that what I felt about Janet was similar to what I feel, currently, about olives.

I have both ordered and eaten olives for the length of my adult life, and yet I lack a clear sense of whether I actually *like* them. They're always there, olives, always on the menu.

Oooh. Yes, I think, Olives would be tasty.

So then I go ahead and order the olives, and then the olives arrive, and then I eat the olives, and *every* time I do I think, I don't *not* like you, olives. But neither are you *as* delish as I always think you'll be.

The mechanics of making out with Janet were similar, and the fact of this kept us stationed in public, in various Greenwich Village dive bars, for the length of our romantic courtship. It lasted one whole month. Lacking pure desire, we needed some other effective motivation, and I was of the opinion that the continued attention from surrounding male bar-goers did an excellent, substitute job.

I also liked having a secret. I didn't keep *Janet* a secret.

On the contrary, I debated buying a pocket-sized foghorn so that I could adequately advertise the news: HEAR YE, HEAR YE! I HAVE MADE OUT WITH A WOMAN. WHAT'S THAT? YES. I AM OPEN AND I'M WILD.

Between us, however, Janet and I said nothing about it. There was no "So: What's all *this* about? Why did *we* start making out?" No discussion of how inexperienced we both were in these, the Sapphic arts. Our conversations were as they had always been: Janet would discuss how she liked being single, how happy it made her. I'd opt *not* to point out that rambling on about how happy you are serves only to convince the world you're repressed and depressed, both. I'd just nod in agreement, maybe mention the ways in which my service skills had markedly improved. Then at a certain point, we'd kiss.

I found it weird—I *find* it weird—the lack of conversation to address the thing between us. But the weirdness lent an air of mystery to the proceedings, and the air of mystery lent it an air of excitement.

Well, show me something exciting, and I'll show you something that's ready to break.

JANET AND I had been at it for two weeks, maybe three, when I noticed our routine had already gotten boring. I felt it internally myself and I knew that Janet felt it too. She'd gotten into this habit where, in the last seconds before a make-out, she would sigh.

And this was not a sexual sigh. This was a rallying energy sigh.

Perhaps I should have been offended, but I was not. I understood on a visceral level where Janet was coming from. The pressure we felt to kiss in public was now akin to the pressure one associates with having to floss.

I really ought to do this. But I do not want to do this.

We were mere days away from ending it. Whatever *it* was.

But then: we did not.

Because then: we got a big shot of adrenaline.

ON TUESDAY, JANET heard through the grapevine that the guy who liked to skateboard had gone and got himself a girlfriend.

On Wednesday, Janet barreled toward me at the start of the Wednesday-night shift.

"Look," she said. "I've been thinking about it, and I think tonight's our night."

"For . . . ?" I asked.

I saw a tremor in her hand. Inadvertently, it shook the powdered sugar off the doughnut she was holding.

"*Us,*" Janet answered, "to, you know, skip the bar. I mean, I was thinking . . . you could . . . just . . . come-homewithmeinstead."

It's a jarring shift, from tipsy French kissing to sober conversation about implicit nakedness and oral sex. But grief caused by an ex-boyfriend who's moved on, this must be managed swiftly and with a strong hand.

I understood that, and obliged.

"Oh," I said. "Okay."

"Really?" said Janet.

"Yes," I said.

"Great," she said. "Well, then. Right. I guess I'll just . . . buy us a bottle of wine. We'll drink it, and . . . just . . . see. We'll just . . . see . . . what happens."

AGE 6

The Pantaloon

Spring of my twenty-fifth year, my friends, and here is exactly what happened: Janet and I ran the bases. WE

RAN THE BASES. Never in my whole entire life have the minutes passed so slowly; imagine sprinting on a treadmill with a backpack filled with dumbbells, for that is the speed at which time passed as I tried to please my girlfriend Janet. It went on for . . . gosh. I don't even know how long. How long are the minutes before you shit yourself in public? How long the minutes before he *finally* texts you back? Things went on for ages, is my point, until finally Janet delivered unto me the most disheartening tap to my shoulder I hope ever to receive. So I stopped. I looked up.

"That's fine," she said. "That's . . . plenty."

"Oh," I said. I sat up.

"Do you . . ." asked Janet, ". . . want me to . . . ?"

"No," I said. "I'm good."

I lack the self-esteem to be sexually demanding. My feelings on the matter go something like *I don't want it if we have to talk about it*. I mean, I like to talk, but just not about, (a) other people's vacations, or (b) what's about to be done to me sexually.

Key word "about."

HERE, I MUST stress: It's not that the *experience* was awful, it's that *I* was awful *at* the experience. These sorts of oral extravaganzas in which we humans engage are occasionally pleasurable, but always ridiculous, and that's under the best circumstances. Experiment on a person for whom you're not biologically programmed, and Godspeed. Because you'll need it. There's no hope of those aspects that do occasionally make it better: getting lost in the moment, getting told you're adept. Nothing so fortifying will occur. You'll only be trapped and alone, plagued with the backbreaking sense you're doing something at which you're really—like, *really*—inept.

AGE 7

The Second Childhood

It was fall, now, of my twenty-fifth year. And was I "good," really? Was I satisfied in the way I claimed to be when Janet asked? Maybe I was, since, well, they say failure isn't the absence of success so much as it is the absence of having tried, at least once, to eat pussy. So I'd tried. I'd run the bases and struck out.

It was difficult, afterward, for Janet and me to look each other in the eye. We did force ourselves to hang out a few more times, but with everything sexual having happened between us, the tension was gone. There wasn't much *there* there. Work became awkward, as you might expect, so thank god I was somewhat briskly fired. It was two weeks after my final encounter with Janet, and I'd been assigned a tableside fish fillet. However, I wound up accidentally stabbing the customer for whom I was doing the fillet *with* the fillet knife. It was just a little nip in the shoulder, really. Nonetheless, I lost my job.

After that, and despite the occasional text, I never saw Janet again.

MY REAL-LIFE LESBIAN encounter had been a failure insofar as it had neither confirmed me as a lesbian nor made me feel adept in the art of experimentation. But rather than let this lack of success motivate me to try harder and better a second time, I chose to let it close a door.

Good-bye, gay, I thought. You were fun, and you were wild, but you were sadly not for me.

The closure felt good, in its way, but it also created a hole.

What would make me cool if not my inauthentic gayness?

And, well, I don't mean to sound too sexual about it, but this hole was a big hole. This was a hole I'd need to fill.

Part II

Renegade

5

Alcoholics Accountable

Prominently displayed on my parents' living-room mantel is my fifth-grade school photo. It's terribly unflattering, but my mother insists on keeping it up.

"It's not that you look cute," she says. "It's just that you look happy."

This much is true. My smile demonstrates the sort of enthusiasm commonly associated with Mormons or Down syndrome. The waistband of my jeans is visible because the way I wore them at the time made it more of a nipple-band, really, than anything relating to a waist. As for my cheeks, they look fat enough to sit on.

Throughout my adolescence, I saw this version of myself more than any other. It left me with the overarching sense that I could stand for some roughening up. I didn't want an authentically challenging experience; I wanted a *veneer* of coolness, a lick of the mysterious about me.

The need had fueled my Sapphic desire for years, and as that desire waxed and waned, I searched for a workable substitute. Something that would project a dark side lurking just below the surface. Which was ironic, actually, because I do *have* a dark side. The problem, though, is that it presently involves peeing in cups in the middle of the night so as to avoid getting up and going to the bathroom.

Such behavior may be darkly slothful, but it does not provide the best fabric out of which to fashion the veil of one's mystery.

"And what about you?" asks a future suitor. He's been drawn in by my unmistakable something. What it is, he knows not. All he knows is that as far as I'm concerned, he smells danger. Complexity. A hypnotically erotic edge. "You're so . . . mysterious," he says. He leans in closer. "I want to know you. *Really* know you."

I inch closer to him. There's a brushing together of knees.

"I pee in cups sometimes," I say. "I do it when I'm tired."

I understand this to be a less than ideal response, evoking a woman Truly Disturbed rather than Alluringly Troubled, and that's not what I was going for. I wanted something in the neighborhood of a Sexy Idiosyncrasy. A head-turning aspect, but one that did not evoke an image of me in a diaper. I was a teenager at this point in my story, and my lesbian aspirations were not looking promising. They'd done nothing in terms of helping me seem *as* enthralling as I would've liked, so I forged ahead with another, better option: I would experiment with alcohol and drugs. I would drink it, and do them. I would seem wild and unique.

I ARRIVED AT New York University in the fall of 1997. Within a month, I attended one of its famously pathetic

sorority parties. God bless my alma mater: Its theater program might waste your money like every under-eye cream
I've ever tried, but its Greek system is one of the worst in
the country. If you join, you *will* be laughed at.

I never drank in high school, owing to a lack of social invitations and a fear of projectile vomit. Once I hit
college, though, I did as young gals do and harnessed a
sense of adventure. I purchased a tube of dark lipstick
and a Blackstreet CD. I told my newly minted friends
and put-upon acquaintances, "Hey there. I'm looking to
party."

I did this for one whole month until finally I heard
about the aforementioned sorority party. I decided to attend, and spent the week leading up to it doing dexterity
exercises in my dorm room. I did wall-to-wall sprints. I
deep-lunged. I quad-stretched. I made an effort to ensure
that if someone did throw up in my general vicinity, I'd be
nimble-footed enough to steal away.

My overall thinking was that the vomit risk was worth
it for the revels that awaited. I'd never been to an alcohol-
laced party before, but I *had* seen a few John Hughes films.
I hoped to go to the party and meet a beefcakey guy who
hoisted girls up above his shoulders. Who'd hoist *me* up
above his shoulders.

"Put me down!" I'd yell.

"Only if you do a shot!" he'd yell back.

So I'd do a shot. And then another. And another.

"You're *crazy*!" he'd shout. "Most girls can't handle
their liquor!"

"But *I* can," I'd say.

"Yes. *You* can," he'd say. "You're a real special lady."

This, in all likelihood, would be the beginning of a
mostly physical relationship in which I'd use the beef-
cake for his body but keep him at arm's length. The new

coolness I possessed from drinking would imbue me with that specific and awe-inspiring skill.

I attended the sorority party with a young lady named Melanie whom I'd met in a freshman-year acting class called Masks of Commedia. Pre-party, Melanie and I had dinner in our dorm's cafeteria. It was during this time that I carbo-loaded so as to prep my body for proper alcohol absorption. I ate one sesame bagel and two plates of refried beans. Having finished, I removed the napkin I'd tucked into the collar of my delicate chemise. I looked Melanie in the eye in much the same way Jennifer Connelly looks Russell Crowe in the eye in the movie *A Beautiful Mind*. I'm referring to that scene in which she says, "I need to believe . . . that something extraordinary . . . is possible." I conveyed a fear of the unknown, I like to think, but also hope. *Hope*. Of meeting men who hoist women up above their shoulders. Of men who get you drunk but make you feel understood.

"We *can* do this," I told her. "I truly believe that we can."

Melanie and I arrived at the sorority party at nine p.m. on a Friday night. I had expected it to take place in some attractive Greenwich Village brownstone, and that is because I thought the sorority scene was made up of refined and wealthy ladies.

Instead, though, it took place in a run-down apartment building just east of Union Square. A total of eight sisters lived on the first and second floors, and to host their party they used their individual apartments, the stairwell *between* the apartments, and, finally, the ground floor entryway. So when you walked in, you walked *in*.

When *I* walked in, the process of doing so felt rather like passing from the natural world, where there was fresh air and reasonable human behavior, into an insane

asylum designated for the treatment of grubby, promiscu-
ous women. People were screaming and flying every which
way. There were indeed a handful of beefcakes, but in person the smell of their cologne was just too much to bear.
My left arm knocked into one of them at one point, and
instantly my hives sprang up.

The experience gave me a sense of not belonging, and
Melanie made it all worse by abandoning me upon entry
to chug a monstrosity called a "forty-ounce beer." She
chugged three in a row before meandering along to the
sorority's mascot, a jumbo stuffed-animal panda. Melanie
straddled the panda, then dry-humped the panda. At that
point, I knew I'd have to soldier forth alone.

I knew I *had* to do what I was *there* to do.

I escorted myself to the bar.

I say "bar," although it is perhaps better described as
a filthy kitchen counter stocked with bottom-shelf booze.
In order to serve myself, I had to squeeze between two
couples that were both French kissing. I was about to tap
one of them on the shoulder to ask them to move, but before I had the chance, one of the young ladies jerked out of
her embrace so she could projectile vomit.

The vomit went *everywhere*. Everywhere except on
me, that is! I used my newfound strength and dexterity
to propel myself at top speed out of the kitchen in the
first-floor apartment, up through the stairwell, and into
the kitchen of the second-floor apartment. There, I found
another filthy counter stocked with the identical bottom-
shelf booze. From the options available, I chose a festive-
looking punch for the singular reason that it smelled like
suntan lotion. It reminded me of a sunny day at the beach,
which, in turn, helped calm me down after seeing someone vomit. The punch tasted like cough syrup mixed with
gasoline. It wasn't great. But it was . . . doable. So I parked

myself in the beanbag chair beside its serving bowl. And I began to drink.

Over the course of the next hour I did so steadily and with negligible interaction from fellow partygoers. At one point I tried stretching my legs out for a more flattering presentation of my figure, but this just caused one of the perfumed beefcakes to trip over my foot and yell, "Watch your fucking feet!" So then I tucked them in again.

I thought, *Sara, you can work with this. Just look prettily forlorn.* The problem with that, though, was that while my face does have its workable angles, Attractive Sadness isn't one of them. If I look forlorn, I just look puffy and deranged. So I kept my face in neutral. If I were to lure in any bait, I'd have to do it with my drinking.

So I drank.

And I drank.

And I drank.

I drank steadily for a total of two hours. After two hours, I was drunk. I thought, Oh, okay. So this is drunk. I felt confused and a little bit sick. Furthermore, I had finally accepted that no one was en route to find my solo drinking sexy. So I pushed myself up out of the beanbag chair and hobbled out the front door and into the stairwell. This should not have been that big a deal, but I'd lost the ability to balance, and to make matters worse, I'd worn a high peep-toe heel for my exciting evening out. Walking normally when sober took some effort. Walking normally when drunk for the first time was simply not an option.

I hobbled toward the staircase, then down the staircase. I made it halfway before I tripped and fell. Which is to say, I didn't walk the rest of the way down the stairs, so much as I *flew* the rest of the way down the stairs. Lucky for me, an emaciated sister was there to break my fall. She'd been standing at the bottom.

"AHHHHHH!" she screamed.

She was awfully loud for someone so teeny-tiny.

So I apologized, like you do, and seeing as how our bodies had landed such that I appeared to be mounting her from behind, I tried to make a joke.

"Buy a gal a drink first, right?" I tried. But the sister was not amused.

"What the *fuck*?" she screamed.

And then I farted in response. It was not intentional. It was merely the choice my body made on my behalf.

The sister screamed again.

"She's farting!" she screamed. "*On* me!"

"Not technically," I said. "Technically, I'm farting *above* you."

One of her male contemporaries charged over and grabbed me by the collar of my delicate chemise.

"You're outta here," he said. "That shit was disrespectful."

I'm not convinced a person does himself a favor by mentioning the word "respect" at a sorority party. He, my molester, held me by the collar of my delicate chemise while the sister lay at our feet huddled in the fetal position. Beside us stood a young woman who'd removed her own brassiere so she could use it as a toilet. People were *applauding* in response, and, I'm sorry, but my feeling is that if one woman is allowed to urinate into her own brassiere—and believe you me: I am *glad* that she is—then another woman should *not* be chastised for a little toot. A little root-toot. A little trumpet de la rumpet.

I made the choice not to argue about it, however, as I was too afraid of my molester. I just asked him—nicely—to please let go of my collar. I tried, for the sake of a smooth exit, to tell him I was sorry.

"I am sorry," I said, and then turned to the sister. "And to you, miss: I am sorry."

Having apologized, I took off my high peep-toe heels

and made my way out the front door. I wasn't wearing socks or pantyhose, but I figured I could walk barefoot the ten minutes it would take to get back to my dorm.

As I walked, I reflected.

I had tried getting drunk—I was still *currently* drunk—and yet I had not been sexily hoisted nor perceived as a lady of wild taste and ability. All I'd been seen as, really, was a woman who farted on better-looking women. And where was the coolness in that? It was mysterious in its way, and possessing of a certain level of darkness, but it was nonetheless the wrong variety of both. Mysterious like *I talk to myself while I shit.* Dark like *I pee in a cup when I'm tired.* It wasn't any inch of what I wanted.

To compound the issue I couldn't relax for so much as an hour once I got home before I myself had to vomit. I threw up in my awful freshman toilet in my awful freshman dorm. As I did, I thought, This is fucking disgusting. I'll never drink like that again.

It's a common enough promise for someone in a regretful situation, but the noteworthy thing here was that I meant it. I never drank like that again. From that day forth—from the moment I left that sorority party—I always drank in moderation. I established a system. I was surprised to see it worked.

Several weeks after the sorority party I was invited to another party thrown by a fellow acting student. Determined not to repeat the trauma from those weeks before, I went out the afternoon of the party and bought myself a stopwatch. I planned to use the stopwatch to keep track of my drinking. I would allow myself one drink per hour, for up to four hours. I would use the stopwatch to time the intervals. I would stock up on bagels prior to the party for proper alcohol absorption, and each time I had a drink, I'd eat a bagel.

What this all meant, then, was that I attended this second party wearing a stopwatch, as well as a backpack that was large enough to carry many bagels. It didn't help me look cool or mysterious, although I nonetheless tried acting cool *and* mysterious. When my stopwatch beeped, I tried turning it off in a "Bond, James Bond" kind of way. When it was time to eat a bagel I tried doing so daintily, in the fashion of an alluringly troubled woman of mystery.

I had this sneaking sense, though, that my efforts weren't successful. At the second party someone said, "Cool backpack," and although I said, "Thank you," I did also intuit that what he meant, really, was, "That is not a cool backpack."

Then someone else said, "Oh. Hey. Where did you get that bagel," and I said, "I brought it in my backpack."

And he said, "Do you have any more? I'm totally starving."

And I said, "I *do* have *several* more. But I have to eat them all."

"You have to eat them *all*?"

"Yes. I have to eat them *all*. I don't like . . . Ooops! Sorry. That's my stopwatch. I can have another drink."

There was nothing cool about this situation as a whole, nor the conversation in specific. Neither parties nor alcohol were helping me look cool. They were rather like a drought to the tiny garden of my mystery. It seemed I'd have to find another way.

6

The Boogie Rhythm

A-toot, a-toot, a-toot diddelyada, toot.
He blows it eight to the bar, in boogie rhythm.
—THE ANDREWS SISTERS

I'd like, for a moment, to discuss the problem of my gas.

I fart with unimaginable frequency and force. That said—and before venturing further—I'd like to acknowledge the philosophical divide.

There are two schools of thought when it comes to flatulence.

"Farts are funny," says the first, propagating the belief that although farts are gross and immature, they are nonetheless amusing.

"Farts are awful," says the second. "They're the easy and pathetic jokes of those with nothing else to say."

It wouldn't stand me in good stead to pretend I don't lock horns daily with issues of originality, with the issue of being disgusting. I acknowledge those components. It's just, I still think farts are funny.

I have always been a problematic farter. My need to fart is constant, and has given me the lifelong sense that I live on borrowed time. *How long until I fart again? How long till that next bomb goes off?* It's a sense of impending doom, and it's with me every second that I'm not alone.

As a kid, I'd overhear complaints of surrounding adults: "That kid just farted. She just farted *loud*, and then kept right on walking." I spent my high school years muscling my anus shut, suffering gas pains that felt (I'd later learn) like exploding ovarian cysts. As an adult, I've been prevented from doing yoga. It's simply too dangerous doing ass-in-air stretches in public.

It is not an issue of what makes it better or worse. It is not like, *Oh, I'll just lay off the broccoli.* The solution is not simple. The problem is never *not* there. Like the stalk is to the broccoli, farts are part of who I am.

My close friends know about my problem, and have, at different stages, described the sound of my emergent gas in different ways. I've been told, "You sound like a screaming ibex," "You sound like an Austrian man blowing an alpine horn," "You sound like a dirt pig who is retarded."

While the sound is impressive, it's got nothing on the odor.

One time I ate an entire fried onion and then went to visit my friend Maggie. While together, I farted nonstop for three hours.

"You smell INSANE," she'd said. "It's like mold and milk have been left to brew in some dank, dark space, and that dank, dark space is your body. I mean, your farts don't even smell like farts, really, so much as they smell like . . . *decay*."

"And sulfur?"

"Yes. There's a sulfur component as well."

AS TO MY point about the philosophical divide, some friends find this funny, while others find it gross. My friend

Kate and her husband, Chris, for example, find me really gross. I spent this one Labor Day weekend with them in a hotel room in the Hudson River Valley. We'd chosen a room with a balcony and two double beds—one for them and one for me—and although we had an okay day of it, I ruined our night with my gas. It was so profoundly bad that Chris and Kate made the eventual decision to pay for a rollout mattress. They put it on the balcony and made me sleep outside.

I had no problem with this course of action. I remember what I smelled like on that day, and it was frankly fair enough.

My issue was just that I thought Kate, Chris, and I should have been able to laugh about it the following morning.

But instead they acted pouty.

"You guys, *what* is the problem?" I asked. "Why are you still in a mood?"

"Because you ruined the hotel room, okay?" said Chris. "Even after you left, it was gross."

Then Kate piped in.

"Honestly, Sara. It was like you rubbed your gas *up* in the fabric or something."

"Yeah, well, I didn't, okay? I did not *rub* my farts *up* in the fabric."

"You know what I mean."

"No, *you* know what *I* mean."

The three of us did not travel together again.

WHILE THE FRIENDS who find it gross can be a challenge, the ones who find it funny are a joy. My friend Rachel, for example, finds it really funny. My friend Rachel is a joy. I've known her since high school, and back in 1995 she made a point of telling me how much she loved it when I farted. She told me never to hold back. She said, "I'll plug my nose if I have to. I just love how hard it makes me laugh."

"*I* love how it hard it makes you laugh," I said, and happily obliged. There was one occasion in particular where Rachel and I were sitting in her bedroom when I felt an explosion en route. I made the choice to let it fly and, if I may say so myself, it was a standout—a real champion—lasting five seconds, and sounding rather like a small machine gun. Rachel laughed hysterically, which made me laugh hysterically, which, in turn, forced the rapid-fire gas out for a victory lap.

This time, though, it emerged in perfect rhythm with my belly laughs:

Ha *fart*! Ha *fart*! Ha *fart*! Ha *fart*!

Rachel laughed harder, which made me laugh harder, which made the cycle carry on for another thirty seconds.

It was a sweet exchange made even sweeter when Rachel's dad called up from downstairs.

"Rach!" he called. "Can you check if the dog took a dump? Something down here smells disgusting!"

It took ten minutes following Rachel's father's request before either she or I had the necessary breath to speak. When finally we did, Rachel lifted her hand to her face. She wiped at her tears. She said, "Your ass-reach is *so . . . wide*, my friend. You *are* the farting master."

IT IS NOT just friends who know about my problem. Boyfriends also know. The issue's too pervasive for them not to. The time always comes when I have to lay it out. I'll say, "I am going to fart," and then I'll fart, and then I'll say, "Yes. So I have farted." This will then segue into a monologue about the extent to which I am plagued by my riotous ass. It's a horrible burden, but at the same time it's an effective bellwether for the relationship itself. If the boyfriend answers, "Oh! Thank *God* we're at that stage!" that means he and I will grow closer. But if, conversely, the boyfriend acts bewildered, that means I've kicked us onto borrowed time.

I had a boyfriend named Jon from '05 to '06, who fell into the first of these two groups. When I told him of my gift, he said, "Well, the thing is, I can top that. I am able to fart . . . *on command.*"

"Really?" I said. "Well, okay. So then fart on command."

"Fart *with* you, you mean?"

"Fart with me, I mean."

And then: *He did.* Jon farted *along with me.* It was . . . wonderful. We felt . . . so close.

Jon was a Boston native and Red Sox fan. During the course of our relationship I lived in a studio apartment in which the bathroom was right beside the bedroom. One morning, I awoke with Jon in bed beside me. I had spent the previous night at a Yankees game. I was not one for baseball usually, but I had accompanied a friend there because it was her birthday—I'd felt atypically obliged—and anyway, in the row in front of us there'd been a gaggle of Japanese tourists. They'd spent the entire game cheering for Hideki Matsui.

"MOTT-SUE-EEEEEEEEEEE!" they had cheered. "MOTT-SUE-EEEEEEEEE! MOTT-SUE-EEEEEEEEEEE! MOTT-SUE-EEEEEEE!!!!!!"

Eventually, the phrase cemented itself in my brain, and that next morning I walked into the bathroom, sat down on the toilet, and went:

"MOTT-SUE-EEEEEEEEE! *Burp* *Fart*"

"MOTT-SUE-EEEEEEEEE! *Burp* *Fart*"

I should clarify: I did not say the words "burp, fart." I made the actual sounds.

I remember the event because the sound *and* smell were the things that woke Jon up that day. He'd said, "First off: fuck the Yankees. Second off: your ass just woke me up."

I DO NOT hide what I am from my boyfriends. I do, though, hide *all* that I am on first dates. It is a challenging task, to be sure. However, after much trial and error I've arrived at a solution to accommodate an inconvenient truth:

You must not hold in your farts if you are dating.

Doing so results only in painful cramps and bloating, and what good does that do in whatever slimming outfit you've got on? So. Your only choice is farting. Not loudly and proudly. But sneakily. Craftily. Cleverly. My time in the field has taught me as much, and—as I am pure of heart and generous of spirit—I will list my tactics here:

1. When asked on a date, suggest an outdoor bar. Rooftops, back patios, and sidewalk cafés. That's if the weather's permitting.
   a. If the weather's not permitting, suggest a crowded bar. You want other people there. You need someone else to blame.
2. Avoid apartments and cars at all costs.
   a. If you cannot avoid a car or an apartment, make sure to keep a window down, or open.
      i. If it's warm outside, great.
      ii. If it's cold outside, say you feel carsick. Or say that you like the fresh air.
   b. If the smell is so intense that the fresh air cannot save you, act as though the stench crept *in*.
3. Gas-X does not work.
   a. Colonic irrigation sometimes does.
4. If, despite your best efforts, you wind up passing gas in the most humiliating way, I do encourage you to

act. Preemptively strike. So you've farted. Fine. Just say, "Wow. Did you just . . . sorry. Never mind." Just like you're appalled. Your date will be thrown off since, as adults, we do not think the one who smelt it *really* dealt it.

Remember—and exploit!—this simple truth.

In conclusion, I'd like to point out that I am not actually pure of heart and generous of spirit. Yesterday, I raced an obese lady for a seat on the subway having figured it'd be good for her to have to stand. I've been feeling guilty ever since, searching for some manner by which to redeem myself. Anyway, I've since admitted farting. I've since explained *stealth* farting. I do believe that, karma-wise, I'm set.

7

The Super Silver Haze

I was not—I *am* not—a true non-drinker. However, my alcoholic consumption is so controlled and infrequent, that
actually, ostensibly, I kind of am. As evidenced by my stopwatch, backpack, and bagels, by my vomiting and farting,
I am poorly suited to drinking and/or partying.

I learned this about myself early at the start of my college career, and while I did accept it, I did not let it lay rest
to any of my old desires. I still craved a means through
which to seem cool and a little bit wild.

In pursuit of my goal, I climbed one rung up the substance ladder. I tried my hand at marijuana.

I'D MADE IT all the way through high school without ever
smoking pot. Because my peers who did, they'd been either

(a) popular, or (b) in possession of a *filthy* head of hair. And I'd avoided the folks with filthy heads of hair, and was myself avoided by anyone/everyone popular.

College, however, changed this situation by widening my social pool. Toward the end of freshman year, I met a guy named Howard through my friend Kate, who, to remind you, is not/was not partial to my gas. Howard was Kate's boyfriend years before Chris, and I absolutely loved him. Howard laughed at my gas and projected an overall air of cleanliness. More to the point, he smoked a lot of marijuana. I felt comfortable around him, so when eventually he offered me a joint, I decided to accept.

I sure was glad I did. Marijuana, as a substance, seemed to suit me. I smoked only joints, though. I never inhaled from bongs. Bongs evoked images of high school students with filthy heads of hair, whereas joints—the physicality of smoking them—made me feel like Lauren Bacall. I liked my pot joints long, so I could hold them like a cigarette. I felt cool in that position, and this coolness helped compensate for the minutes following the inhalation when, without fail, I would eat huge amounts of cereal and suffer minor hallucinations. I would hallucinate any number of the following:

1. That my throw pillow had come to life.
2. That I was a duck.
3. That I was on a boat decorated in an eighteenth-century baroque style.

These hallucinations were pleasant and entertaining, and though I lacked the confidence and dexterity to do what's called "packing a bowl" or "rolling a joint," I nonetheless called myself "a pothead." The term conveyed a wild side that juxtaposed nicely with my Lauren-Bacall-smoking-position elegance. I claimed the title despite never smoking pot more than once a week. I'd find myself in the path of Howard's extra-long joints, and I'd accept them, saying, "Thanks. I'm a pothead. I love a toke."

"Do you mean *to* toke?"

"Yes, exactly."

The process of me actually going out and *buying* drugs was less feasible than the second coming of Christ. Despite my growing experience, I still could not determine how much marijuana was "an eighth," nor interact with dealers of drugs, nor sellers of pipes. Such activities connected me to the illegality of the drug, and despite my previous experience shoplifting packaged ham, illegal activity made me really anxious. I could handle smoking pot in Howard's dorm room. Or maybe—*maybe*—in a park if there were other people smoking too. Handing over a wad of cash, however, in exchange for a tiny plastic bag was another thing entirely. I was too afraid of being caught. I imagined that if ever I let a drug dealer into my dorm room, I'd be arrested by the SWAT team that would follow in behind.

An unwillingness to buy pot and/or its related paraphernalia puts a cap on the seriousness of the relationship that develops between a pothead and her pot. At least, that's how it was in my relationship. The two of us lasted six months.

IT WAS THE summer between freshman and sophomore year of college, and I spent it back home in suburban Chicago perfecting my recipe for chocolate-covered pretzels. The only scheduled break in the routine was a visit from Howard and Kate. They were in the midst of a cross-country summer drive and had included a stop in suburban Chicago as a personal favor to me.

Kate, Howard, and I decided we ought to spend our time together in Chicago doing something festive. We researched various activities and learned that the night of their visit would correspond with the Illinois leg of the Lilith Fair tour. As we all loved the artists of the Lilith Fair, we all promptly purchased tickets.

Kate and Howard were slated to arrive at my parents' house in the early afternoon, but then they hit traffic on the way and arrived three hours late. We had very little time before we hopped back in the car to drive another hour to where the concert was in Tinley Park, and so ran frantically around trying to remember the various items we wanted to take with us.

As we ran, my mother ran around after us. She carried with her a large bag of trail mix.

"Someone take some trail mix!" she yelled. "I made too big a batch!"

So we took the bag of trail mix. We started our drive to the show.

En route, Howard said, "It's good your mom gave us that trail mix."

"Why?" I asked.

"Because," he answered, "we're about to get the munchies."

Slowly, seductively, Howard pulled a bag of marijuana from his pocket. "Sara," he said, "meet the Super Silver Haze."

Howard's hope was that he, Kate, and I would all smoke the Super Silver Haze together. Kate, however, refused. Like me, she was a delicate flower and had suffered hallucinations the one time she'd smoked previously. Unlike me, she hadn't enjoyed her hallucinations. Mine had been almost soothing. They'd felt like, *Oh, I'm a duck. I get to sit in a waterfall,* or *Oh. I'm a rich lady. I own a boat.*

But Kate's had felt otherwise.

"The one time I smoked pot," she said, "I hallucinated that I was stuck in a real-life version of the musical *The*

King and I, and that the king was trying to kill me with a machete."

"Wow. Sounds scary. How did you cope?"

"By climbing in the bathtub. I was in there for hours. I ate *a lot* of pretzels. I wasn't right for days."

With Kate down for the count, Howard focused his marijuana pitch on me.

This is a thing about potheads, or as I am now wont to call them, the Marijuana People. In the style of the truly self-loathing, vast numbers are forever rambling on about the merits of their actions. They are a prideful, proselytizing people. And boy, oh boy, they *love* to dish on product quality.

"The Super Silver Haze is a top-notch product," Howard explained. "It won first place at this year's *High Times* Cannabis Cup."

I had no idea what it was, the *High Times* Cannabis Cup. Nevertheless, the phrase prompted stirrings of nausea within.

"What *is* it?" I asked. "What's it even *mean*?"

"That you will get high," said Howard. "Like, very. Like very, very high."

I looked to Kate for approval. She said, "As someone who shares your sensitivity to marijuana, I hope you'll hear me when I say: I don't think you should smoke this."

Howard scoffed. "Jesus. Chill," he said. "Sara will be fine."

"Yeah. Chill," I repeated. "I'll be fine."

The word "chill" hadn't previously appeared in my personal lexicon, but there I was on a madcap adventure in the fine town of Tinley Park. I figured I'd give it a whirl.

HERE'S WHAT I remember:

That after smoking the Super Silver Haze my head felt fuzzy. I also recall that I was hungry for a hot dog. So I went to a nearby food vendor, and bought myself a hot dog. A jumbo one, as a matter of fact, since being at a concert in this heretofore unknown bit of the Midwest felt like a celebratory occasion. I remember eating the hot dog and thinking, This is *delicious*. I remember looking at my friends swaying in rhythm to Paula Cole's "Where Have All the Cowboys Gone?" and thinking, This is the life. This *is* the life.

That whole scene took all of twenty minutes, at which point I remember feeling like a vise had been placed on my head. I'd returned to Kate and Howard by this point, and I remember saying, "Excuse me. I have to lie down."

"Now?" Kate asked. "Are you sure? I mean, Paula Cole's playing."

"Yes," I said. "I'm sure."

I remember hearing Howard tell Kate, "Maybe she's just hungry."

And I remember hearing Kate tell Howard, "Did you not see the hot dog she just ate? It was, like, *really* big."

And I remember lying down.

HERE'S WHAT I'VE been told happened next:

That I passed out one-third of the way through the show.

I've been told that my body lay sprawled on the grass in an unflattering position. I've been told, "Your belly was out. It was just . . . *all,* like, out."

I've been told I stayed unconscious only briefly, however, before getting up.

I've been told that after getting up, I had renewed energy with which to express a wide range of emotions.

"You told me you loved me," said Kate. "You said that if anyone was ever rude to me you'd 'break all sorts of bottles on their heads.' You were holding a Snapple bottle when you said this, which you then hurled at a nearby garbage can."

I've been told that after hurling the Snapple bottle at the nearby garbage can, the Snapple bottle shattered.

I've been told that, once the Snapple bottle shattered, I did a series of seven deep lunges.

I've been told that *as* I performed each one of these lunges, I yelled out one letter of the word "victory."

I've been told that once I'd spelled out all of the word "victory," I did a cartwheel-into-demi-split.

I've been told that once I hit the demi-split, I yelled, "Oof! My thighs are *tight*!" and that this, finally, drew the attention of Tinley Park Security.

I've been told that as Tinley Park Security approached, I told them, "If you guys gotta problem, you can stick it where the sun don't shine. Hey! Where the sun don't shine means a butt!"

I've been told that despite their attempts to look surly, Tinley Park Security laughed when I said this, and that I clocked their laughter, and then broke into a rousing version of "Let Me Entertain You" from the musical *Gypsy*.

I've been told that after I finished the song, I asked Tinley Park Security, "Do I *seem* like a star? Because I *feel* like a star!"

I've been told that a member of the security team responded, "No. You don't seem like a star. You just seem off your face."

I've been told that I was then dragged toward the exit.

I've been told that Howard and Kate were given the choice to join me or leave me.

I've been told that Howard could not offer an opinion, because Howard, too, was very high.

I've been told that Kate, alone, was forced to decide what to do.

I've been told that what Kate *wanted* to do was lock us both in the car while she returned to the concert to enjoy it on her own.

I've been told that the only reason Kate *didn't* do exactly that, was that she thought we both might vomit.

I've been told she cried tears of frustration.

I've been told she thought, My night's beyond repair.

I've been told that we all left together.

I've been told we missed most of the show.

WE WERE BACK at my parents' house by the time I finally regained consciousness. It happened in the middle of the night, when I was jerked awake by a horrendous wave of nausea. It kept me up for hours, and then at six a.m., I puked.

Kate, Howard, and I had made a standing date for breakfast the following morning. My mother had promised to make us pancakes if we all promised to eat some of her trail mix too. She'd begged us, pretty much, and so we'd felt obliged.

My appetite was back by mid-morning, which was good. Nonetheless, I maintained an overall sense of foreboding. Although I did not know yet what had happened, I knew it probably wasn't good.

Kate, my mother, and I all arrived in the kitchen at ten a.m. Howard, however, was nowhere to be seen.

"So, ladies: trail mix?" asked my mom.

"Thank you, but no thank you," Kate answered, and then she turned to me. She said, "We have to have a talk."

"Now?" I said.

"Now," she said.

"So no trail mix?" asked my mom.

"Sorry, Lynn. No," answered Kate.

"Well, then here," said my mom, and handed Kate a one-pound bag of trail mix. "You can eat it on the road."

Kate thanked my mother for the trail mix. Then, again, she turned to me.

"Go outside," she said, "while I go wake up Howard."

"Outside?" I said.

"Outside," she said. "I think we should go on a walk. We'll go on a *nice* little walk and have a *nice* little talk."

I nodded in agreement, and with an increased sense of foreboding, went to wait outside. Minutes later, Kate arrived with Howard, who looked groggy.

"All right. So let's go," she said. "You'll walk, and I'll talk."

So that is what we did. We walked while Kate talked.

"The first thing I want to say is that I am enraged. And that if I don't express my rage *before* we're in the car, then, Howard, I will kill us. I'll be totally unfocused and I'll drive us both into a pole."

Howard and I both nodded yes. Okay. That all sounds good. Whatever you want, Kate. Whatever you say.

"Do you remember what you did?" she asked.

"Me?" I said.

"Yes, you," she said.

"Well, no," I said. "I *don't* remember what I did. But I *do* remember throwing up. Because I threw up. This morning at, like, six o'clock. And, well, awful, right? You know how much I hate that."

"Poor baby," she said.

"Are you being sarcastic?" I said.

Kate inhaled through her nostrils. She exhaled through her mouth.

"Oh, *yes*," she said. "I *am*."

Kate went on to explain my antics from the night before: the passing out, the belly out, the waking up. The telling her I loved her. The Snapple bottle breaking. The singing, the expulsion. The missing two-thirds of the show.

She chastised Howard for providing the Super Silver Haze, and me for electing to smoke it.

"Do you guys even *know* what I've dealt with this summer?" she asked. "I've watched my grandfather's Alzheimer's advance. I've watched my mother sob in the face of my grandfather's advancing Alzheimer's. I've babysat my nephew, and he's a fucking *asshole,* by the way, because my sister's husband is two hundred pounds of bitterness and unlikability, and he's passed those qualities on to his kid. He's ugly, too, although not overweight. Which *is* good. Anyway, my nephew spits. He's a *spitter*! He spits *in my face*! I've been spit at by my ugly, shitty nephew *all* fucking summer, you guys! And the one thing I had to look forward to amidst it *all,* was a road trip I *thought* would include Paula Cole. But *you, Sara,* collapsed *during* Paula Cole. And you, Howard, could not have been less of a help."

"I'm sorry," said Howard.

"Me too," I said.

And although I was sorry, I was not, like, *crazy* sorry. I thought Kate could've cut me more slack, seeing as how I'd said all that loving stuff about her *while* blacked out. Guilt didn't overwhelm me so much as regret overwhelmed me, and that regret was owed less to Kate than it was to one specific fact that she had shared:

I'd collapsed with my belly "all out."

My belly, exposed, is but a Russian doll of doughnuts: a doughnut in a doughnut in a doughnut.

That other people would have seen it *un*-sucked-in was just too much to bear. It was just so *un*-Bacall.

Kate saw how sad I looked. She sighed and rolled her eyes.

"Jesus," she said. "It's not *that* big a deal. Just don't let it happen again."

I nodded in agreement.

"I won't," I said. "Not ever."

And true to my word, I did not. I did not let it happen again, because I didn't ever smoke pot again. Never ever. Never once. Sure, the drug and I had had our easy start, but the cumulative effect of the vomiting, the minor guilt, and the major regret had proved a powerful means of dissuasion. Pot had robbed me of my sense of self-control, and that's a thing I need in order to act my way around my honest self. Without it, I will not appear naturally cool. I will just fart or puke or sing or lunge, and these actions form a foghorn. They proclaim, "I AM NOT COOL."

Perhaps I should've listened to the foghorn. But people who are cool *never* listen to the foghorn. People who are cool always learn to shut it out.

8

Appetite for Destruction

At the age of twenty-three, I found myself single, as usual, and convinced I would remain so until my early death at fifty-four. The death fixation was owed to a recent annual physical at which I was diagnosed with poor circulation. When I went home to research the condition online, I discovered that one in twenty afflicted *may* die prematurely.

So I was anxious and lonely overall, and one otherwise uneventful afternoon it came to my attention care of an *Empty Nest* rerun that a good way to get a boyfriend was to hang out in a dog park. Dogs, apparently, are conversation starters. And women who own dogs and go the length of engaging with them are, by and large, considered interesting, kind, and attractive.

I didn't own a dog, however, and that is because I take

no genuine delight in the species as a whole. Rather, I feel about dogs as I do about plantar warts: Fun to play with, yes. But at what cost? People run their mouths about unconditional love and what have you, but that's not of interest to me. Not unless the individual in question has the capacity to verbally articulate a thought like, "You are special, Sara Barron."

But just because you don't own a dog, that doesn't mean you can't stand *near* a dog run and *ogle* the dogs. So I packed up a bag of Pepperidge Farm Goldfish, threw on a sundress and a pair of wedge sandals, and walked myself to the one in Union Square. The sundress was to make me look feminine, the heels to elongate my legs, the Goldfish, to solicit canine attention. I hoped to come across as a younger and more comely Bird Woman from *Mary Poppins,* but with dogs instead of pigeons and Goldfish instead of birdseed. I would gain a dog's attention, then trick him into thinking that I cared.

"Hello, sweetheart," I'd say as he groveled at my feet. I would scratch behind his ears, which would be gross, yes, but a necessary part of the performance. "What a good boy. Are those some yummy Goldfish? Do you like those yummy Goldfish?"

His virile owner would approach.

"Wow," he'd say. "He really likes you."

"I like him too," I'd say. "I mean, I love dogs, generally. And dog parks. It's the smell that does it. Of man. And beast. Together."

"I know what you mean. And also, well, I know this is forward of me, but would you like to grab coffee sometime? Maybe take Keaton for a walk?"

"Who's Keaton?"

"My dog."

"Oh, yes. Of course. And I think coffee sounds divine."

So I stood at the fence and started throwing Gold-fish. When the dogs did not respond, I started eating the Goldfish myself. I was getting toward the bottom of the bag, deep in consideration of the merits of cheesy carbo-hydrates, when a man arrived named Charlie. I knew his name was Charlie because he was wearing an oversized polo shirt, and pinned to that oversized polo shirt was a large plastic name tag.

CHARLIE, it read. T-MOBILE REPRESENTATIVE.

Charlie did not appear to have a dog. He was meander-ing around, looking at the women *with* the dogs. He sidled up beside me.

"Dogs . . ." said Charlie. "Right?"

"Right," I answered. "Dogs. They're . . . so friendly. They . . . make such good companions."

Charlie nodded. He said, "That's what I think too."

Charlie and I founded a three-month romance on this, the fact that we both thought dogs made good compan-ions. We shared the requisite attraction, too, of course. Charlie had that attractive urban swagger of someone al-ways in oversized polo shirts and mid-butt-slung jeans. He lived on Long Island with his parents. For our first date, he suggested meeting at his local Papa John's.

"We could grab a pie and head back to my parents'," he'd said. "I know it sounds lame, but the thing is, I've got the basement all to myself. It's big down there. I have a mini-fridge, a couch, and a treadmill."

Papa John's was just the ticket, the worm to my naïve and eager fish. I'd been waiting tables at the time at this upscale pizzeria, and every godforsaken thing was "locally sourced" this, and "house-cured braciola" that; there was one pizza in particular that featured dried fish roe and cheese that smelled distinctly of a human asshole. Peddle enough of that stuff, and I promise: a night at Papa John's will be cause for celebration more than it is a chance to consider where in your life you went wrong.

Charlie and I, once established as a couple, ate Papa John's pizza almost every day. People like routines, and this was ours: Charlie would finish work at T-Mobile, and then we'd meet at Penn Station to catch the Long Island Rail Road back to his parents' house in Huntington Station, New York. We'd order Papa John's, eat it in the basement, have sex, and go to sleep.

You will be *unsurprised* to hear that I gained weight from this routine. I owned a pair of boyfriend jeans at the time that fit more like denim leggings with every passing day. I knew it was happening *as* it was happening, but I couldn't find the will to care.

AN EPISODE OF *Oprah* jumps to mind in which Kirstie Alley examines her relationship with food. Oprah asks, "Why do you use food to avoid feeling feelings? Why don't you prioritize your health?"

And Kirstie Alley answers, "Because I'm always putting other people first."

They go back and forth like this for a while, and then some other stuff happens, and then Oprah surprises Kirstie Alley with a kitchen renovation care of Nate Berkus. The idea is that a more beautiful kitchen will help inspire healthy eating.

The segment ends with Kirstie in tears in her new, fancy kitchen.

"I just want to be good . . . enough," she cries. "Good enough . . . for my kitchen."

I've referenced the clip so that I might compare it to the response *I* had to Charlie's basement. So that you will have the proper context when I tell you: Charlie's basement had a dissimilar effect on me. That is to say, it *inspired* obesity.

There was wall-to-wall blue carpet. Posters of Derek Jeter and Bob Marley Scotch-taped to the wall. There was a TV set and a pleather couch in the center of the room, while the treadmill and mini-fridge had been placed in opposite corners.

I'd be down there and I'd think, The world's a lonely place. I think I'll have more pizza.

Charlie, unfairly, did not gain weight from our routine. He responded to it differently insofar as he started falling asleep during sex. The habit took a month to gain momentum, but once it did, look out: *It did not stop*. There were two weeks over the course of which we engaged in a smattering of intercourse, and Charlie stayed entirely awake for none of it.

"I'm embarrassed," he said.

"Don't be," I said. "I like the chance to pee or watch TV. Honestly, it's fine."

"It's not," he said.

"It is," I said.

"Sara, it's not. I want to apologize. I'm taking you out."

Being taken out was an odd thing to consider in my relationship with Charlie. We only ever appeared "out" together on that stretch of the Long Island Rail Road that ran from Penn Station to Huntington Station. And, of course, the Papa John's.

"Out?" I asked. "What do you mean by 'out'?"

"What do you mean, 'What do you mean?'" he asked. "*I* mean we're going out."

Charlie put his hand in his pocket and pulled out two tickets.

"Are we going to a show?" I asked.

"No," he said. "We're going out for hot wings."

Charlie had purchased two tickets for an all-you-can-eat buffet serving an assortment of hot wings. It was part of a "Hot Wing Festival" taking place at his neighborhood bar.

"And that's not all," he said.

"It's not?" I said.

"It's not," he said.

Charlie then put his other hand in his other pocket. He pulled out two white pills.

"I thought that for dessert we'd do some ecstasy."

"As in . . . the drug?" I asked.

"As in the drug," he answered. "I thought we'd go eat *lots* of hot wings. And then take a walk to this park."

Charlie leaned closer in when he said "this park." He put his mouth against my ear. He said, "And then we'll take our tablets, babe. And then I'll stay awake . . . to *do* you."

MY MOTHER WOULD tell me, as a child, that the only thing she regretted about her marriage to my father was that he never called her "babe."

"Don't get me wrong," she'd say. "I love your father. I know I'm lucky to have a husband who does the dishes as well as all the rest of what I tell him. It's just, sometimes I wish I had one of those husbands who would walk into the kitchen, all five-foot-nine of him, and say, 'Hey, babe! What's the problem with the dishwasher?' And then just *fix* it, you know?"

I was nine and so I didn't. However, the statement repeated over the course of my childhood had left the impression that to land a man who called one "babe" was a rare and precious victory. "A keeper," let's call him, regardless of whether he says, "I'm gonna stay awake to do you." Regardless of whether his polo shirt fits him like a nightgown.

THE ECSTASY WAS a bigger step toward psychosis than I had ever planned to take. I was now several years into the stopwatch-and-bagel-based moderations to my drinking. I had not smoked pot in years. My regimen for substance experimentation had fallen to the wayside simply because I had never stumbled across another opportunity, and I had been too traumatized by my previous experience to aggressively chase one on my own.

And yet now, here one was. Here *he* was, in his basement. In his big ol' polo shirt.

"Ecstasy." I said the word again. "I mean, like, *wow.* Right? Like, *ecstasy.*"

Charlie shrugged. "Yeah," he said. "I thought it'd be fun."

Charlie thought it'd be fun, but my instinct disagreed. My instinct told me that a jump to an ecstasy tablet from my tailor-made drinking regimen was just too huge, the gap too wide. Working against that instinct, however, was not just Charlie, but my still-burning desire to have that bit of edge about me, and that's to say nothing of my new convincing silhouette. I'd put on quite a bit of weight since getting together with Charlie, and while the fact of this was depressing, it was also fortifying. It made me feel, if not resilient, then absorbent. As though my new physique could take an ecstasy tablet and hide it in its far and distant corners.

"Well, then . . . okay," I said to Charlie. "Let's eat some wings. And . . . take some ecstasy."

ONE WEEK LATER, Charlie and I attended the Hot Wing Festival at Punches! bar in Huntington Station, Long Island. While the first hour was fun enough, we got thrown out in the second. Charlie got belligerent on promotional vodka samples, and when the overweight lady bartender cut him off and told him it was time to leave, he screamed, "You're a fat fucking cunt, you know that? You're really fucking fat."

It was awful hearing him talk this way. I mean, I enjoy a joke about incest, rape, farts, Hitler, pedophiles, September 11, Columbine, midgets, bestiality, pediatric cancer, wealthy Russians, spousal abuse, the word "Mongoloid," the mentally disabled, homosexuals, hookers, dead hookers, anything pertaining to Jewish culture, and a large portion of race-related issues as long as the audience for whom the joke is performed isn't entirely white. I like fat jokes too, if I'm being honest. It's just, this wasn't a fat joke so much as it was authentic rage directed at the overweight.

Awful as it was, though, I said nothing to Charlie about it. I didn't want to make the already tense mood even worse. On the contrary, I wanted to ensure we were both in a positive state of mind for the ecstasy portion of events.

Over the course of the previous week, I'd convinced myself I could not only handle the drug but enjoy it. I'd worked myself into a state of genuine excitement. Charlie and I had been together three months by the time the hot-wing festival rolled around and already we were shouldering the dual issues of my weight gain and his sexual sleepiness. We felt similarly ambivalent toward each other, I think. I found Charlie both likable *and* pathetic for his willingness to be with me, and I was pretty sure he felt the same toward me. I liked him fine and hoped to like him more. I had therefore identified the ecstasy as a sexual spark plug. A sexual savior, if you will. Doing ecstasy with Charlie would mean I'd shared something with him that I had shared with no one else. The fact of this would forge a bond between us to make up for the overall lack of chemistry. I would take the ecstasy, and I would do some sexy, crazy thing. In the sand, under the stars, I'd twirl Stevie Nicks–like before the inevitable onslaught of an overwhelming sex drive to facilitate rousing sex with my now highly conscious boyfriend.

HAVING BEEN THROWN out of the hot-wing festival, Charlie and I made our way to "this park." When we arrived at "this park," I noticed a playground, at the center of which was a slide (for babies) with a tree house (for babies) attached to its top. Charlie and I climbed up to the top of this slide for babies, and into the tree house for babies. We did this for the privacy, and despite the fact that the dimensions were such that we could not stand upright.

We sat down Indian-style instead.

Charlie took out the ecstasy tablets. He swallowed his tablet. He fed me my tablet, which, as a process, I did not enjoy. Having it fed *to* me felt rather like living inside a poorly staged version of the musical *Hair*. It felt much more grimy than sexy, and the griminess undermined the excitement I had so far managed to drum up. It undercut it with a strong case of anxiety.

"Charlie," I said. "I am feeling very anxious. Do you hear me? *Can* you hear me? *I AM FEELING VERY ANXIOUS.*"

Charlie had been sitting on the opposite side of the tree house. He looked dazed. He'd told me that yes, he could hear me. He told me to sit back and relax.

I tried doing as instructed, and although I did manage to sit back, I don't think I quite relaxed. I took a few breaths, and over the course of . . . I don't even know how long . . . twenty minutes? Maybe thirty? . . . I swam through alternate waves of nausea and sexual longing. I waited for the waves of nausea to pass, until I was secure in the zone of sexual longing. And then—and even though I lacked the space to stand upright, and even though Charlie himself was now lying on his back, rigid and wide-eyed—I slid toward him on the doughnut-in-the-doughnut of my stomach.

I reached him. I straddled him. I made a polite request for sex.

"Would you like to have sex?" I asked.

"No," he answered. "I feel too depressed. I called that fat girl 'cunt.'"

"You *did*?" I asked.

And not because I myself did not remember. Rather because I wanted Charlie off the subject of his own self-loathing, and onto the subject of wild baby-tree-house sex.

"I did," Charlie said. "I called her a cunt. I told her she was fat."

"Which, okay, was maybe not the *best* thing, but it wasn't the worst thing either. Anyway, would you like to have sex?"

Charlie shook his head. "I'm a loser," he said. "I live in a basement."

I reminded Charlie that it was in this very basement that he had space for a treadmill, a TV, and a mini-fridge. But these facts were cold comfort. He curled up into a ball.

"Will you stroke my hair until I fall asleep?" he asked.

I knew the cause was lost.

"Sure," I said, and did as he'd requested. However, as my own little treat to myself I pretended that it was not Charlie's hair at all, but rather the silky, voluminous chest hair of a handsome Viking.

Charlie required a half hour of hair stroking before he fell asleep. As I'd been straddling him throughout that half hour, my hip sockets felt overstretched.

I dismounted, massaged my hip sockets, and decided to slide down the slide. I took off my pants before doing so, however, for I had Spanx on underneath, and I figured sliding down a slide in Spanx would facilitate a swifter and more adventurous descent.

The only problem with my plan was that I was now a larger lady on a baby slide. So once I was actually on the slide, I traveled mere inches before getting stuck. Nothing a little elbow grease couldn't fix, of course, but I'd been wiped out by my self-administered hip massage. I decided to stay where I was. I stared at the sky for a while. I thought about the Viking with the chest hair. I, too, fell asleep.

WHEN I AWOKE the following morning, the first thing I saw was Charlie, who was perched at the top of the slide. He seemed to have pulled it together. His torso blocked the sun.

"Where are your pants?" he asked. "And why are you sleeping on the slide?"

"I wanted to slide down it," I explained, "and I thought it'd be faster if I wasn't wearing pants."

I paused. Charlie said nothing.

"But then I got stuck on the slide," I continued, "because, well, I'm fat."

"*You're* not fat," said Charlie. "That bartender last night was fat."

"*She* was morbidly obese," I said. "And I am standard-issue fat."

Charlie shrugged. "Here," he said. "I'll push you."

Charlie pushed, although his doing so did not prompt the glorious descent I had imagined. I had to nudge myself the whole way down.

We reconvened at the bottom.

"Wanna come back to my basement?" he asked. "We can order in some Papa John's?"

Strangely, I did not want to go back to Charlie's basement and I did not want to order in more Papa John's. The sentiment surprised me. For I loved Papa John's. And while the same could not be said of Charlie's basement, it could be said that I loved to be *invited* to his basement.

Prior to getting together with Charlie, all I'd wanted was a boyfriend. And then I got one. At a dog run. He'd offered access to his basement, coital time in which to pee and wash my face. What more could I want? What more could I *need*? Why wasn't it enough? Was I afraid? Was I a snob? Was I wrong to turn my nose up at a carpet in a basement?

I was, and had been, ambivalent where Charlie was concerned. And although ambivalence *will* grow into disappointment, the great thing about it is that it's easy enough to ignore. At least for a while. You can distract yourself by eating. You can remember what it's like to be alone. Such techniques are effective, but they are never foolproof. They will not, for example, hold strong for you through ecstasy. Lost endorphins are a pin to their balloon.

"I think I'll skip the pizza," I told Charlie. "I think I'll just go home."

Charlie shrugged. He said, "Okay."

I said, "Okay."

He said, "Do you want to put your pants on?"

I said, "Oh, right. Yes. Of course."

So I put my pants on and Charlie and I walked together to the Long Island Rail Road station. We waited for the train. When finally it came, I said, "Okay, well . . ."

And Charlie said, "Okay, well . . ." and then we kissed good-bye.

I GOT BACK to my apartment and lay down on my bed. Eight hours had passed since I'd taken the ecstasy. Now, suddenly, I felt awfully depressed. By which I mean I felt *so* depressed, and also that it was awful how depressed I felt. But it was only eight a.m. There was still time in the day to turn my frown (as it were) upside down. I thought maybe it'd be good to be alone in my apartment. I thought maybe I'd find joy in tweezing or watching TV. But sequestered as I was, I just kept feeling sad. I just could *not* get off my mattress. I did try a few times, to do some bare minimum activity. To get up and watch TV. The problem, though, was that in order to watch TV, I had to get up and go to my couch. And I could not lie flat on my back on the couch *and* also see the TV.

I felt compelled to be flat on my back.

So I returned to my mattress. I put on a Jewel CD. I played it again and again, and as I did—as time went on—I decided to break up with Charlie. I felt it was time. I just felt *so* low. And if *I* felt so low, maybe Charlie did too. And if Charlie did too, maybe he'd break up with me. And if *he* broke up with *me,* well, I was not equipped to cope.

Charlie called me the following day. When he did, I channeled Jewel.

"These foolish games," I said, "are tearing me apart."

"What?" asked Charlie.

"The foolish games?" I said again. "Are tearing me apart?"

Nothing.

"Anyway," I continued, "*since* they're tearing me apart, I think we should break up."

"Oh," said Charlie. "Well. Okay."

"Okay?" I said.

"Okay," he said.

We shared an awkward pause. We both hung up the phone.

It was summer at this stage, and I lay sweating on my mattress. I took off my Spanx, wiped at my brow, and with the dandruff that accumulates from a week without a shower, formed little thoughts to myself on my mattress, impermanent letters of note.

Dear drugs, please stay away from Sara.
Dear Sara, you must now stay away from drugs.

9

Forever Yours, Flipper

On the path toward artful, attractive rebellion, one must consider a tattoo. Tattoos give their owners a new energy, a sexier aura. Tattooed women have an air about them that says, "I have lived."

We all have, of course, it's just that my unexceptional variation on the verb involved frequent masturbation and a deep-seated fear of throwing up. My history was written in my arch-support sneakers and boot-cut jeans. A tattoo would be a counterbalance.

The impulse to get a tattoo did not come about easily for me. As a child, I found tattoos repulsive. They struck me in much the same way a meth den strikes me now. That is, when I'm watching *Breaking Bad*.

They seemed foreign, dirty, and depraved.

I *think* that about meth dens. I *thought* that about tattoos.

If, as a child, I saw a tattoo, I saw its backstory. I saw the victim strapped into the awful chair, staring down the awful needle. That a person would voluntarily subject herself to such a thing seemed entirely psychotic, and for years I struggled to trust the people who had them. For years, I found these people filthy.

As I got older, however, I outgrew the opinion. I began to feel less afraid of both tattoos and *the tattooed*. This was due in part to the fear swap that occurs as you pass from childhood into adulthood: You get better with things like monsters, the dark, the sense that tattoos are disgusting. In their place, though, comes a flood of other issues: how you'll afford it, that thing on your toe. I went from thinking tattoos were disgusting to thinking they were not so bad to finding them attractive.

There was not a specific moment in which the shift occurred. Rather, there were a few occasions wherein I enjoyed riotous intercourse with gentlemen who had tattoos. This helped me form a new opinion. I began to think tattoos were sexy, and then, eventually, to think that *I'd* be sexy if I had one. Some residual horror surrounded the actual application process, but I chose to ignore it. I thought it'd be worth it for the increased desirability. For *my* increased desirability.

I decided I would get one. Before I did, though, I had questions.

What might I get?

And where might I put it?

And where might I go to get it put?

ON WHAT I MIGHT GET

Because I live alone and am often described by friends and family as "challenging; but not in the way that's that rewarding," I have on various occasions been encouraged to get a pet. People think a dog or cat would do me good, to which I respond, "If by 'dog' or 'cat' you mean 'affordable cleaning woman' or 'Djimon Hounsou blow-up doll,' then yes." Otherwise, I'm not in the market for things that can't converse yet whose vomit I'm expected to dispose of.

I do, however, enjoy animals when they're part of a design aesthetic. Anthropologie sells beautiful bird-shaped coat hooks, for example. A friend's kitchen features swaths of owl-themed wallpaper, and every time I see it I think, What a charming and whimsical touch!

It therefore stood to reason that an animal etched on my body would deliver unto me a vibe that was equally charming and whimsical.

I narrowed the vast kingdom down to one: the dolphin. I liked the dolphin's reputation for intelligence, as well as the fact that they always look as though they're smiling. But then I voiced my idea to various acquaintances and learned the overriding opinion is that dolphin tattoos are moronic.

"Why not just write 'ANUS-FACE' *on* your face?" asked one. "That sends a subtler message."

Another told me I'd be better off shaving my head.

"Really?" I asked, and felt a flutter of excitement. "Would I look like I had cancer, do you think?"

But the friend just shook his head.

"No," he said. "You weigh too much to look like you have cancer. My point is just that a dolphin tattoo is deranged. So if you want to look deranged, then why not shave your head? Aesthetically speaking, it's less of a commitment."

My brother Sam offered yet another perspective: "If someone says 'dolphin tattoo,' the first thing that jumps to mind for me, personally, is a condom."

"As in, you'd find it attractive? You'd want to have sex?"

"No." He shook his head. "More like, 'Dirty hippie. Wrap it up.'"

So I dropped the dolphin idea and went a different route entirely, designing a hieroglyphic-like entity comprised of my mother's initials, L.H.B. It sounds extreme, I know, but at this stage I was willing to do whatever I could to offset her guilt trips:

"You don't call."

"Yes, I do."

"No. You don't. You do not call *enough*. And on those rare occasions when you *do* call, you never talk to me about my health."

"About *yourself*?"

"About my *health*."

"You see a doctor a week, Mom. I just can't keep up."

"And you never visit, either. And *when* you visit, you never rub my feet. You used to rub my feet when you were little. You never do that anymore."

I was at a breaking point, forced to wonder whether etching her initials on my person might not be the way to go. Might not stave her off for a while, express devotion in a manner *not* involving foot rubs.

It seemed like a good idea to me, and so I shared it with my friend Amanda. I've known Amanda since college. The first time we met was in a dormitory hallway and she was wearing a nightgown she'd fashioned into a viable dress with a belt and a series of brooches. Holistically speaking, Amanda is/was informed and creative in the ways of fashion. I did/do value her opinion.

"I'm thinking of getting a hieroglyphic-y tattoo comprised of my mother's initials," I said.

Amanda furrowed her brow.

"Did your mom die?" she asked.

"Excuse me?" I asked.

"*Did your mom die?*" she repeated.

"No," I answered. "You *know* she didn't die. You saw her last week. You told her she needed new jeans."

"She does," said Amanda. "But my point is that you—that *one*—can tattoo someone else's name on your body if and only if that person has already died. Or, alternately, if that person has frequent exposure to gang-related activities."

"What? Really?"

"Yes. Really. Furthermore, you may *not* tattoo someone else's name on your body just because she pays your health insurance bill."

"It was more, like, to get her off my back. She says I don't rub her feet as much as I used to."

Amanda sighed as if to say, *Whaddya do.*

"Regardless, Sara, the bigger issue has nothing to do with gangs, or alive-versus-dead, or foot rubs or whatever. The bigger issue—the *biggest* issue—is your whole my-mom-is-my-best-friend routine."

And therein lay the point. The real point.

I am loath to endure the company of individuals who describe their parents as best friends.

My mom and I are just so *close. She is truly my best friend.*

These declarations seem always laced with undue pride, always rife with subtext.

"*I* value *my* family," says the subtext. "*I* bridge generation gaps."

I'm supposed to be impressed. But I am always unimpressed. If I hear a mother's a best friend, I don't think, Wow. That's just so lovely. No. I think, Find someone to like you who doesn't *have* to like you. And Amanda's point, I guess, was that a person who espouses such beliefs has no business etching her mom's initials on her body.

I decided Amanda was right, and dropped the idea of the hieroglyph just as I'd dropped the idea of the dolphin. I spent the next couple weeks backing and forthing on various other options. I considered the Chinese symbol for "Alone," as well as the Palestinian flag. However, nothing so eccentric seemed to suit me. So I tried thinking in terms of something more basic. Something more steeped in tradition.

That is when the answer finally came.

When it hit me, I knew instinctively that it was right.

My tattoo would be . . . a butterfly. But not just any butterfly. *My* butterfly would sit . . . atop . . . *a heart*.

It was pretty strange, actually, that I hadn't thought of it before. Because, well, a butterfly *atop* a heart communicated the very essence of what I myself was trying to project: sweet, sexy, daring. I thought, Tattoos say "sexy." Butterflies and hearts say "sweet." Therefore, a butterfly atop a heart says that I am super-sexy. And also that I'm sweet!

It didn't hurt, of course, the way in which the whole thing scratched the unmitigated itch for an animal theme.

ON WHERE I MIGHT PUT IT

If there's one sure thing besides death and taxes, it's that I will not age like Helen Mirren. I therefore had to consider which part of me would . . . advance, if not well, then not badly, either. I was twenty-six at the time, and already my knees had sagged to the point of resembling lumpy, gelatin-stuffed pillows. My breasts would've done the same had they possessed the necessary volume, but lest I be spared any indignity in the general region, my décolletage was but a compressed accordion of skin. Other joyous changes were surely forthcoming, and so it seemed the smart course of action would be avoiding my face, back, hands, torso, buttocks, and the length of all extremities.

The only viable option, then, was the back of my neck. It was on frequent display owing to the up-do hair phase I was in at the time that, in turn, was owed to my recent battle with female baldness.

Now, technically, I wasn't bald. The issue was that I am—and have always been—plagued with a horrendous cowlick on the crown of my head. Combined with the strawlike texture of my hair, it is *the* thing that's offered unto me the Garth Algar Triangle Shape.

As I've gotten older, my hair has behaved as so much hair is wont to do: it has begun the tragic process of a gradual but distinct thinning-out. Therefore my cowlick is now on more evident display, and what it looks like from the back is a series of sparse hairs running *away* from other hairs. It looks as though the sparse hairs are sort of, like, *fleeing* the crown of my head.

I might've stayed in the dark about the whole thing, but then my mother felt obliged to point it out. She got in the habit of sending me clippings on the subject. Not of cowlicks, but of baldness. *Lady* baldness.

She would scrawl her own notes in the margins.

"Do *you* think you're struggling with this?" asked one.

"*I* think you're struggling with this," said another.

Sometimes she'd circle phrases like "iron deficiency" or "thyroid problem," "testosterone," or "women should not be ashamed."

I should've liked the attention brought to me via an ailment. But the ailment was too ugly for my liking. So I didn't like the ailment, and neither did I argue with my mother *about* the ailment. I did not say, "Mom. Lay off. I've got a cowlick, not a bald spot," and that is because—in accordance with idiotic superstitions I never *want* to believe but cannot *help* but believe—I felt like claiming *not* to have a bald spot would be the thing to condemn me to a bald spot. I received my mother's literature and read my mother's literature and worked with various hand mirrors to examine the crown of my head. Over time, I decided, *yes*: In point of fact, I had a bald spot. I *absolutely* had a bald spot, and any person who said otherwise—"Your mom's projecting some weird shit onto you, okay? I promise you. You are *not* bald"—was just being polite. They were protecting me from the bitter truth, and that bitter truth was this: I had a massive, raging bald spot. It looked, from above, like a plowed and barren field.

I knew I needed to solve the problem somehow, and had therefore started gathering what hair I did have into a strategically placed—if sadly flaccid—knot. Doing so covered the bald spot but left the nape exposed.

"Ink me, girl," it said. "Ink me with a butterfly that's perched atop a heart."

ON WHERE I MIGHT GO TO GET IT PUT

I decided to get my butterfly-atop-a-heart tattoo at a spot called Venus Modern Body Arts, and that is because Venus Modern Body Arts was next door to a Taco Bell.

Once, as a follow-up to what I'm *not* ashamed to tell you was an impressive bit of sexual maneuvering, I was affectionately choked, then ordered: "Tell me what to do to you. Tell me what you want."

I am also not ashamed to tell you that the answer that came to me was Taco Bell. There was one next door to the gentleman's apartment, and I could smell its chemical fiesta through the walls. So when, in effect, he asked me what I wanted, I remember thinking, Taco Bell.

I *love* Taco Bell, and I mention this because, despite where I was in my life in terms of wanting a tattoo, despite the progress I'd made in terms of finding them disgusting, I was still terrified of the actual parlors. I was under the impression they would smell sterile, but unsettlingly so: the sterileness of a stripper pole, not a nicely tiled bathroom. However, with a Taco Bell next door, I could take my fear of odor off the table. The Taco Bell would permeate the parlor, and this, in turn, would help to calm me down.

I ARRIVED AT Venus Modern Body Arts in the early afternoon because the early afternoon is a non-satanic time of day. I thought I'd be the first customer in there, but in what appeared to be a dentist's chair lay what appeared to be a prostitute. Maybe she wasn't a prostitute, but if it walks like a duck and it's in bike shorts and knee-high boots, it's probably a prostitute. A whirring needle buzzed at the prostitute's abdomen. And while, yes, it *did* smell like Taco Bell, it did not smell *enough* like Taco Bell to distract from the iguana. It was perched on the shoulder of the presumed employee, who had a beard—I *swear*—that was long enough to braid.

"Need any help?" he asked. "Have any questions?"

"No thank you," I said. "I am just here to browse."

Of course I was not just there to browse. But the iguana unnerved me, and I lost control of what had been said and of how I had hoped to respond.

"Okay, cool," said the man, and handed me a book of design options.

He crossed back toward the quasi-prostitute in the quasi–dentist's chair.

Between them, a conversation started on the subject of a musical band.

Someone said, "Rough, wild sound."

Someone else said, "Trish got kind of raped, if you ask me."

I hadn't felt this out of place since I'd gone to dinner with a thirty-year-old friend and her fifty-something boyfriend only to discover the fifty-something boyfriend liked to feed my friend her food. As a manner of eating, this one is never pretty, but throw in a fat age gap for good measure, and you'll find yourself praying for the impending apocalypse. You'll be like, "Now, please. I'd like *my* impending apocalypse *now*."

Well, I didn't bolt from that dinner, and I should have, seeing as how the dessert course involved the fifty-something boyfriend saying, "It's nice, for once, *not* to date an Asian."

You live and you learn, though, right? You learn enough to know it's time to leave.

I returned the design book. I strolled toward the door.

Now, strolling toward a door may mean that a lady is *leaving*, but it does not mean she's *left*.

If you talk about her, she can hear you.

"These girls, man. Jesus Christ."

"We ought to shove Iggy in her face. Be all like, 'Oooga booga, oooga booga!' You too scared now for your tramp stamp?"

There was laughter. Iggy, I figured, was the iguana.

"Seriously. I wanna be like, 'It's a tat shop, little princess. Not the Gap.'"

I wanted to be like, *Your valid point is no match for my fear of braided beards. I'm just not meant for this. I'm too afraid.*

Not being "meant for this," however, means confrontation is beyond you. It means you get defeated by your princesshood. It means you go silently into your day. I had planned to spend the rest of mine in tattoo-recovery mode, but now I had nothing to do. I wandered around. I bought myself a jumbo pretzel. I decided to see a movie. I saw *Notes on a Scandal*. I listened as Cate Blanchett explained her minor dance with pedophilia to Judi Dench:

"Well, you see, I was always *so* good. I had always

done *everything* proper. And finally, I just needed . . . to be bad . . ."

I heard the explanation. I looked at gorgeous Cate Blanchett. I thought, Now *there's* some cool rebellion.

Of course, pedophilia is a bigger commitment than even an ink stain.

I stuck with the rebellion of no tattoo instead.

10

How Long Till My Soul
Gets It Right?

I've *been* dumped more often that I *have* dumped. I am, if not happy to admit this, then certainly willing, and the reason I bring it up is this: I was somewhat recently dumped. Nothing would thrill me more than speeding along into another doomed relationship. However, friends and family have suggested "focusing" on myself as an alternative. Which sounds nice, but isn't, really. Since self-involvement is like sex: more fun when you've got someone to focus *on* you, *with* you.

So instead of focusing on myself, I filled out an online dating profile for the sole purpose of e-mailing a guy whose online name was I_am_a_Spanish_Bagel. He'd been advertised by my Yahoo! homepage as a "Brooklyn single," and claimed in his profile to like the book *The Kite Runner*.

Well, I *also* like the book *The Kite Runner*! Realizing we were thus destined to marry, I sent along a clever quip and awaited a reply. None came, however, and while this threw the obvious wrench in the works of our marriage, I was consoled by the fact that I thought I knew why: I had been too honest when describing my musical taste. The website had asked, "What kind of music do you like?" and rather than journey down my usual path of feigned sophistication, I thought, I have to tell the truth. My future perfect boyfriend must love ALL of me.

And so I wrote what follows:

"I like Paula Cole, the Indigo Girls, and Tori Amos. I like Alanis Morissette, Sarah McLachlan, and Jewel."

I HAVE BEEN plagued my whole life with unfashionable taste in music. It's a fact I've hinted at already: There's been Jewel and Paula Cole. And Lisa Loeb and Lilith Fair. What I admit to you now, though, is that such references are not just nostalgic facts. No. They are part of my present, the fabric of my current taste. This might not sound so bad, but it is. I've spent my adult life living off again, on again, and *on* again in hipster central: Northern Brooklyn. And this, in turn, means everyone I meet has expert taste in music. I might fare okay elsewhere, but here, I do not. Here, it is *bad*. It's a message I've absorbed for years, and it's played a large part, I think, in fueling my ambition to be cool in other ways. To have some other edge about me.

"What's that? Well, I'm *sorry* I like Jewel. But perhaps you haven't noticed THAT I'M GAY."

"What's that? Well, I'm *sorry* I like Meredith Brooks. But perhaps you haven't SEEN ME DRINK THREE BEERS."

These goals of mine, while impressive, still failed to serve as effective antidotes to my musical taste. Not a single one was realistic or achievable, and the fact of this led to the eventual conclusion that I ought to keep my taste in music under wraps.

As with any secret, mine requires upkeep. It has therefore facilitated a low-boiling but chronic anxiety. Whatever fear unfolds for grown illiterates when asked to read aloud, so unfolds for me when I'm out on a date and I'm asked, "So, what kind of music are you into?"

Over time, and with the assistance of friends and loved ones whose goal it is to have me married off, I've learned to lie. I'm told of bands with names like Arcade Fire, Fleet Foxes, Blonde Redhead, the Helio Sequence, the National. Because, you see, unimpressive musical taste is one thing, lack of preparedness another. I'm nothing if not crafty. I know how to play it on a date.

> **Me:** I am into *all* sorts of music. I enjoy many different bands. For example: the Blonde Redhead, the National, the Helio Sequence.
> **A date:** What'd you think of their last album, though? I was a little like, "Meh. I'm underwhelmed."
> **Me:** As was I. That is exactly how I would describe my own feelings toward the Arcade Fire.
> **A date:** I've heard good things about the National, though. Do you have a favorite song?
> **Me:** Could Sophie choose between her children? Please. I love them all.

THE TRUTH COMES out eventually, though. Keys get exchanged, and I'm walked in on singing in the shower. I'll be singing "Bitch" or "Cornflake Girl."

GROWING UP, MY brother and I listened mostly to musical theater. Over time—and in much the same way a literal palate could be fed fast food and adjust to fast food—my youthful mind registered "good" music as that which lacked nuance. I liked a bold message, loudly expressed. I liked Caucasians bemoaning affairs of the heart. Sam did too, but for reasons unclear and unjust, he eventually outgrew the taste. Newly adolescent, he found this one band called the Who, and another called Pink Floyd, and then there he was: set on the path to acceptable taste. Moreover, the musical-theater affections of his past have not only *not* hurt him, they've helped. They've been offset by an air I've heard others call "macho." (Sam and I were at a bar once, when a woman leaned drunkenly toward me and slurred, "Your brother looks like what I want all firemen to look like.") He's considered empirically manly, is my point—a quality that's effectively juxtaposed against his knowledge of the American musical theater canon from 1945 to 1982. The female population finds the contrast attractive in much the same way they find a masculine cry attractive: He looks all at once hard but soft; tough but tender.

"I'm saying, I get *action*," Sam will say, "and that this action is due to knowing, for example, *Hello, Dolly.*"

"That's so not fair."

"No. But it *is* awesome."

Sam used his tween years to broaden his musical horizons, his macho flair to contrast cutely against his early, effeminate tastes. But I was not so lucky. If, at the age of sixteen, someone had asked me my favorite song, I would've said, " 'Last Night of the World' from *Miss Saigon*," and it was at this impressionable age, in this impressionable state of mind, that my parents forced me to get my first real job. I'd done the water-aerobics assistance thing a couple years before, but that had been only an hour a day for the sum total of twenty dollars a week. Now here I was, a young woman with international travel under her braided leather belt.

"You can't just sleep all day," said my mom. "It's depressing. Don't *you* think it's depressing?"

"By 'depressing,' do you mean 'relaxing'?" I asked.

"I don't," she said. "Go get a job."

I did as instructed, and wound up working the to-go counter at a local restaurant called Bino's BBQ. Bino Steinberg, owner and proprietor, was a middle-aged man who wore a golf-ball-sized Jewish star around his neck. My primary responsibility was answering his three-line phone system whenever customers called in to place an order. Additional tasks included taking the attendance of the all-Hispanic kitchen staff, filling mayonnaise containers, and keeping up appearances by wearing a plastic visor that read BINO'S BBQ: WE'RE SMOKIN'.

There were pros and cons to my new job.

Pros

1. The kitchen staff was kind and welcoming, bestowing unto me a nickname: Sweaty Sara B. (pronounced SweatEEE Sara BEEE), because whenever I entered the kitchen I'd become instantly, profusely sweaty.
2. The guy whose job it was to prep the sides—sautéed spinach, baked potatoes, etc.—who *looked* Hispanic, but his name, weirdly, was Olaf. Olaf had the appearance of an amateur bodybuilder insofar as his physique was *so* athletic, it walked the line between sexy and grotesque.

In Olaf's case, I felt the sexy side won out. I was therefore thrilled when he began to flirt with me *about* my sweating.

"Here she is, amigos: SweatEEE Sara BEEE! Lookin' good today, *amiga*. You want for me to wipe you off? For to be using my bandanna?"

I felt an attraction between us, and eventually asked

Olaf if, in light of his advances, he might not like to take me out. But Olaf just laughed and put a hand on my shoulder.

"What? Ha! No, Sara BEEE. My SweatEEE Sara BEEE. I am being only funny. You and me, we no go out. For you, you are too sweaty. For me, I have too much wife at home."

Despite the romantic rejection—or, perhaps, because of the guilt it inspired—Olaf continued to shower me with attention. I, naturally, continued to love it. He called me by my nickname, he kept up with his flirting. And, yes, now I knew the flirting itself was an empty promise, but I didn't care, really, since in addition to the flirting, Olaf took up the daily habit of sneaking me a twice-baked potato. Out of guilt or affection, I didn't know and didn't care. One must never look a gift horse in the mouth.

Con

1. One of the prominent features at Bino's BBQ was Bino's wife, Sharon. Sharon was angular of feature and very mean, and she'd come in every day to yell about how no one was working hard enough. The waiters were "fuckups," the cooks were "lazy." The specific issue with me was that I watched too much TV.

My to-go station came equipped with a cable-connected, large-screen version, and as most of my job involved waiting for the phone to ring, I spent most of it leaned against the cash register staring at the TV screen. In any given shift, Sharon was guaranteed to wander through the to-go station and see me in a state of repose. And then she would scream, "GET OFF YOUR ELBOWS! WE'RE RUNNING LOW ON RANCH DRESSING!" or "GET OFF YOUR ELBOWS! GO WINDEX THE FRONT DOOR!"

The thing was, though, the cable access made it worth

it, enduring Sharon's rants. As the TV at my parents' house had only six channels, I spent my first weeks at Bino's BBQ delighting in the vast cable array. I'd enjoy one channel, then hop caddishly on to the next. Nothing compelled me at first, for there was too much to explore.

But then one special day, I found one special channel.

Her name was VH1.

Once we found each other, I could not channel surf again.

MTV I'd heard of before, but found it rather hard—too *rock*—for my sadly honed tastes. But oh, VH1. She was my glass slipper of channels bestowing unto me an embarrassment of riches: Lisa Loeb, Tori Amos, Natalie Merchant. Sheryl Crow, Sarah McLachlan, the Indigo Girls . . . I felt as though my life up until the moment of finding these women had been but a preparatory course in learning to love them. Their lyrics were so far up my alley as to be pornographic, possessing as they did all the nuance of Bino's golf-ball-sized Jewish star.

They spoke to me directly:

So you found a girl who thinks really deep thoughts / What's so amazing about really deep thoughts? / Boy, you best pray that I bleed real soon / How's that thought for you?

That is an excerpt from a wonderful song called "Silent All These Years" by Tori Amos. A tale of a woman loved and left. I heard it for the first time when I was still a virgin, and thought, She *is* me. She gets me. I bet she'd really like me.

I will call it a homecoming, my discovery of VH1 and its featured female artists. For in finding them, I felt I'd found a place where I belonged.

I do believe Jewel said it best:

You were meant for me / and I was meant for you.

I REACHED A stage in my relationship with VH1 wherein I'd memorized almost all its songs. This, in turn, became the stage in which I had to sing along. It happened fast, over the course of a month. I'd do it inadvertently sometimes. The to-go station was its own little air-conditioned room set apart from both the kitchen and the larger restaurant; it shared the storefront with the restaurant, with the kitchen in the back. The layout fostered a sense of isolation and made it easy to forget I was within earshot of the staff. Having forgotten, I would belt unself-consciously along.

Other times, though, my belting was more conscious. My hope was to be overheard and then discovered. I had this fantasy that Olaf doubled as a music executive, and that our flirtation was but a covert test to see how I would handle the attention once he made me a star. Or I'd imagine that a customer would wander in, and although he would be conservatively dressed, he would turn out to be a talent scout.

"Hello. How do you do? I happen to be a talent scout."

"Really? Because you look like an insurance salesman."

"I know. But I am not. What I am, actually, is a talent scout, and I am looking for a girl like you. With your body type exactly. Although . . . Hold on: Are you open to fattening up?"

"I am."

"Great. Then I'm looking for a girl like you—*or fatter*—to cover songs by Tori Amos."

ONE AFTERNOON I was leaning against the register, throwing all my energy at a sing-along to Lisa Loeb's "Stay," when Bino wandered in. You'd think someone with a Jewish star as big as Bino's would have a lead-footed swagger about him. But Bino did not. He crept in silently. Gentle like the breeze, but with a hint of CK One.

"*YOU TELL ME THAT YOU WANT ME THEN* . . . Oh. Hi Bino. Sorry. Sometimes I forget I'm not alone."

"No problem," said Bino. "You sure do like to sing."

"I do," I said.

"That's good," he said.

"It is?" I said.

"It is," he said.

"Well . . . great," I said. "But why?"

"Because," he said, "I'd like *you* as my opening act. For my night of karaoke."

What it wasn't: an album of Tori Amos covers.

What it *was:* some vaguely positive attention. Some recognition that my talents were deserving of a bigger "stage."

I used the quotation marks on "stage" just then because in my turn of karaoke-kicking-off, I never—not once—saw a stage. I stood exclusively on a section of carpet. A section of *green* carpet, in a corner of a restaurant.

Bino explained that his overall plan was to improve his Tuesday-night business. Tuesdays had been slow, he said, and he thought he could lure in more customers with the classic two-for-one customer bait: dinner and a show for the price of dinner alone.

Bino considered which of his options would have the lowest overhead and decided on karaoke.

"People will get into it eventually," he said. "But they'll need someone else to kick it off."

"Me," I said.

"Yes," he said. "Every Tuesday, you'd do a song to get us started."

Just prior to this conversation with Bino I'd read an

article in *Seventeen* magazine. It had been a profile on Claire Danes in which she discussed the degrading commercial work she'd done prior to *My So-Called Life*, and it had left the conveniently timed impression that every step toward glory was a step worth taking.

If she, Claire Danes, could preach the merits of Velveeta cheese or Ford Motors, then I, Sara Barron, could be the kick-off act in a night of karaoke.

I told Bino I would do it.

MY DUTIES BEGAN the following Tuesday. I was nervous, but only to the point of a loose pre-show bowel movement. I had been craving an audience for ages, after all. I was mostly just excited.

When six o'clock rolled around, Bino introduced me to his customers.

"Hey, everyone. Hey," Bino said. "We've got some fun stuff for you tonight. *Good* stuff. Here's Sara. She answers the phones. She's gonna get us started."

There was a smattering of applause. I took the microphone from Bino.

"Hello," I said.

I then stayed silent until the opening chords of the song, which, for my first performance, was "Memory" from *Cats*.

Once I'd finished singing, there was another faint smattering of applause. I did try basking in its glory; however, this was the equivalent of trying to scrub myself clean in a faint morning dew. It wasn't bask-worthy applause, really, but I thought, Well, that's okay. I've got time in which to grow.

TUESDAY-NIGHT KARAOKE LASTED eight weeks in total, and during those eight weeks neither Bino nor I ever wavered from our opening routine. Bino would introduce me. There'd be a smattering of applause. I would say hello, and then stand in silence before the opening chords of my song. After that, I would sing.

With each passing Tuesday, I established a more powerful carpet-corner presence. I walked toward that carpet corner with an increased level of confidence. I would swagger toward it. I would tell myself how good I was.

You're a star in the making. A gift to those who get to hear you sing.

I was able to indulge these delusions in part because I'd convinced myself that wanting an audience was proof enough that I deserved one. Moreover, my audience was made up mostly of middle-aged parents, and these types, as a group, are inclined to be supportive. They were never rude or mocking. They would just avoid eye contact by staring at their plates.

I perceived their discomfort not as discomfort at all, but as reverence. I thought that they were *in awe* of my talent. I thought that they'd been wowed by the boldness of the songs I chose. Ideally, these would've been the songs of my new lady idols, but sadly they were not. Bino's karaoke songbook did not include my favorite songs, so I sang duets instead. I would sing them on my own. I loved the chance to play two parts: "Suddenly Seymour," "Summer Nights," "Beauty and the Beast," "A Whole New World," "I Got You, Babe," "Opposites Attract."

I enjoyed the acting challenge of conveying the dual roles through the use of shifting focal points.

The above duets were the only ones I knew well enough to do at karaoke. I ran out of options as time went on, and so at the eighth week decided to scrap the duet format entirely, as well as the karaoke machine. I decided to sing a cappella "Behind the Wall" by Tracy Chapman. Recently,

I'd seen Chapman's video for her more current song, "Matters of the Heart" on VH1. I had loved it, memorized it, and made a point of going to the library to check out her other CDs. I listened to these other CDs until they too had been memorized. My hope was that any number of her songs might be featured in the karaoke songbook. When they were not, I recalled that "Behind the Wall" off her eponymous album was done a cappella. It didn't need a backing track. In which case, *I* didn't need a backing track. I could do it on my own.

"Behind the Wall" is a story of domestic violence: a wife abused. A police department ill adept at keeping her protected. I chose the song figuring my community would appreciate the issues being brought to light, and performed it in a style that was less song singing, than it was spoken-word poem reciting. To my carpet corner I brought a similar delivery to what you'd see years later on Russell Simmons's *Def Poetry Jam.* I thought the content of the song and the style in which I performed it were not only Progressive, but Important.

On this point, however, neither my employers nor my audience agreed.

Usually, it was during my performance that my audience would look away. Usually, after my performance they would clap or tentatively smile. However, when I performed "Behind the Wall," the audience didn't look at me even once it was over. Perhaps this was because there had been no backing track to signal that it was over. Or perhaps it was because they'd felt too . . . inspired to look me in the eye.

THREE DAYS FOLLOWING my "Behind the Wall" performance, Bino received a letter of complaint. It had been sent by someone who'd been there, and had cited my "insensitivity to race."

I knew about it only because Bino chose to tell me about it. He carried the letter with him into the to-go station and told me what it said. He told me that *because* of what it said, he was taking me off karaoke detail. He told me he was scrapping the night as a whole.

"But why?" I asked. "I thought it was all going good."

"It wasn't," Bino answered. "I hoped it would, but what I realize now is that karaoke makes people eat less instead of more. Besides which, now here I am with a letter of complaint."

"But I don't even get it. *What* was her complaint?"

"That you were 'acting black.' She wrote"—and Bino grimaced—"that you were being . . . *racist*."

If you live in a mostly white suburb—and I lived in a mostly white suburb—you learn the lesson fast that there is no worse thing than being racist. One mentions that word, one cuts close to the bone. You learn to be defensive on the subject, and it is this defensiveness that clouds your judgment. It makes it hard to consider the validity of any racist accusation. For example: Maybe a sixteen-year-old who does a certain style of performance is in fact latently racist. Then again, if a grown adult thinks there's such a thing as "acting black," well then, maybe *she's* the one who's racist.

Regardless of whether my unknown accuser had a valid point, her accusation followed by the loss of the karaoke gig had the cumulative effect of making me *really* depressed. When Bino left the to-go station, I made a mad dash for the employee bathroom for an impromptu clutch-'n'-sob. (In which I clutched myself. And sobbed.) "Possession" was playing on VH1 when I got back, but I couldn't enjoy it. I just sulked through the rest of my shift, left work, and went home.

My bad mood carried through into the next day. I arrived

at Bino's BBQ in the early afternoon only to discover that I was atypically *uninterested* in Olaf. He'd brought me my potato as usual, and all I'd said was, "Okay. Whatever, Olaf. Thanks."

Olaf looked confused.

"Sweat-EEE Sara BEEEE," he said. "Today you be some bitch? Why come you be some bitch?"

Speaking of some bitch, Olaf asked me why I was being some bitch at exactly the same moment Bino's wife, Sharon, wandered in. Sharon was in an equally bad mood. Sharon was never in a good mood really, but today's was especially bad. Earlier in my shift, I'd heard various grumblings about something to do with the employee bathroom. Something about how someone had gone in and drawn Sharon with a penis in her ass. Something about a caption *beneath* the ass that read, *"Tengo muchas ganas de morir."*

This translates roughly from Spanish to English to mean, "I really want to die."

Sharon had discovered this drawing of herself, and now here she was mere minutes later with Olaf and me. She'd walked in on Olaf giving me a potato, and me leaning against the cash register. VH1 blared from the TV set behind us. It was one Ms. Tracy Chapman. She was "Talkin' 'Bout a Revolution."

Over the several months I'd worked at Bino's BBQ, Sharon had been successful in instilling within me a certain amount of fear. Normally when she entered the to-go station I would jump to attention to feign a modicum of respect.

This time, though, I didn't care and didn't want to. *This* time I had been accused of being racist, I had been stripped of karaoke stardom, I had been told by Olaf not to be some bitch.

This time, when Sharon barreled in, I stayed exactly as I was.

"WHAT THE **FUCK**?!" she yelled. "YOU ALWAYS WATCH TV!"

And that's when I said it:

"Fuck you."

I was not usually so mouthy. But I had been pushed to my limits, and Tracy Chapman was there for support. Tracy Chapman was talkin' 'bout a revolution. And so was Sara Barron. Sara Barron—*finally*—had the will to take a stand.

And, therefore, a reason to be fired.

There was no fanfare and no time for good-byes. I said, "Fuck you," and then Sharon shouted, "WHAT? WHAT? WHAT?" and then I shouted, "Nothing! Nothing! Nothing!" and ran straight for the door.

I was high on fear and excitement for twenty-four hours. Then, though, I had to call work to see whether or not I was supposed to come in. I was terrified to make the call, and to disguise myself I affected a British accent. Which meant I then had to say who I was. *In* a British accent.

"Oh. Bino. Cheerio. It's Sara Barron. I . . . um . . . *Well.* I do beg your pardon, but I'm . . . supposed to work today. At four p.m. So, well, should I? Come in?"

Bino was silent for a moment.

Finally, he said, "You told my wife to fuck herself."

Then I was silent for a moment.

Finally, I said, "No I didn't. I just said, 'FUCK YOU!' "

With that, I slammed down the phone.

WHERE WAS IT all coming from? Such boldness! *Such* aggression! I guess my recent exposure to so much articulately expressed female anger had had its positive effect.

And now here I was: standing on the shoulders of giants. On the shoulders of *my* giants. Of Tracy, and of Tori. Of Lisa, and of Sarah, too.

I MISSED MY job after losing it. I missed Olaf, my potatoes, and the overall sense of camaraderie. I felt the sting of these losses but I also recovered quickly from them. I was mostly just happy not to have to work. I had lost my job one week before I was due back at high school, and was grateful for the extra time in which to relax, as well as for the wealth of new music I'd discovered. I put my personal knack for lyric memorization to good use, singing aloud whenever location permitted: in my bed, in the shower. On long, private walks to the beach. I sang so I would not forget. When finally my last Bino's BBQ paycheck arrived, I used it to purchase the albums on which all my favorite songs appeared. When Hanukkah rolled around, I requested a cable subscription, promising my parents that if they bought it for me, it would preclude them from further present requests for a minimum of six months.

"Make it a year," said my mom.

"Agreed," I said, and as a woman of my word, did not complain when, the following May, I turned seventeen and received a jar of Clausen pickles.

Impressed by the trustworthy teen I'd become, the universe gifted unto me a woman by the name of Alanis Morissette.

She wrote a song called "You Oughta Know."

The amount I enjoyed "You Oughta Know"—the sheer number of hours I spent seductively pressing my hands against the full-length mirror in my bedroom while singing its lyrics *at* myself with a zeal to suggest I'd suffered a very real mental breakdown—cannot be overstated.

———

I KNOW I'M not alone in behaving as I did. So many others knew and loved these women and their music. The difference, though, is that these others—the ones I know, anyway—have matured and moved on. I had a friend in high school who *died* for Lisa Loeb. Now, though, she's a painter-cum-sculptor. Now, though, she dies for Grizzly Bear. Which is a guy, I guess. Or a band? I honestly don't know. The point is that *now* she likes him/them. For she's matured, you see. So many do. They're happy to revisit aural haunts on occasion, for theirs is a journey driven by nostalgia.

Mine, though, is not. My love remains dangerously true. When I listen to Alanis Morissette's "Ironic," it is not, uh, ironic. It is not for some jaunt down memory lane. It is because I've opened up iTunes and seen it sitting there beside some other thing called Morrissey, and I have very truly thought, But I *love* the song "Ironic." Why force my way through the unknown?

My tastes, exposed, may have made me a pariah. But they have fostered self-acceptance. They have made me finally free.

My name is Sara Barron. My favorite album ever made is *Little Earthquakes*.

My name is Sara Barron. My workout mix is Jewel and Meredith Brooks.

I don't know Bob Dylan.

I don't know The Smiths.

It may have taken time to get here. But in the end, I got here: In my bones, I am uncool.

Part III

Roommate

11
Mole Woman

Before I moved to New York, a roommate, like a bouquet,
struck me as a lovely addition to one's living space. I'd
put in eighteen years at home with my parents and my
brother. It hadn't been bad, but it hadn't been great, either.
Certainly, it had not been great *enough* to slay me with the
bittersweetness as we all four reached the end, as I inched
toward my college departure. I did not mourn the day-to-
day loss of my family. I was too excited for a roommate.
A proper gal pal. She would laugh with me in good times,
cook for me in bad. I'd be new to New York, exhausted by
the intellectual rigor of studying acting, and she'd be there
for me, my rock: a full pant size bigger than I was, and
dying to hear about my day. I'd come back from class and
she'd already be there, already waiting.

"Hi!" I'd say.

"Hi!" she'd say.

"You've *got* to hear about my day!" I'd say.

"I *want* to hear about your day!" she'd say.

We would speak only in exclamations and we would be almost always happy.

I held on to this fantasy for six months before I left for college.

I let this fantasy go six days after arriving *at* college. This was thanks to a freshman roommate who tweezed her pubic hair while seated at her desk. It was not an ideal practice, but at least it was quiet. The more significant problem was the whining that followed the tweezing.

"My neck is sore!" she'd moan. "I need a massage!"

There's a limit to how many times a person can hear this before offering advice. Mine was ninety-five. Finally, I said, "It occurs to me it might be helpful if you stopped staring at your twat like it's a fucking mirror."

And she answered back, "Yeah, well, it occurs to *me* it might be helpful if you went and fucked yourself."

From an objective distance, I now can see we both had solid points. I can see we both suffered through the other's idiocy, and I don't begrudge doing so, frankly, since the process taught me an important lesson early on:

A roommate is not there to be a bestie, she's just there to split the rent.

Thus was my metaphor forcibly switched.

From: Bouquet.
To: The process of a *most* unpleasant puke.

From: A lovely contribution to a living space.
To: Something awful you endure because you have to.

And so did I endure: one new roommate for each new year of college. In the end, the pubic-hair tweezer *did* turn out to be the worst. But the others weren't great either.

THE HARM IN ASKING

None of them would talk about how wonderful I was and/ or ask about my day.

AS I INCHED toward college graduation, I became increasingly obsessed with the prospect of living alone. I'd look in the window of every real estate office that I walked past. I'd learn all that I could about the apartments that I saw. Dimensions, street names, price. If you told me the size of the place and the street it was on, I could make a pretty good guess at its cost.

400 square feet. Morton Street: $1,800 a month.
300 square feet. Christopher Street: $900 a month.

I was usually right. But the breadth of my knowledge was narrow. Each one of my college dorms had been in Greenwich Village, and so I'd walked mostly past Greenwich Village real estate offices with Greenwich Village listings. These meanders were the extent of my research. It was 2000–01 by this stage, and while I was aware of the Internet, I did not yet *live* on the Internet. I did not yet have the wherewithal to research any options farther out, and was therefore under the impression that a studio apartment—that *any* studio apartment—cost around fifteen hundred dollars a month.

You might as well have told me it cost around fifteen *million* dollars a month.

There were cheaper options out there in the farther reaches of the outer boroughs. But that would take some time to figure out. All I knew for now and for sure was that I'd need a place to live.

And that in that place, I'd need a roommate.

COLLEGE GRADUATION CAME and went, my parents informed me that they would no longer be paying my rent. As a gift, they gave me a check for $1,000. My mother was the one to hand it over. When she did, she said, "This is very, *very* generous. Do not insult us by asking for more."

I promised I would not, and then promptly used a significant portion of the money to book a one-way flight to London. I was in the midst of a fledgling romance with a British student. He'd decided to move home to London, and I'd decided it might be nice to join him. I thought I might go for the summer and share his apartment and see how it went. I knew it was impulsive, but I was very much in love. And this, my blinding and impulsive love, fought through the fact that he, my beau, looked *just* like Marty Feldman.

Picture those crazy, bulbous eyes. Picture that *tiniest* of tiny hunchbacks.

Imperfection be damned, though, he "shagged" and also "snogged" as though every day might be his last. And we shared a worldview. We agreed on the stuff that's important:

1. The sunny side of the street causes headaches.
2. Pets are disgusting.
3. Chronic lateness is indicative of self-absorption.

Things went along okay for a while, but then one afternoon he and I were enjoying a luxurious afternoon nap when he turned to me to say, "Listen: I *do* love you. But I've thought a lot about it, and come to the conclusion that I could love someone else . . . more."

"Who?"

"Well, I don't know *who,* exactly, I'm just speaking in general terms."

A decade later, I calmly reflect on this exchange—on the romance as a whole—as one of youthful misadventure. I rejoice in the gentleman's current status as a waiter/unpaid blogger on the indie-music scene.

At the time, though, my brash American temper got the

best of me. I reached for the bedside pot of tea and tried scalding bits of his anatomy. Then I hopped the next flight to New York. Which isn't a cheap fuck-you, by the way. I used up most of the rest of my graduation gift to do so. I had no money left over, and since my parents had the ridiculous idea that college graduates ought to pay their rent themselves, I went ahead and chose the least-expensive option: I moved into the walk-in closet of this guy I knew named Wayne.

Wayne and I had met three years prior in a college elective called Valuing Self: Solo Performance Through the Ages. Within days of my New York return, he and I ran into each other in Tompkins Square Park. I'd gone there to consider whether the homeless lifestyle might be negotiable by any stretch, and Wayne had come to power-walk.

"Sara? Barron?" he'd asked.

He'd seen me crying while lying prostrate on a bench.

"Why are you crying on a bench?"

Wayne's question was the perfect inroad to a conversation on the injustices of postcollegiate life. I told him, "I just got dumped by that English guy you said looked like Marty Feldman! I have no money! I slept at a youth hostel last night, and when I showered there this morning I stepped in a pile of someone else's hair! I swear to you, it looked *alive*!"

"I hear you," said Wayne. "*My* dad cut *me* off after graduation. It's totally unfair."

Wayne's dad was a wealthy businessman who'd built his fortune on savvy participation in the Indian hair trade.

"He still pays for this class I'm in called Script Yourself, *and* for my rent *and* for a gym membership so I can work on my pear shape. *And* he pays for groceries and a weekly cleaning service. Nothing else though, and I'm like, 'Well, I can't *create* art, if I can't afford to *see* art.'"

I nodded sympathetically. I said, "Struggling *is* the destiny of the artist, though. Just like they taught us in Valuing Self."

Wayne and I tossed around solutions to our respective problems, like that I could sell my eggs or that Wayne could get a job. But these were not realistic options. I lacked the necessary generosity of spirit, and Wayne lacked a willingness to interrupt his PACT.

PACT was an acronym from Valuing Self.

It stood for Personal Art Creation Time.

Eventually, though, and after enough rigorous debate, we arrived at a potentially brilliant and mutually beneficial solution: I could move into Wayne's apartment, but then in lieu of paying rent, I'd do the cleaning. I'd shirk homelessness this way, and Wayne would free up a portion of his budget.

"But what if your dad finds out?" I asked.

"He won't," Wayne answered. "I get a lump sum every month. And all he says is, 'Just *please* go to the gym. Just *please* work on your pear shape.'"

The plan felt perfect to the both of us. The only downside was that Wayne was homosexual, and that this, in turn, meant no hope of trading sex for further amenities. It was a shame, really. I would've loved the occasional romp if it meant un-begrudged access to Wayne's high-end foodstuffs. But as Wayne himself would say, "Why shove a lemon up your asshole if you're drinking lemonade?"

Why, indeed? I would opt to keep my asshole lemon-free.

Wayne lived in the East Village, which, as a neighborhood, can shift on a dime. Or rather: *in* a block. From idyllic to disgusting. From brownstones and boutiques to bongs and belly-button rings. The apartments do the same. Some are tiny as a shoebox. They are weirdly arranged

with showers in kitchens and toilets in communal hall-
ways. Others, however, are dream-worthy brownstones.
They look like how New York looks in the movies. By
which I mean like a rom-com kind of movie. Not a gritty
drama.

By which I mean *When Harry Met Sally*. Not *Kids*.

Wayne, as I said, was still supported by his parents. Not
a little by his parents. Completely by his parents. The situation surprised and confused me: How had Wayne coerced
them? How and why had they agreed? I could only imagine that they had done so begrudgingly, and that if Wayne
lived in the East Village, he did so on a grimy street, in one
of the shoebox apartments.

Please, then, try to imagine the surprise I felt the first
time I saw Wayne's *actual* apartment. His *actually* perfect
East Village apartment. For it was not a grimy shoebox.
No. It was a gorgeous, light-filled unit in the newest building on the street.

"Jesus *Christ*," was all I could say when I saw it.

Wayne shrugged. He pointed to a nearby gym. I could
see it through a floor-to-ceiling window.

"My dad liked the look of that gym," he said, "since he
likes when I work on my pear shape."

Wayne then pointed to the balcony. Because there was
a balcony.

"I, however, like the balcony," he said. "I like to use it
when I'm PACT-ing."

I nodded. I said, "I can see why you would."

The apartment was beyond my wildest dreams. Nevertheless, it was still a one-bedroom. It offered everything in
the way of, well, everything, but not much in the way of
space. Wayne thought the best way to solve the problem
would be to put me in the closet.

You would think I would not want to be put in the

closet. But I *did* want to be put in the closet. Because Wayne's closet was not just any closet.

Wayne's closet was . . . a *walk-in* closet.

We're talking *in* Manhattan. We're talking *very* big.

"We'll make it your own little room," Wayne said.

"Sounds perfect," I said. Because it genuinely did. The closet was big enough for me to stand upright or lie lengthwise on my air mattress. I plugged a "desk"-lamp into the outlet and nicknamed the space "A Room of My Own." That is, until Wayne told me my nickname was ill chosen.

"Why?" I asked.

"Because," Wayne answered, "Woolf's point was that a woman should have a space that she has paid for, for herself. And you don't pay for this yourself."

"Who's Woolf?" I asked. "I'm quoting the Indigo Girls."

This, here, was a nice thing about Wayne: He might not have exchanged intercourse for foodstuffs, but at the same time, he knew enough about '90s chick rock to help me unravel the threads of my own ignorance.

Wayne explained, "The Indigo Girls were quoting Virginia Woolf. Which is why they called the song 'Virginia Woolf.' She believed that for a woman to be an artist, she had to have a space that she, herself, has paid for. A space she'd use for work."

"Oh. I'm *using* it to work," I said, and this was essentially true. Lacking a TV for my walk-in closet, I set to work on a solo show that detailed this first year of my postcollegiate life. Its working title was *Mole Woman,* and the process of writing it did the job of a TV insofar as it could alternately entertain me and lull me into sleep.

In my experience, art that puts you to sleep does so because it's either especially stupid or especially complex.

Mole Woman was especially complex. If you doubt me, here's a sample:

> Her future stretched before her like a wide, open meadow. She knew she'd live a big and vibrant life.

WAYNE AND I lived happily together for a full six months. During those six months, I scored a job as a greeter and shirt-folder at the Banana Republic store in SoHo. Since I wasn't paying rent, I managed to squirrel away a portion of my income while simultaneously treating myself to my own high-end foodstuffs. I'd do the occasional after-work jaunt through the Dean and Deluca at Broadway and Prince. I'd buy artisanal chocolate bars or loaves of Asiago cheese bread. I would share these treats with Wayne, who in turn would share his treats with me: a mint-scented Kiehl's exfoliant. A body butter from Laura Mercier.

I was grateful to Wayne for this exciting first go at non-student housing. My gratitude was manifest in the zeal I brought to my cleaning. Wayne, in turn, was grateful for my zeal. We had such a good balance. Such a perfect give-and-take. Our relationship was like my initial roommate fantasy from several years before, and it convinced me, for a moment, that living with a roommate could be better than living alone. It *could* be better, but only if Wayne was that roommate. Only Wayne. Perfect Wayne. Always and forever: *Wayne.*

And by "always" and "forever," I meant until we both had boyfriends.

And by "until we both had boyfriends," I meant until *I* had a boyfriend.

SO YOU CAN see, then, why I perceived it as a problem when Wayne got a boyfriend first.

Wayne's boyfriend was a young man named Tomas. (Pronounced, not "TAH-miss," but rather the immeasurably more annoying "Toe-MOSS.") Tomas was, in personality, the Antichrist. He was a hellish man for a wide variety of reasons, but perhaps the most telling one of all was that he called himself an actor/dancer.

If you said, "What is it that you do, Tomas?" Tomas would say, "I am an actor/dancer."

Nowadays, this slash ("/") in one's job title is a common thing to see. The folks who like to use it, they like to seem, well, what exactly? Diverse in their talents? Successful in multiple fields? Ironically, the use of the slash undermines what they're after, since it mostly confirms a lack of success. A lack of achievement in more than one field. An actor/dancer. A writer/painter. An actor/writer/director. A photographer/painter/designer. The sign of the slash does not mean you do it all, or more than one. It means that you wait tables for a living. Or temp. Or have a parent, wife, or husband who funds the things you say you are. It shows you have a hobby, a thing you're hoping or trying to be.

In keeping with this idea, Tomas called himself an actor/dancer, yet to earn his money he taught fifteen spin classes per week. Well, combine the self-delusion inherent in slash ("/") exploitation with the self-discipline involved in fifteen spin classes per week, and it's like, of *course* Tomas was awful. The first time I met him, I'd recently arrived home from a shift at Banana Republic. I'd been back for, I don't know, twenty minutes, let's say, and already I had changed into my cleaning-woman outfit so that I might scour hardened ketchup off a counter.

Suddenly, there was Tomas.

I heard a door and a voice. And turned around. And he was there. And he was *gorgeous*. Tomas had that level of attractiveness that can really bowl a person over.

Wordlessly, it suggested that I should smooth back my hair and set down my scouring pad.

Tomas had a movie-star face and what are often referred to as "washboard" abdominals, and these, the latter feature, were on display care of the white-ribbed tank top he'd worn and tied in a knot at the base of his chest. For my part, I'd been outfitted in wide-legged sweatpants, kneepads, and a roomy sports brassiere. Such was my uniform for cleaning.

I set down my scouring pad and dried off my hands.

"Tomas, Sara," said Wayne. "Sara, Tomas."

"Hello," I said.

"Hello," said Tomas.

"Sara is my friend," Wayne said. "The one living in the closet."

"Weird," said Tomas. "I mean, like, why? *Why* are you living in the closet? And, like, *why* are you even dressed like that?"

This first question from Tomas did not help me like Tomas. On the contrary, he questioned my living situation and my cleaning outfit, and I thought, I know for a fact that I'm going to hate you. But, of course, that is not the kind of thing one can say without looking psychotic. So instead of telling Tomas that I knew that I hated him, I just mumbled, "It's comfortable. I clean a lot," and then scurried away to my closet, to a safer place where his evil abdominals could not stare me in the face.

I sat there, alone, in my closet, and channeled my feelings into my work.

"Times were tough," I wrote. "Tough times were fast becoming my best friends. But I could take it. I was resilient. In other words: I was just a common woman."

I hadn't yet decided on the ideal format for *Mole Woman,* and reconfigured the sentiment as a spoken-word poem.

I wrote, "There I was at the School of Hard Knocks / Droppin' rocks / Of negativity / Rocks: That were holdin' me down / Bring it, world / Bring the pain / It's my gain / It makes me tough."

A week went by, and by the end of that week, Wayne and Tomas were a Couple. They were in a Relationship. How this sort of thing happens at the drop of a hat for everyone other than me, I'll never know. But the point, for the moment, is just that they were a Couple, and that by the end of *one* week, Tomas had ostensibly moved in.

Wayne, Tomas, and I managed the cramped quarters with a pair of noise-canceling headphones. Wayne bought them off eBay, and left them for me in my closet with a note attached that read, "Hi! I was hoping you'd wear these at night from now on. Just for privacy and stuff. Thanks!"

I told Wayne no problem, and wore the headphones when I slept. It wasn't the most comfortable thing in the world, but neither is sleeping ten feet from aggressive intercourse, anal or otherwise. Which is what I did, countless nights a week. Wayne and Tomas would do a lot of intercourse at night, and in the afternoons they'd watch TV. Tomas would leave whenever he had his spin classes, and Wayne would go with him. When they returned, Tomas would set up two yoga mats in the communal living space, and lead Wayne in a series of yoga poses. The schedule was such that Wayne and Tomas would do their daily yoga at the same time that I would do my daily cleaning. Often I would clean around them. Sometimes Wayne would invite me to join in on the yoga, but more often than not, I would've just finished a bag of beef jerky, and doing a child's pose in that condition would've been like waving a red flag at the bull of my cataclysmic gas.

"Oh, gosh," I'd say. "I shouldn't."

Wayne tried to include me on a number of occasions, but I always declined. These declined invitations appeared always to offend Tomas. One day, two months into their relationship, Wayne, as usual, invited me to join them. I, as usual, said thank you but no thank you. Tomas, as usual, rolled his eyes. But then in an unprecedented manner, he wanted to discuss the issue further. He asked, "So, like, what *do* you do for your body?"

I thought it rude to use so hostile a tone in response to so selfless an act. My first impulse was to give Tomas a piece of my mind, but the blatant rudeness had thrown me off guard. I'd been holding a bag of beef jerky at the time, and instead of any verbal retort, I brandished the jerky in his face.

"*That's* your defense?" he said. "That you clutch a bag of jerky like a blankie?"

"It's good for me."

"It's not, actually. The nitrates and sodium trigger water retention and, over time, can cause obesity and diabetes."

"Well, congrats," I said, "on knowing stuff about beef jerky. For your job."

"Yes, well," he said. "My career *is* going awesome at the moment."

"Yeah, well," I said. "If we all taught gym class, then we all could have awesome careers."

It is scary to speak *so* directly to someone *so* attractive. I have this fear these types can use their beauty to . . . I don't know . . . like, *melt* my lesser face.

Tomas glared, although, in truth, he did not melt my lesser face.

"I am an *actor* and a *dancer*," said Tomas. "*That* is my career."

"It's not," I said. "Maybe it will be at some stage, but for now, it is your hobby. Gym instruction's your career."

"What-*ever*," he said. "Like you're one to judge. *You* work at Banana Republic."

"True," I said. "But I also have a hobby. I'm also working on a show."

"What show?" he asked.

"A show I wrote," I said. "It's called *Mole Woman*."

Tomas's eyes lit up. They danced with the evil unique to those with zero body fat.

"Do you even know what a mole person *is*?" he asked.

"Of course," I said.

"Someone who lives in a subway tunnel," he said.

"I *know*," I said. Although, in fact, I had not known. Despite the blow, I carried on. "Anyway, I'm reappropriating the term."

"To mean . . . ?"

"A struggling artist."

"Who mooches off her friend?"

I stared back blankly. I collected my thoughts. I said, "Excuse me, but *I* am not mooching off my friend. *I* am cleaning so *I* can stay in the apartment."

"How impressive," he said.

"It is," I said, "compared to you. I clean so I can stay in the apartment. You have sex so you can stay in the apartment."

Tomas gasped. He said, "*You're* calling *me* a hooker?"

"No," I said. "*You* are calling you a hooker. I'm just pointing out the facts."

I *was* just pointing out the facts. However, there was one I had omitted and it was the whole entire point: Wayne and Tomas, as a couple, looked *bizarre*. Tomas looked every inch the high-end hooker, whereas Wayne, as previously discussed, looked like a human-sized pear. He had asymmetrical eyes to boot, and a nose you could hang your hat on. And sure, it was possible that Tomas was the kind of guy who cared about what was on the inside. It was also possible that *Mole Woman* was bound for a Broadway debut. Wayne was (1) a human-sized pear with (2) a fabulous apartment. And I knew—the *world* knew!—which one of those two things had kept Tomas around.

I wanted to say as much, but Wayne had been standing between Tomas and me throughout our fight, staring at the floor.

I turned toward the refrigerator, opened the door, and took out my cheese bread.

"Oh. *Classic,*" said Tomas. "Your friend, Wayne, is using her cheese bread to escape. Wow. I'm so, like, *totally* surprised."

Wayne, still, said nothing. I chewed some cheese bread. I swallowed the cheese bread. I turned back toward Tomas.

"I hate you," I said. And, with that, I walked away. I went inside my closet.

It felt exciting to tell someone I hated him. But that excitement was quickly undercut with a fear of being asked to leave. And fear can unhinge you a bit.

I grabbed my phone and called my mom.

"Hi, Mom," I said.

"Hi," she said.

"I was wondering if I could have some money," I said.

"What?" She laughed. "'Some money'? Ha! No. You cannot have 'some money.'" A pause. "Unless, of course, you're sick." A pause. "Sara, are you sick?"

"No," I said.

"Then why would you ask for 'some money'?"

"Because Wayne's boyfriend moved in. He's here all the time."

"And?" she said.

"*And,*" I said, "I think it could be good for me, creatively, if I could live in my own place."

"Good for you."

"Yes."

"Creatively."

"Yes."

I could hear my mother breathe.

"Well, good chat," she said, and then hung up the phone.

I considered other options.

I had a little money of my own saved up from my job at Banana Republic, but I crunched the numbers and realized it was nowhere near enough to help me afford my own place. All I could afford was another apartment with another roommate. It was not what I wanted. What I wanted was to live alone or, barring that, I wanted Tomas to slip during one of his spin classes and rupture his anus on his bike seat.

But dreams do not always come true. Tomas was too steady on a spin bike. I was too poor to afford my own place.

I sat in my closet feeling despondent. I stared at my "desk"-lamp for a while. I got bored and chose to do a little writing. I wrote a scene in *Mole Woman* in which she, the Mole Woman, is discovered at Banana Republic and asked to star in a movie for which she receives a comprehensive makeover.

As I wrote, I dreamed that Wayne would come knocking on the closet door.

"Sara," he'd say, "I am here for three reasons. One, I need to apologize for the way Tomas has treated you. Two, I've broken up with him because of it. Three, I need to know what you are working on. Please. May I read aloud an excerpt?" and then he'd read aloud an excerpt.

" 'Art is the battle of YOUR LIFE! Fight for what you believe. BE A BADASS, AND TAKE! NO! PRISONERS!' Oh my God. Did you write this?"

And I would say, "I did."

And he would say, "Sara: *It's* amazing. Sara: *You're* amazing."

SEVERAL HOURS LATER, Wayne did, in fact, come knocking on the closet door.

"Come in," I said, and repositioned myself so that Wayne could see my script.

"Can we talk?" he asked.

"Sure," I answered.

"Outside of the closet?" he asked.

"Is Tomas here?" I asked.

"No," he said.

"Then sure," I said, and came outside.

"So," he said.

"So," I said.

"*So,*" he said. "You were just, like, psychotically rude to my boyfriend."

"*Because,*" I said, "your boyfriend was psychotically rude to me first."

"Tomas was not rude," he said, "Tomas *is* not rude. Tomas is direct. I think it's refreshing."

"Refreshing?" I asked.

"Yes," he answered. "I think it's a brave way to live."

Over the course of two months, it had never once occurred to me that Wayne thought of Tomas as anything other than a horrible human he liked having sex with. True, he'd never said as much. True, they never spent any time apart. Perhaps, then, I should've been clued in to the fact that Wayne might actually like Tomas, might actually care about him in a more substantial way. But I was not. I had written the inseparability off as the sustained intoxication that came with looking *at* Tomas and knowing, soon, you'd *have* Tomas. I could not believe that in a coherent moment in which one gentleman was separated from the pheromones of the other, Wayne would describe Tomas as "brave" or "refreshing." Wayne used those words, and it felt like looking at an old friend from across a wide distance. The details were fuzzy, but the outline was clear.

"I should probably move out," I said.

"I've been thinking that'd be best," Wayne said, "and so I went on Craigslist. I've got a few options picked out."

12

Can't You Help a Person Who Is Sick to Wash Her Back?

Wayne and I riffled through the Craigslist options until I found a suitable place in Park Slope. If you know this section of Brooklyn, if you're familiar with its manicured flower boxes and local food–fed Caucasians, the fact of my doing so might surprise you. Under normal circumstances, Park Slope is outside the price range of the average Banana Republic employee. But then, it wouldn't be a normal circumstance, living in the basement of a deranged diabetic.

WE HADN'T BEEN on Craigslist long when I saw the Park Slope option in my price range. Its ad read: "I am renting my extra bedroom. It has its own bathroom. I have diabetes. Good price for location. —Jan."

I thought it was odd to mention diabetes in an

apartment posting. But Wayne, eager as he was for me to leave, did not.

"Really?" he'd said. "I think it'd be weird *not* to."

When I called the number listed, a woman answered who sounded very angry.

"THIS IS JAN!" she screamed. "WHO IS *THIS*?"

"Hi. I'm Sara," I answered. "I'm calling about the apartment."

"ARE YOU A FREAK?" Jan asked.

An occasion jumped to mind wherein my nipple was tweaked to the point of bleeding. I hadn't enjoyed it.

"No," I said. "I'm not a freak."

"Good," said Jan. "'Cause I got diabetes. I'm looking for a nice girl."

"Well," I said, "that's pretty much me in a nutshell."

I went to see the apartment later that afternoon, and when I did, I was greeted by a frail woman in her mid-sixties, crowned with a mop of graying, disorganized hair. But the apartment. *Oh,* the apartment. It was the home of my dreams, of *all* our dreams: a Cosby-esque, two-story brownstone complete with back deck and vaulted ceilings. The living room featured a bay window alongside a series of ornate sconces, and in the kitchen—the separate sit-down kitchen—a Restoration Hardware Farmhouse Collection table. The bedroom itself, the one I hoped to rent, was huge. It could have fit ten air mattresses, and came complete with its own private bathroom.

It was the Caesars Palace to my shack of a previous abode. More to the point, it was magnificent enough to make up for the presence of another roommate. And not just any other roommate: Diabetic Jan. She could've answered the door with a loaded gun and shouted, "Forget my diabetes! How's about Russian roulette?!" and still: I would have begged to live there.

I assumed Park Slope had a higher happiness standard than the East Village. I based this assumption on the fact that Park Slope was, quite simply, a prettier place to be. The East Village had some good blocks; Park Slope had all good blocks. There were more trees, more cute coffee shops. Fewer frat boys at the bars, fewer heroin addicts in the parks. If I lived in Park Slope, I would live near a beautiful corner market. I would go there every morning to buy organic produce, and I would cook it in Jan's gorgeous, sit-down kitchen every night. In time, I'd start to run. Prospect Park was nearby, and its proximity would inspire me. I'd be on the Park Slope diet of outdoor running and organic produce, and I'd become altogether more fabulous than I'd been on my East Village diet of jerky and rage.

I was therefore lucky that Jan liked me as much as I liked Jan's apartment. She offered it to me on the basis of my hair.

"I like it," Jan had said. "It's funny like a wig."

And I accepted the offer despite the nagging sense that being offered an apartment on the basis of one's hair *does* tend to indicate that one is gaining an unstable landlord. Jan's instability was something I thought I could handle, however, and that is because I thought real estate could buy happiness. Jan may have been a far cry from my gal-pal roommate fantasy, but you know what? So was everyone else. At least Jan had a bay window and an expensive kitchen table. At least Jan was not Tomas.

We shook hands and signed a few papers. We settled on a move-in date.

I was excited by the prospect of my new apartment. At the same time, though, I felt a minor apprehension. I blamed this apprehension on three unanswered questions:

Why does Jan mention her diabetes all the time?

How did someone so seemingly bizarre afford such a nice kitchen table?

Why did Jan pick a new tenant on the basis of said tenant's hair?

Asking these questions is fun, but getting the answers is less so. But that's what roommatehood is all about, right? You think, What the fuck is *your* problem? and then get your answer.

QUESTION: Why did Jan mention her diabetes all the time?

ANSWER: Jan mentioned her diabetes all the time because doing so manipulated certain spineless individuals into doing things for her she could easily have done herself.

I didn't know much about diabetes at the time other than that it sometimes involved orange juice. I thought it was like rheumatoid arthritis insofar as it severely limited movement. And that was because Jan presented it that way. And *that* was how I wound up washing her back. I washed it nine times in the nine months that we lived together. The first time she asked, the request had followed a string of others, and I'd been thrown too off guard to tell her no. I'd been asked to roast a chicken, snake a toilet, and fix her television set.

Jan: Sara! Fix the TV! *I* can't do it! *I* got diabetes!
Me: Jan, I'm sorry. Electronics are hard for me to understand.
Jan: Well, *I'm* not doing it. I need *you* to wash my back.

Do you see how if it were asked that casually and on the tail end of a conversation you already wanted to be over, you'd say yes? Although I didn't say yes, really. What I said was, "You want . . . me to . . . *what*?"

And Jan responded, "CAN'T YOU HELP A PERSON WHO IS SICK TO WASH HER BACK?"

And *that's* when I said yes. Or, more specifically, "Oh. Okay. Sure. Should I just . . . go run the water . . . now?"

What I was thinking at the time was this: Yes, it's weird to wash your roommate's back. But I love my new apartment. I don't want Jan to throw me out.

I wondered whether or not the back washing might not be an unspoken condition of my tenancy agreement. Additionally, I had this bizarre flash wherein I felt like if I *didn't* wash her back, it would mean I was cruel to the elderly.

So I ran a bath. I left Jan alone to get in. After a time she yelled, "Ready!" and that was the point at which I entered the bathroom myself. I squeezed a little liquid soap on a Buff Puff. And then I washed my landlord's back.

If you manipulate me into washing your back once, shame on you. If you manipulate me into washing your back nine times, shame on me. After the fifth or sixth time, these activities came up in conversation with my friend Maggie, who was of the opinion that washing my landlord's back was "fucked up" and that I was "fucked up" for doing it. "What? Are you, like, *into* it or something? I mean, you can tell me if you are."

I told Maggie no, that I didn't think I was subconsciously aroused by washing the backs of the elderly. Of course, one never knows what motivates her on the baser levels, but what it felt like consciously was that washing Jan's back was not as horrible as having her yell at me or kick me out if I refused.

So there were eight more times Jan asked me. And eight more times that I said yes.

QUESTION: How did someone so crazy afford such a nice kitchen table?

ANSWER: Someone so crazy affords such a nice kitchen table by virtue of being a trust-fund baby, all grown-up. Jan explained this situation as a cleverly manipulative wind-up to getting me to snake her toilet.

I'd been in my bedroom with the blinds drawn one weekday afternoon. I'd given up on *Mole Woman* and was now spending most of my free time masturbating. Jan had walked in unannounced to find me on my air mattress reading *Sabbath's Theater* by Philip Roth. (If you, like me, struggle with most available pornography, if you've exhausted the lesbian fantasies of your tween/teenage years, allow me to recommend pages 214 to 220 of *Sabbath's Theater*. You'll see what I mean when you get there.)

"What's going on?" Jan asked. "What are you reading in the dark for, in your underpants?"

"I get headaches from the sun," I said.

"Weird," she said, and then she leaned against the doorframe. "I know what you're thinking, you know. You're thinking, How can Jan afford this place? Jan wears pajamas all the time."

Mostly, I'd been thinking about how vulnerable I felt conversing in my underwear. Second to that, though, I had been thinking exactly what Jan suspected me of thinking.

It's always a mistake to think the seemingly deranged are not perceptive.

Jan went on to explain that her father had invented a brand of calculator so successful that she, his daughter, had been forever freed from work.

"And I never got married or had children," she continued. "So who knows where all that money goes."

"Well," I said, "where do you *think* it will go?"

Jan shrugged. "Don't know," she said. "Probably just to someone who's been nice to me."

Jan stared me square in the eye when she said that last bit—"someone who's been nice to me"—and I had, I *swear*, to actively suppress the urge to scoop her up into my arms and rush her to the bathroom for her bath.

It's true that since moving in with Jan, my own financial situation had improved. I had transitioned from greeting and shirt-folding at Banana Republic to waiting tables at a Midtown Olive Garden, and what this meant, financially, was that I'd moved from living at the poverty line to living one inch above the poverty line. The upward mobility was impressive, I know. However, at the rate I was going, I was still several lifetimes away from earning the kind of money I would need to live alone and/or achieve other long-term goals. I had just two:

1. To afford to buy a home instead of just renting a home.
2. To afford various fertility treatments (for when I tried to conceive at the age of forty-five and it didn't go so great).

These had been my long-term goals. But on the day my diabetic landlord talked around the word "inheritance," two blossomed into three:

3. I would care for Jan until she died. She would reward me with an inheritance as a result, which I could then put toward my home and impending fertility issues.

It would not be an easy task. Jan was a difficult person and being nice to her was hard. That was true if we were talking week to week. But year to year? How long did she have? Ten years? Maybe twenty? Could I carry on that long? And *if* I could, well, would she *really* leave me any money?

Jan continued, "Anyway, my toilet's clogged. But you'll make sure to fix it, right? Since I've got diabetes?"

I pictured it, this mountain of the future. This mountain of immeasurable wealth.

"I will," I said, and proceeded to Jan's bathroom with a bounce in my step and, in my hand, an unwound wire hanger.

QUESTION: Why did Jan pick a tenant on the basis of said tenant's hair?

ANSWER: I don't know why Jan picked me as a tenant on the basis of my hair. But what I *do* know—what we *all* know—is that doing so signifies an unorthodox approach to life. To go a step further, doing so signifies that a person's approach to life is indisputably psychotic, and that that indisputable psychosis will show its face at every turn.

Here it bears mentioning that I enjoy a bit of robust shower singing. I always have, and I did it a lot while living with Jan for no other reason, really, than that I've done it a lot always. But shower singing with Jan around was different because Jan liked joining in. I'd be singing in my shower and since Jan rarely left the apartment, she'd hear me singing every time. If she knew the song, she'd come to my bathroom door, throw it open, and sing along.

"*'THE RUM TUM TUGGER IS A CURIOUS CAT / AND THERE ISN'T ANY CALL FOR ME TO SHOUT IT!'* Good song, Sara. *Good.*"

Jan's sing-alongs were consistently shocking, which is to say I was never *not* surprised. I'd hear her voice, panic, and say, "Jan? Is that you?" and she'd laugh and shout, "What? No! It's the *real* Rum Tum Tugger!" Or—musical song choice depending—"What? No! It is *really* Eponine!"

JAN AND I lived together for a total of nine months. During those nine months, I had sex once, which is to say there was significantly less sex than there was back washing of a certain special someone. The event felt terribly precious, and this was in light of the fact that my partner in crime was a Burning Man enthusiast who measured in at five-foot-four.

I'm not talking shorter than I am *if I'm in heels,* I'm talking shorter than I am. Done.

The Burning Man and I had been set up by Gwen, a mutual friend, and although Gwen had good intentions, she had horrific matchmaking skills. The Burning Man showed up to our date late and wearing a backpack, and then proceeded to talk almost entirely about Burning Man. On the rare occasions when the Burning Man permitted me to speak, he wouldn't look me in the eye. He preferred scanning the room as I spoke.

Now, in fairness, the Burning Man surely had complaints of his own about me: Like that I showed up in an unsavory thrift-store ensemble. Like that I slapped myself to stay awake as he spoke incessantly about Burning Man.

All in all, it was an unpleasant evening out. The thing was, though, our mutual disdain was this weird sort of turn-on, and that, I think, was how we wound up having sex.

A little booze, a lot of self-loathing. You wind up having sex with people you despise.

The Burning Man and I arrived in my bedroom. We got on with the usual business of things, but not before I forgot to draw the curtain on my window. It faced the street. Things went relatively well for, I don't know, eight minutes? Maybe ten? But then I noticed the Burning Man watching himself in the mirror. It was all very *American Psycho,* that scene in the movie where Christian Bale is having sex with the prostitutes prior to bashing their heads in with some sort of radiator part, and he makes a face in the mirror that's all like, "Well, aren't *I* the sexy king?"

It was an unsettling thing to have evoked, and it wasn't helped by the frequent knocking of the small man's forehead against my chin. Nevertheless, I'd hoped to forgive and forget. However, this proved difficult when I noticed his expression shift from "Well, aren't *I* the sexy king?" to "What is going on outside the window?"

"Is that the landlord?" he asked. "The one who's diabetic?"

I looked out the window. And there, at midnight, was Jan. I couldn't tell you what she was doing there other than staring and waving.

"Hi, Sara!" she mouthed through the window.

"Hi, Jan!" I mouthed back.

If I am walked in on in a public bathroom stall, and if we, as humans, are to be divided into two distinct groups—those who shout, "Someone's *in* here!" versus those who shout, "Sorry! I'm so sorry!"—I'm a "sorry" type, no question. If any portion of my body is to be involuntarily seen naked, I can't shake the feeling that I'm not the victim so much as I am the one who's committed the crime. So it is that when my landlord stares me down and waves at me mid-coitus, when she appears jovial in lieu of annoyed, it is simply *in* me to wave back. I prefer repressing my annoyance. I prefer to let it bubble to the surface later on.

Jan and I exchanged greetings, and then she stood there for a moment, and then came back inside.

Well. You can just imagine where the sexual momentum was at that stage. There'd been the mirror gazing, the chin knocking, the cherry-on-top that was the verbal interaction with Jan. I could not have felt any less engaged, and so was delighted when the Burning Man did an awkward slither of a dismount and said, "Uh, well, I should get going, I guess. I've got a full day of work tomorrow. *And* I've got all my Burning Man photos, which I have to edit down and post to Facebook."

I slapped myself in the face.

"That sounds . . . rewarding," I said. "But also ex-hausting. So, well, like you said: it's probably time to go."

TWO WEEKS LATER, I was out for a power-walk through Prospect Park. I had originally planned on a run, but quickly I learned that I am not actually capable of breath-ing *while* I run. And this, it turns out, is a problem. So I stopped with the running and shifted into power-walking.

I power-walked into the park, past the band shell, the long meadow, and into the woods. It was there in the woods that I saw a homeless man asleep beneath a tree. He had scored himself a mattress, and the setup, as a whole, had the look of a canopy bed.

Seeing the homeless man lying there in his canopy bed was sort of like stumbling upon Sleeping Beauty. I do not mean that he looked drugged, just that he looked peaceful.

I stared at the homeless man for a minute or two before he awoke to see me staring.

"Hello," I said.

He pointed at my power-walking shoes.

"Dyke shoes," he said.

"I'm sorry?" I said.

But the homeless man had already fallen back to sleep.

The confusion I felt over the shoe exchange did not mit-igate the jealousy I felt over the sleeping setup. The home-less man had looked so peaceful there in the woods, on his mattress, under his tree. Surely he had his own trials and tribulations, but at least he could have intercourse in peace if the chance for intercourse arose. At least he didn't have to wash another person. At least if he had the chance to wash himself, he didn't have a landlord singing at him.

At least he didn't have a landlord.

The moment you envy a homeless man is the moment you must facilitate personal change.

In a rational moment, I knew I couldn't cope with Jan long-term. Or short-term, for that matter. It just wasn't worth it. I could not endure, and earn an inheritance, and pay for my own fertility treatments. I knew I had to move. Which meant I knew I had to get another roommate. Which meant I had to ask myself the painful but inevitable question:

Who next?

If I may, for a moment, presume that you have *not* undergone an emotional battering at the hands of a male almost-model, only to follow it up with Diabetic Jan, I'll report that the experience leaves a dramatic impression of roommates, and their capacity to top one another. It raises the questions: What worse roommate options are there? Would they continue to get worse? Would they ever *not* be awful?

These questions caused me terrible anxiety. The anxiety loosened my grip on reality, and that loose grip on reality had me thinking weird, unlikely things:

I am jealous of a homeless man.

Perhaps my mom will help me out.

So I left the homeless man alone. I raced home to call my mom.

"Hi, Mom," I said.

"Hi," she said.

"How's it going?" I said.

"Fine," she said.

"I'm having a hard time with my roommate," I said.

"The diabetic?" she said.

"Yes," I said. "So could I maybe have some money? It would help me move out."

"You have a *job* to earn money, to help you move out."

"But if you gave me *more* money, I could get my own place."

I heard her sigh: the audible eye-roll.

"Sara, *I* don't have my own place. I'm in the basement at the moment, hiding from your father, who's annoying."

My mother hung up the phone after that, and in the moment she did I heard a crash in Jan's bedroom. And then:

"SARA! COME FIX THE TV!"

I knew that leaving Jan was but a step down the rabbit hole toward some impossibly worse option. But that was just the risk I'd have to take.

I made a mad dash from my bedroom to the kitchen. I rummaged around for an onion, which I promptly sliced and sniffed. I walked toward Jan's bedroom with tears in my eyes. I knocked lightly on her door.

"Jan?" I called. "Are you in there?"

Jan opened the door.

"What?" she asked. "The hippie dwarf stopped calling?"

"No," I said. I wiped at my tears. "It's my mom. She's . . . she's . . . she's just been diagnosed with diabetes."

Jan paused. "What kind?" she asked.

I paused. "The bad kind," I answered. "So I need to go home. I mean, I need to *move* home. To be with her. I think it's the right thing to do."

Honest communication *is* important, but only for those in lasting relationships. With landlords and tenants, it's better to lie, to preserve someone's feelings. It's better to have an effective way out of your lease.

13

Not All Italians

I lied about my mother having diabetes, and doing so proved effective: Jan let me break my lease. The impending freedom was nice, but the downside was that Jan felt rejected. She stopped talking to me in those last weeks we lived together, and while this made for an uncomfortable at-home dynamic, it also meant no more washing of the back. This, in turn, meant I had some extra time to spend on Craigslist. I'd search the "Rooms/Shared" section, and then I'd scan the studios. I still could not afford a studio, but it felt like a treat just to look.

I was shocked to find the odd, affordable option. Nothing *in* my price range, to be clear, but the odd scrap of an apartment that wasn't quite so wildly *outside* my price range either. Were they hellholes? They were hellholes. Still, though, it was nice to know that they were out there. I studied a handful of options located in previously unknown neighborhoods: Woodside, Sunnyside, Rockaway. Bed-Stuy, Bushwick, Brownsville. I crunched some numbers. I determined that if I saved a small amount of money every month for one year, that by the end of that year, I could maybe—just maybe—afford one. Of course, I could maybe—just maybe—be raped or pillaged if ever I walked around outside in such affordable neighborhoods. But wouldn't that be worth it to avoid another roommate? I thought that it would, and returned to the "Rooms/ Shared" section. I searched for another apartment complete with another roommate. Something "for now," you see, so I could set aside the necessary money for the hellhole of my future. For a hellhole to call my own.

I MOVED FROM Park Slope to Astoria, Queens. There were several key reasons why the neighborhood appealed. It was a quick commute to my Olive Garden job, for one thing, and for another, its rents at the time were comparatively cheap. This made my studio goal more manageable. Astoria lacked the wealth and beauty of a place like Park Slope. The apartments were all short and squat, and the large Greek population meant that all privately owned businesses smelled a little bit like feta cheese.

I've always enjoyed acclimating to neighborhoods by endearing myself to local deli owners. Some people like doing this at bars, but I find delis less intimidating. Days after my Astoria arrival, I popped into a local spot called Athena's Face to order a sandwich and apple turnover. The man behind the counter, busy though he was undermining his Omar Sharif resemblance with a knee-length jean jacket, met my sandwich order with the question, "Sheep? Lamb? Goat?"

To this, I replied, "Oh. I'm sorry. A sandwich? May I have a sandwich?"

He of the Jacket of Jean sighed the exasperated sigh of those forced into repetition. "*Yes,*" he said. "So: Sheep? Lamb? Goat?"

I settled on lamb and sweetened, dehydrated beans in lieu of my apple turnover. I gazed out the deli window at a row of squat apartments, and told myself that this new and foreign culture would more than make up for the less than scenic surroundings.

My new Astoria apartment provided me with a new Astoria roommate, a young man named Roy. Roy, like Jan, I found on Craigslist. He worked for the New York City Fire Department, and the fact of his employment struck me as odd at first because Roy was emaciated. I'm talking, like, he had one of those physiques you want to lay across your knee and snap in two, and use as chopsticks. Further inquiry would eventually reveal he was not, in fact, a *fireman,* he simply worked for the Fire *Department.* And although I would remain forever unsure of his job title, Roy's firehouse responsibilities seemed to categorize as either secretarial or what-a-cleaning-man-does; he did something with phones, I think, a bit of picking up about the place, a bit of cooking.

"I cook," he'd say. "For the guys. Casseroles and stuff. With peas. Maybe chicken. That's what they like."

Roy and I didn't do a lot of talking. His work schedule was such that he spent half the week—twenty-four hours a day for three days straight—at the Kew Gardens firehouse so as to have the following three days off, three days he'd log locked in his bedroom, acting alcoholic. During his three-day stints at home, Roy would engage in certain habitual behaviors. Roy would:

1. Bring a six-pack into the bedroom.
2. Watch the TV in the bedroom.

3. Come out of the bedroom only to urinate, recycle, or restock.

This may sound bleak, and in theory, it was. However, in practice it meant I had the rest of the apartment to myself. And there was nothing bleak about that. On the contrary, I recall those first months with Roy as an idyllic period in my life. It felt like living alone, save for the asking price of being made aware of someone else's taste for self-destruction.

The joys of a *quiet* alcoholic roommate are too numerous to count. Therefore, I'll focus only on the one that's most important: I had control of the living room TV. I celebrated by watching it obsessively, like it was some crippled, dying animal that needed my attention to survive. Hours a day I worked to bolster my knowledge of everything from Tim Gunn's sex abstention to Tyra Banks's wig collection. From Jonathan Antin's water-purification system to the vast array of women who don't know they're pregnant until they have a baby in their jeans.

One evening I stumbled upon a show I had heard about, but never seen. It was called *The Sopranos,* and it was a rerun episode in which a character named Carmela sobs in a therapist's office after being forced to confront her husband's moral code.

Carmela: But Tony's a good man. He's a good father.
Therapist: You tell me he's a depressed criminal prone to anger, serially unfaithful. Is that your definition of a good man?

If an obsession can be born in an instant, then my obsession with *The Sopranos* did just exactly that. I loved everything about it: James Gandolfini, Edie Falco. The presentation of therapy as brave instead of self-involved. My attraction to John Ventimiglia.

I saw *The Sopranos* for the first time and joined Netflix immediately after for the sole purpose of watching every episode sequentially.

From that point on, the structure of my average day included eight hours of sleep, eight hours of waiting tables, and four hours of watching or rewatching *The Sopranos*. The remaining four hours were spent showering, eating, commuting, and so on, but it's important to note that throughout those remaining hours, I *thought* about *The Sopranos*. I thought about the character relationships. I thought about mob culture in general. I thought about how nice it would be to have a lot of cousins. I thought about David Chase's own personal therapy sessions, and also about the physical and emotional experience that would be hugging Tony Soprano. At a certain stage, I grew fearful of becoming a civilian casualty in a mafia-related crime, and became all at once admiring *and* scared of anyone I met who looked Italian American.

I wondered if this was potentially racist, but then I thought, Nah. I'm white. They're white. It's totally fine.

OVER TIME, MY *Sopranos* obsession had a dramatic effect. It left me with the sense that the Sopranos were real, that the mafia was everywhere. I might wind up unwittingly involved if I wasn't careful, and while this would be good insofar as I liked feeling protected, it would be bad insofar as I didn't want to die. Perhaps Roy, as my roommate, could have been my grounding influence. But his unobtrusive drinking kept him otherwise engaged.

One day Roy arrived home from work earlier than usual. His doing so prompted an atypically lengthy exchange.

Me: Oh, hi.
Roy: Hi.

Me: How come you're home?

Roy: I was fired.

Me: What? Really?

Roy: Yes.

Me: Wow. I'm sorry.

Roy: Thanks. (A pause.) I guess I'll make dinner. You want some? You like a casserole?

Me: What kind of casserole?

Roy: Chicken casserole. I'll throw in some Del Monte peas.

Roy made the casserole, we ate the casserole, and I am here to tell you that it was *the* worst thing I've ever eaten in my whole entire life. It tasted as though he'd thrown a gallon of week-old water onto a masticated, chicken-stuffed croissant. It was so disgusting that I gagged. I hadn't wanted to, but the reaction was not to be stopped.

Roy was drunk at this stage, and offended by my gagging.

"Jesus!" he screamed. "You are *welcome*! For your *dinner*!"

"Roy," I choked, and made up a story about being allergic to peas. "And when you said 'peas,' I thought you said 'cheese'!" I lied. "And that is why I gagged! Please don't be offended!"

Roy slammed down his beer can. He did this thing I'd seen in *The Sopranos* called "getting up in someone's face."

"Don't treat me like I'm dumb," he said.

"What?!" I yelled. "I *don't*!"

But Roy had already stormed out of the kitchen, down our meager hallway, and out toward our front door.

The apartment was quiet now, save for the half-dozen beer cans that stirred in his wake. I took the moment of quasi-silence to reflect on this first occasion of having someone *up* and *in* my face. It had been scary and threatening, but if the upshot was that I no longer felt pressured to eat the Del Monte casserole, then fine.

I debated wrapping the casserole in Saran wrap and putting it back in the refrigerator. But then I thought, No, Roy. You should not have gotten *up* and *in* my face. I will not reward such bad behavior by graciously preserving a casserole.

So I left the casserole out, exposed, atop the kitchen counter.

After that, I watched *The Sopranos.*

After that, I went to bed.

BY THE FOLLOWING morning, Roy still had not returned. I did not feel nervous in his absence. I rather enjoyed the luxury of having the place so fully to myself. I fluttered about. I whistled *The Sopranos* theme song. I imagined that if e'er I lived alone I'd keep a vase of flowers here, set a pedicure station up there.

I sipped my morning coffee. I gazed out the kitchen window at the car wash across the street.

And then I heard the noise.

It sounded very much like intercourse.

It came from behind Roy's bedroom door.

So. He *is* home, I thought. He *is* home. And he *is* having intercourse.

I debated whether to masturbate along, but decided instead to drown it out with an a.m. episode of *The Sopranos,* the one in which Janet Soprano steals Svetlana's wooden leg.

I watched half the episode before the noise stopped, and Roy's bedroom door swung open. A woman emerged who looked exactly like Snooki Polizzi. Mind you, this was before Snooki Polizzi blasted into public consciousness, so

I didn't see this woman and think, She looks exactly like Snooki Polizzi. Rather, the revelation came years later. I'd be watching *Jersey Shore,* see Snooki, and think: Wow. She and Gina are THE SAME.

"This is Gina," Roy said, and this new woman, Gina, responded by slapping her hand against Roy's chest.

"*Whatta man,*" she sang to no one in particular. "*Whatta man, whatta man, whatta man, whatta man, whatta mighty good maaaaaaaaan.*"

Gina, I gathered, was in her clothing from the night before: jeans and a mesh-lace halter top, as well as one of those bracelet/ring combinations that clamps onto the wrist, snakes up to the finger, and into a gargoyle ring. Accessory-wise, it's two for the price of one. Two for the price of looking like you belong at New York City's most repulsive rave. And, I'm sorry, but were we at a rave? No. We were standing in my kitchen.

The first thing I thought to consider was whether Gina was a one-night stand or a previously unseen girlfriend. Or a one-night-stand who would become a *much*-seen girlfriend. Instinct told me Gina was a one-night-stand who would become a much-seen girlfriend, because, as previously demonstrated, I have a bizarre and hugely annoying habit of attracting people who slip into relationships like they're slipping on a pair of well-worn jeans.

The second thing I thought to consider was whether Gina might have mafia connections. Because, well, she did seem *as* Italian American as any human could. I was both excited and terrified by the idea, and made a promise to myself that come hell or more audible sex with my roommate, I would work to stay on Gina's good side. I would not piss Gina off.

"Well! Hello, Gina!" I said, just as warmly as I could. "It's really nice to meet you! Would you like some *pro-SHOOT*? Or perhaps some *ri-GOT*?"

Gina grimaced.

"Nah," she said. "I'll just have cereal or whatevah. It's too early for *pro-SHOOT*."

"Totally," I said. "I'll just *fuhgeddaboudit* then."

GINA, LIKE TOMAS, appeared one day, and then just pretty much moved in. I thought things could go differently between us, however; that in the case of Gina and me, the deference I showered upon her would preemptively put her in a headspace to be kind and respectful toward me. But as the days and weeks progressed, it seemed rather that Gina wanted to challenge my deference by being annoying. Her personal habits included nicknaming Roy's forearms her "nibble sticks," as well as making frequent reference to her levels of vaginal moisture. When I asked her how she and Roy had met, she'd said, "I'll tell ya. I was atta bar, and I sawr him, and I said to my girl, Adriana, 'Oh my *gawd*, Adriana, check him *out*. Get me a paper towel *now*.' And Adriana was like, '*Why?*' And I was like, 'Because: My snatch is floodin', bitch! I wet my seat! I need to wipe!' "

My main point of interest here was not Gina's physical response to the emaciated Roy. It was rather that Gina had a close friend named Adriana. Which, I'll remind you, is the name of Chris Moltisanti's ill-fated fiancée who (spoiler alert) IS KILLED BY THE **MAFIA CAPTAIN** WHO IS SUPPOSED TO BE HER **FRIEND**.

Hello.

I had become the kind of person who cannot separate the characters in her favorite daytime soap from the real-life actors who play them on TV. When Gina said "my girl, Adriana," what I heard was "I have a friend who's engaged to the protégé of the head of the New Jersey family."

In which case:

1. Gina, Roy's girlfriend, was two degrees removed from the New Jersey mafia.

And also:

2. I, Sara Barron, was *three* degrees removed from the New Jersey mafia.

In light of points 1 and 2 above, I considered how at *any* second of *any* day I might find myself in the inconvenient path of a stray bullet. Civilians who move near those mafia circles *can* be harmed in this way, and so did I consider whether to treat myself to a bulletproof vest.

Gina went, "My girl, Adriana . . ."

And I went, Maybe I need a bulletproof vest.

I considered it. Not a lot, but a little. Eventually, though, I realized I was jumping to conclusions, and that the money I'd put toward a bulletproof vest could be used to more practical effect if I put it toward sanitary wipes instead. In light of Gina's excitable vagina, I figured they'd be good to have around.

Gina discussed her vagina nonstop. Everything was "my snatch" this and "my snatch" that.

"My snatch gets swamp damp when I see my boyfriend."

"My snatch is a horny jellyfish."

"My snatch is wet 'n' wild. LIKE THE LIP GLOSS!"

Now, I am nothing if not a woman who loves a little vaginal comparison now and again. But it was just too much when combined with Gina's other affections: vanilla-scented Yankee candles, as well as a Jessica Simpson home spray called Fancy Nights. The candles were always burning, and as for the home spray, anytime anyone made a bowel movement—or rather, any time Gina *thought* she *smelled* a bowel movement—she would shout the phrase

"Fancy Nights! Fancy Nights!" and grab the spray, and spray it everywhere within ten feet of the toilet.

I felt about this behavior as I felt about the vaginal comparison: enjoyable in the right circumstance, and from the right person. But a woman living rent-free in my apartment is neither. Not when she has a boyfriend and I myself do not. Under this particular circumstance I am destined to be less receptive. I'll hear her Fancy Nights turd alarm and become thoroughly annoyed.

I AM HAPPY to tell you that things did turn around eventually between Gina and me, and that I owe that turnaround to the excessive length of Gina's vagina.

Yes. The excessive length of Gina's vagina.

Six months into Gina's relationship with Roy—which, then, was six months into Roy's stint of unemployment—Roy was busy drinking in his bedroom, while Gina and I sat chatting in the kitchen. We'd been discussing those more scenic sections of Weehawken, New Jersey, when suddenly a light snow began to fall. In response, Gina shouted "HOLY SHIT! SNOW!" and then tried hoisting herself onto the kitchen table—it sat right beside a window—in the hope of getting a better view. However, her jeans were too tight to allow her to do so, and so she removed them, as you do. She took off her jeans and was therefore in only the snuggest of underpants when she succeeded in getting herself up there on that table. Gina perched there, squatting froglike, watching snow.

The view from behind was astounding. Just . . . astounding. A large tongue, was what it looked like, sandwiched by a puffy bun. I have to admit that I loved it, and by this I mean that I loved the experience of seeing it. What with my limited real-life lesbian experience as well as my general pornography aversion, it was the first occasion wherein I'd struck that delicate balance between distance *and* proximity—in other words, the balance one needs to get a proper look. When finally I did, I was delighted. For I thought, Well, I might be hefty of neck, waist, and ankle, but at least *that's* not happening. Then it occurred to me that maybe it *was* happening, it was just that I didn't know it was happening since I don't ever see myself from that particular angle.

Ultimately, though, I abandoned that line of thinking, and that is because occasionally—and for reasons unknown—I manage effective steps toward self-preservation. Sometimes I think, Sara, you don't need a bulletproof vest just because you live with an Italian girl who has a friend named Adriana. Or, Sara, let it go. Your vagina length is perfect.

The knowledge of the long vagina did a lot to improve my relationship with Gina. It provided me with a much-appreciated bump to my self-esteem and, as we all know, a person who makes us feel good about ourselves is a person we enjoy. Furthermore, it helped to humanize Gina. This was the natural side effect of seeing her in so raw and vulnerable a state. Something shook loose in my head, and I got it. I was like, Oh. Gina's not some scary mafioso. She's just a nice girl, with a long vagina.

I felt less afraid and was therefore able to be more direct. So when, for example, Gina started hand-washing her underpants and hanging them to dry on the shower rod, and when this particular action resulted in water dripping on my person from the crotch areas of Gina's underpants whenever I entered or exited the shower, I was empowered to say something about it rather than cower in fear. I said, "Hey, Gina. Can you do me a favor and hang your underpants somewhere else after you wash them?" and Gina answered, "Huh? Oh. Sure," and started laying the underpants across the kitchen chairs instead. It wasn't the optimal location, but the point is that we were communicating, and that that communication was helping our relationship.

The same could not be said for Roy and Gina. Their honeymoon period was over by this stage, and the sound of their intercourse had been replaced with the sound of inebriated attempts at conversation.

"I wanted a cone."

"What? I don't know you."

"You know me, baby!"

"Fuck it. Want a sandwich?"

"What? No! I wanted a *cone*. Ice cream is *fun* in a *cone*."

Most of the time, these exchanges would start out drunk and relating in some way to food, before devolving into something hostile, and relating in some way to money. Gina was angry because she'd lent Roy an indiscernible amount and he had failed to pay her back. He also drank too much, although I'm paraphrasing by writing it that way. What Gina said exactly was, "Roy! Ya' too drunk! Ya' don't take the snatch no more! Just *take* it! Be like, 'Who's your boss, bitch? *Roy's* your boss!' "

I myself had overheard this particular argument countless times, and had taken it upon myself to devise a solution. The old me might've warned Roy that an unpaid debt to an Italian was a really bad idea, but the new me was direct with those around her, and not at all beholden to Italian American stereotypes. The new me had mature solutions, and wondered whether Gina, who was living with Roy and me full-time, should perhaps forgive the debt as repayment for the previous months' rent. More to the point, I wondered whether she should pay rent moving forward.

I returned home from work one night and decided to be bold, to bring up my idea. Roy was in his bedroom drinking. Gina was in the living room watching TV. I said, "Oh, hey, Gina. How are you?" but she did not respond. So I walked closer to her. I could see that she was drunk.

I tried again.

"Hey. Gina," I repeated.

"Whaaa?" she slurred.

"Oh! Good! You're awake," I said. "I thought maybe you were doing that thing where people sleep with their eyes open. Have you ever seen it? It's super weird! Anyway, care to chat? Woman to woman?"

Gina, still, said nothing.

"Well. So. Here's the thing," I said. "I've overheard you and Roy these past few weeks discussing how he owes you money for . . . a case of beer, I think it was, and tickets to see Coldplay. But seeing as how you've been living here full-time, I thought maybe the thing to do would be to call it even on the money. I thought that maybe moving forward, you'd pay a portion of the rent."

Gina looked confused at this stage, and backed her head into her neck. This had the overall effect of giving her a double chin.

She belched loudly in my face.

"Bless you," I said.

"*Fuck* you," she said. "Just, like, fuck. *You*. I ain't givin' you money. Or Roy money. Or anybody money."

The "fuck you" felt out of left field and unnecessarily aggressive. Nonetheless, I chose not to make an issue.

"You've had a long day," I said. "I can see that, and I blame myself, as a matter of fact, for choosing a stupid time to bring this up. Let's discuss it in the morning, maybe, when you're in a better frame of mind to—"

"JUST SHUT *UP*!" she screamed. "JUST LEAVE ME ALONE! WHY CAN'T *EVERYONE* LEAVE . . . ME . . . *ALONE*?"

I threw my hands up, not in exasperation, but so that I might convey an overall mood of compliance.

"Yes, okay," I said. "I am leaving you alone."

Gina took a deep breath, marched toward Roy's bedroom, and slammed the door behind her.

I took a deep breath, sat down in the living room, and watched *The Sopranos*. It felt different this time, though, as I felt atypically distracted. I kept reviewing what Gina had said:

"Why can't EVERYONE leave me alone?"

I found the sentence disconcerting. Who did she mean when she said "everyone"? On instinct, I pictured a sociopathic brother with a chip on his shoulder who'd be angry at his sister's deadbeat boyfriend. I pictured someone who would swing by soon to beat Roy up. Or, if things went wrong, to shoot him. And he'd shoot me too, by the way. He'd shoot Roy because Roy had been disrespectful, and he'd shoot me because I had seen him shooting Roy.

I was jumping to conclusions and I knew it.

Sara, I told myself. *Lemon. Asshole. OUT.*

There was no reason to be nervous. I channeled the better version of myself, the one who knew that this was not how people behaved just because they were Italian American. I reminded myself of the progress I'd made in my relationship with Gina. She was someone with whom I had a rapport. Gina was no one to fear. Gina was almost a friend. And if she, a friend, made reference to an unspecified "everyone," well, then she probably meant, like, I don't know . . . her mom? Yes. She probably meant her mom. Her totally normal, nonthreatening mom.

I was smart enough—now—to understand this. I was rational. I was *mature*.

THE FOLLOWING MORNING I slept in, treated myself to a bacon breakfast, and went to the bathroom for an on-schedule morning movement. As I exited the bathroom, I prepared for Gina's usual Fancy Nights turd alarm, and was therefore surprised when I heard a loud knock at the door. Gina went to the door, opened the door, and there before her stood a man—shirtless—wearing only tracksuit pants.

This man, I would learn, was Gina's brother, and his name was Dinosaur Dante. Why? you ask. Because he had stegosaurus back plates tattooed along his spine.

"Dinosaur Dante!" screamed Gina. "Whatta ya doin' here! Whatta ya doin' in my home?"

In *my* home? IN *MY HOME*?

I would've found the phrase more audacious, but I was too terrified by a certain aggressor who had just been allowed in my home.

In *my* home. Because I, of course, paid rent.

Dinosaur Dante did some nasal breathing.

"Get outta my way," he said to Gina. "Just tell me where to find that skinny bitch."

One thing I don't evoke is "skinny bitch." If Dinosaur Dante had come to our apartment looking for a "skinny bitch," then he was surely there for Roy. He had surely spoken to his sister about the status of her current relationship, and was surely here to seek revenge.

I write "surely," although what I mean is "presumably." Because I could only presume. I could only use my knowledge of *The Sopranos* and, therefore, of all Italian American families, to make an educated guess as to what had happened. Gina had presumably complained about Roy in front of Dinosaur Dante. Gina had presumably mentioned Roy's continued unemployment, or the fact that Roy had borrowed money, and failed to pay her back. And in light of Dinosaur Dante's proclivity for fits of shirt-removing aggression, shouldn't Gina—presumably—have thought that through a little more?

Why, yes, indeed. Why, yes, she should.

Dinosaur Dante barreled past me—I'd stood frozen by the bathroom door—toward Roy, who was sipping a beer in his bedroom. Dinosaur Dante announced that he had come to fight. Not with his words, but with his actions. Which is to say he kept repeatedly jamming his sternum against Roy's chest concavity while alternately smacking him in the face.

"I'm an Ultimate Fighta, okay?" he told him. "*That's* who you fuck with when you fuck with Gina Bogadelli. An Ultimate. *Fighta.*"

The unbridled anger combined with the sight of Dinosaur's namesake tattoos left me with the distinct impression that someone was going to die. And who could say for sure who that would be? Roy was the obvious choice, but my understanding of a certain type of hostile individual is that their targets can shift on a dime.

Consider, for a moment, the relationship between Tony Soprano and Georgie, the bartender at the Bada Bing. Georgie's a nice guy, sure, but he rubs Tony the wrong way. And since Tony's always angry about one thing or another, Tony's always beating Georgie up. I'd seen it happen a million times and felt instantly, viscerally concerned that something similar could happen to me with Dinosaur Dante. That if I wasn't careful, I'd wind up the Georgie to his Tony.

As for Roy, I thought he handled himself well. By this I mean that he did not cry or shit his pants. He just kept telling Dinosaur Dante to "chill."

As for Gina, she passed the time pleading with Dinosaur Dante on Roy's behalf.

"DINOSAUR, STOP! PLEASE STOP! ROY'S FRAGILE! HE'S FRAGILE!"

I wanted to tell her it would all be okay, but I couldn't

get a word in edgewise, and anyway, I wasn't so sure. I tried making my way from the bathroom to the kitchen for a serrated knife with which to defend myself *in case,* but then Dinosaur covered Roy's face with his hand and slammed Roy's head against the wall, and instinctively, I shouted, "OY!"

And Dinosaur Dante whipped around.

"Back up, bitch," he said. "Back. The Fuck. Up."

"I WILL!" I screamed. "I'M BACKING UP! I'M VERY SORRY!"

I ran for my bedroom and blocked the door with my bookcase, bed, and dresser. I searched for weapons. I grabbed a bobby pin and earring post. I stood at the ready in what is commonly known as Warrior II.

Prepare, I told myself. *To fight.*

I'VE HEARD IT said that you can't know how you'll respond in a crisis until that crisis arrives. What *I* learned in *my* crisis was that I would respond with both a yoga pose and an ineffective weapon. I'd do this as I basked in the perverse glow that is being right when you cannot *believe* that you are right . . . when you wanted, for once, to be wrong.

I learned that I would promptly call my mom.

"Mom," I said. "It's me."

"Where are you?" she asked.

"At home," I answered.

"Why are you whispering?" she asked.

"Because," I answered, "Roy's girlfriend . . ."

"The one with the underpants? The underpants she lays across the chairs?"

"Yes," I said. "Her brother came over, and he wasn't wearing a shirt, and he was acting really angry, and I said, 'OY!' . . ."

"*Why?!*" she yelled. "*Why* would you say 'OY' to a very angry man?"

"*Because!*" I said. "He was pressing Roy's head against the wall, and he threatened me and called me 'bitch'!"

A pause.

"Mom? Did you hear what I said? HE THREATENED ME AND CALLED ME 'BITCH'!"

A pause.

"How much?" she asked.

A pause.

"Eight hundred," I answered. "At the absolute most."

Let me here return to the issue of my savings.

In the year I'd lived with Roy, I had saved up almost enough for one of those hellholes of an affordable studio apartment. The operative word, though, is "almost." On the day of Dinosaur Dante's arrival I lacked the necessary funds to move out, for I lacked the necessary funds for a security deposit. I was on the path toward saving the money myself, and would've gotten there in just a few more months. And was there value in that? In getting there myself? I did believe there was. But now—in this moment—I had a maybe-killer in my home. Now—in this moment—I was literally squatting as my form of self-defense.

"Eight hundred . . . *dollars*?" asked my mom.

"Yes," I said.

"You're out of your mind," she said.

"Mom," I said, "I'm really not. I swear I'm not. I'm asking because I might die."

"You will not die."

"But I *could* die."

"You couldn't die."

"I *could* die."

"It's unlikely that you'd die."

"Yes, well, it was unlikely that that hemorrhoid I had

last spring was a tumor. But you paid for the out-of-network doctor because it *could* have been. Because I *could* have died. I could have died from cancer, and I could still die at the hand of the aggressive man!"

A pause. An exasperated breath.

"Eight hundred dollars, Sara. Fine. I swear to god, though, if you ever do so much as . . ."

"I won't, Mom. I promise. I won't ever ask again."

THE MINUTES PASSED by. Ten. Twenty. Thirty. I heard neither a gunshot nor a skull go through a wall. I relaxed slightly and got off the phone with my mother. I came out from under my bed, where I'd gone to make the call, and back into my Warrior II. I stayed there for a moment. I moved from my Warrior II to the top of the dresser that I'd pushed against the door. This new position was a more vulnerable position, but I was desperate to hear what was going on.

I heard a bit more yelling and a bit more sternum-bumping.

I heard a loud smack and a scream.

I heard the cops arrive.

I heard everyone go quiet.

I heard the cops ask what the problem was.

I heard Gina and company respond.

"Nothin'. Nothin'. We're cool, sir. We're good."

I heard the cops say, "Well, keep it down then, all right?"

I heard the cops leave after that, and I heard Dinosaur Dante leave with them. He was not handcuffed or, as I had expected, arrested on sight for the murder of someone named Don Giovanni. He was just escorted nonviolently out.

Gina stayed behind with Roy. I stayed locked in my

bedroom for hours. I came out only when I had to go to work. I gave myself a little extra time, though, for a little talk with Roy.

I found him slumped on the couch beside Gina. They looked drunk and very tired.

"Hey, Roy," I said, "I'd like to talk."

"Whaaa?" he slurred.

"I'd like to talk," I said.

"Okeydokey," he said. "Talk."

"Well," I said. "It's a difficult topic. But sometimes, well, it's important to be honest, don't you think?"

Gina grabbed the remote. She increased the volume.

"*Anyway,*" I said (over the increase in volume), "Roy, I think it's important to be honest. And the reason I bring it up is that I'd like to be honest with you. There's something, well, difficult that I would like to talk to you about."

"Whaaaa?" he slurred.

"There's something difficult that I would like to talk to you about."

"O-*kaaaay,*" he said.

"The thing is, Roy—and this is hard for me to say—but I need you, as my roommate, to know."

Gina, again, increased the volume.

"ROY, IF YOU CAN HEAR ME, THERE'S SOME-THNG I NEED YOU TO KNOW."

"WHAAAA?" he asked. "WHADDAYA NEED ME TA KNOW?"

I paused. I said, "I WAS AROUND A LOT OF VIO-LENCE AS A CHILD."

In truth, the only violence I was around as a child took place this one Fourth of July weekend, when my parents took Sam and me to a water park in Wisconsin. While there, I'd seen another kid get spanked. That had been the sum total of my childhood violence exposure, however my last lie about family had worked pretty well. I figured I should try my luck with it again.

"ANYWAY, YES," I continued. "THAT IS . . . ME. AND MY . . . STORY."

"OH. YEAH?" he said.

"OH. *YEAH*," I said. "AND I MENTION IT BE-CAUSE TODAY WAS JUST . . . TOO MUCH. FOR ME. YOU KNOW? I THINK I HAVE TO MOVE."

"MOOOOOOOOVE," he said, contemplative.

"YES," I said. "MOVE."

Roy closed his eyes and shrugged. He stayed there for a moment. He opened them again.

"FINE," he said. "YOU GO DO WHATEVAH. YOU GO SEE IF I CARE."

I'D HAVE MONEY in the bank. I had the blessing of my roommate. It was everything I needed. It was time to live alone.

14
Eleanor Barron

Although I myself have never been married, I know a few women who have. Who have craved it, and gone on to get it. I have known these women and spoken to these women, and they have told me what it feels like, getting the thing they wanted so badly for so long.

For a moment, it *is* great. But then it mostly isn't great. It is precisely what it feels like to finally live alone.

I LIED TO Roy about my early exposure to violence, and two weeks later I moved from Astoria, Queens, to a thumb-sized studio in the Bushwick section of Brooklyn.

Bushwick, at its worst, was a series of warehouses interspersed with chain-link fence and the odd, abandoned lot.

Bushwick, at its best, had a certain industrial charm.

There was a supermarket with a comprehensive "World Food" aisle, and a coffee shop that sold sandwiches without too much mayonnaise. There was a Laundromat with a good deal on stain removal and a corner bodega where—if you were so moved—you could buy the dried ears of a pig.

Bushwick covers a wide stretch of Brooklyn, and is home to a diverse population of Hispanics, blacks, and whites. The whites are mostly hipsters. The blacks and Hispanics are not.

I moved to the part that was hipster and Hispanic.

When I saw someone Hispanic, she'd be going to or coming from work.

When I saw someone Hipster, she'd be in a crazy outfit.

These generalizations are sweeping. But they are also mostly true.

The hipsters were always all "'sup, dude" this and "peace, man" that. One time, I was power-walking through the supermarket, when I heard a woman in a cowboy hat and full-length mink say, "Art's what I was born for."

I found this behavior all at once ridiculous and intimidating. I'd run my Bushwick errands in the same sweatpants ensemble I'd favored for my Astoria errands. No one thought much of it back in Queens, but this was not the case in Bushwick. I was at the coffee shop one time, when the guy behind the counter asked, "I'm sorry, but are you sick?"

And I said, "No."

And *he* said, "Then how come you're always in sweatpants?"

I will point out that at the time of this exchange, the guy behind the counter was wearing a onesie he had belted with a headscarf.

Lacking the confidence to stay true to myself and my

sweatpants, I purchased a pair of knock-off Ray-Bans and a used, waist-length fur of my own. But then I got gnats from the fur and the weight of the Ray-Bans gave me a headache. So I threw them both out and purchased instead a handful of plaid, lady-lumberjack shirts. I paired the shirts with jean shorts. I paired the jean shorts with ripped tights. I thought I looked good. Or rather, I thought I looked appropriate, considering.

I was madly in love with my new apartment, for it was mine and mine alone. And sure, it was small, but I mostly didn't care. The bedroom was the kitchen, which was also the den. The bathroom was its own separate thing, which was good, although the toilet didn't flush.

That's an exaggeration.

It would be fairer to say that one in five times the toilet *wouldn't* flush.

In a different situation this might have upset me, but in this one it did not. If you are literally starving, you will find yourself willing to eat human flesh. If you have lived with Wayne and Tomas, Jan, and Roy and Gina, you can watch a turd *go nowhere* up to seven times a week. You can watch a turd go nowhere and feel lucky while you do.

I would not have believed it if I myself had not lived through it.

I loved living alone as much as I have ever loved anything else in my life. There was a good, long stretch of time in which I felt . . . I think the word is "happy." The experience suited me. I smiled more. I slept better. I had that glow that comes with exercise, but without having to exercise.

My favorite part of each day was now coming home at the end of it. After waiting tables for eight hours, the silence upon entry was like a massage, relaxing and luxurious. I set up a pedicure station smack in the middle of my bedroom/kitchen/den. I would sit there and give myself a pedicure. I would pass gas like it's what I was paid for. I would feel, in a word, content.

Such was my life alone in a studio apartment: mostly good, if uneventful.

But then something happened.

It was *very* bizarre.

I had been living alone for approximately one year the first time I noticed it.

I write "approximately" because it was the sort of thing that goes on for ages before you even know you're doing it. The sort of thing you catch yourself doing offhandedly one day, and think, Oh. Wait. I've been doing that a *lot*.

I had been feeding an imaginary dog.

While living alone I had developed the habit of eating always on my couch or in my bed. Once I was done eating, I would not walk the plate back to the sink. To avoid getting up, I would leave it on the floor, and there was a point at which I started coupling this behavior with the affectionate encouragement of a nonexistent dog.

"*Good* dog. *Good* girl. Lick up all the scraps so Mommy doesn't have to clean the plate."

Or: "Okay, sweetie. Here's the rest of Mommy's popcorn. You can have it as a treat."

I knew instinctively that the creature was an English bulldog named Eleanor Barron. I knew she was withholding from everyone other than me.

I HAVE ALREADY mentioned that I do not like pets of any kind and, as a result, have never had any conscious ambition toward dog ownership. The neediness, the odor. The chewing, the mess. It all just annoys me, and that's to say nothing of the fact that the only thing that's ever made me *truly* gag is the smell and gelatinous texture of wet dog food.

Eleanor emerging from my subconscious was therefore surprising. But it was also, strangely, not surprising. As a child, I invented some orphan teen models. As an adult, I came up with a dog. The manifestations were different, but the motivation was the same: I was lonely, and it helped to have someone around.

I did not feel ashamed of my bulldog. I rather felt resourceful *because* of my bulldog. I had found a solution to the loneliness with all of the benefits and none of the problems. Eleanor never puked or emptied her bowels. She never needed to go out unless I myself was going out. So it was that having Eleanor around never felt like "Oh. I'm having a breakdown." It was more like, "*Well.* Aren't *I* the lucky duck? I've got a brand-new friend who doesn't cost me any money."

Eleanor became my frequent bedmate and travel companion. I noticed her in early October, and by the time Thanksgiving rolled around, I'd taken to inviting her into my bed. The reason I know it was Thanksgiving was that I'd been at my parents' house in Chicago. I remember I was in my childhood bedroom, and I remember I whispered, "Do you like it in Chicago? Here, Eleanor, come cuddle up with Mommy!"

We had a lovely time together that holiday weekend, although over the course of it I made the intelligent choice not to introduce her to my parents. They're just not animal people, you see, and furthermore I was not up for the possibility of being labeled schizophrenic. Talking to myself is and was an enjoyable part of my day. I did not care to have it sullied by parental disapproval.

One afternoon, I went out for coffee with my friend Maggie. It was winter now and I had recently gotten into this new habit of using a hot water bottle to keep myself warm. Not only that, I had taken to projecting Eleanor *onto* the hot water bottle. So instead of existing as an un-defined air mass, she now existed as an object. I debated whether to buy her one of those dog-shaped hot-water-bottle cases, but eventually decided against it. I thought doing so would make the whole thing too bizarre, and was now leaning (hot-water-bottle-wise) toward something in the teal family. Something patternless.

"So," Maggie said, "what have you done today? Any-thing?"

"I read *Seventeen* magazine," I said. "And . . . I have a dog I've been talking to. So I talked to her for a while."

Maggie looked up.

I continued, "I've been doing this thing where I pretend my hot-water bottle is an imaginary dog."

"Are you having a breakdown?" Maggie asked.

"I don't think so," I answered. "I mean, I understand that she's not real. I know that she's not there. It's more like . . ."

"You need someone around," she said. "You need someone to talk to."

"Yes," I said. And Maggie shrugged.

"Well, then I think it's nice," she said. "Then I think it's probably good."

The chance to talk about my situation made me feel good about it, even better than I had before. I felt en-couraged and understood, and two weeks later wound up treating myself to the dog-patterned hot-water-bottle holder after all. I thought, What the hey: it's *really* cute. Not long after, I treated myself to a throw pillow upon which was an embroidered bulldog face. The pillow I kept on the couch while the hot water bottle stayed on my bed. This way, Eleanor was everywhere.

When I left the house without her, I'd see other dogs —real dogs—jumping up on people, barking, peeing, and pooping like they do. And I would whisper, "Eleanor would never." Or, "I have raised Eleanor better than that."

ELEANOR NOT ONLY *was* my dog, she *is* my dog. She has stayed with me, my loving companion. She has remained forever true. We get along great, and it's not surprising, really, since Lovable Master with Zero Responsibility is the job that I was born for. The companionship's good too, I think. It's the bare minimum required to keep me feeling sane.

15
Talk to Her

It had been two years since I had moved into my studio apartment in Bushwick. It had been one year since discovering—and then embracing—the bulldog, Eleanor Barron.

It was summer, and I was sweating. Every day, I sweat *a lot*.

I had graduated from waiting tables at the Olive Garden and was now waiting tables at a trendy, more upscale pizzeria. This had provided me with my second blip of a wage increase, and I was putting the extra money toward living in a more extravagant style. Which is to say I was putting it toward this Lancôme under-eye cream that did not nearly enough for me, but that I continued to buy because I wanted to believe it did. I had nothing left over for any additional treats. When finally I accrued a week's worth of vacation, I had no choice but to stay on in New York.

My initial plan was to spend the time exploring the city in a budget-conscious way. I'd do all the touristy things you never get around to when you live here. I'd visit the Statue of Liberty, followed by a stroll up the West Side Highway, followed by a visit to TKTS to see if there were any $30 seats to *Mamma Mia!* But then that first morning of the scheduled staycation my alarm went off at nine a.m., and I weighed my plans against the prospect of sleeping two more hours, getting a bagel and cream cheese, and watching *The View*.

The second option beat the first.

I chose it, and stuck with it. For four days in a row.

I slept, I ate, I watched TV.

I slept, I ate, I watched TV.

The time went by and I spoke to no one. No one other than Eleanor, that is, who (I'm sad to say) faltered in her duties. She was usually so adept at mitigating the pitfalls of living alone, but that was when I spent forty hours a week at work among my fellow human beings. That was when I had coworkers to talk to. Without them, an imaginary dog was very much the Band-Aid on the gunshot. Very "Who needs the epidural? Try a Tylenol instead."

After four days without human interaction my need for conversation had become so hugely overwhelming that I left my apartment and went to the corner deli for the singular purpose of chatting to the man behind the counter.

"Hello!" I'd said. "How are you? What time did you start work today? Shit! That's really early! I live around the corner. I think this deli's really nice."

The man found my neediness alienating, as men so often do, and it hurt my feelings when I clocked it, when

I saw him give the ol' widening of the eyes to his co-worker behind the register. They were all, like, *HELP,* his eyes. They were all like, *RING HER UP AND GET HER OUT.*

So then I walked back home. I decided maybe I'd call my parents, but then I remembered they were visiting Sam at college in New Orleans. So I called my mother's cell phone. She didn't pick up. She did, however, respond via text message two hours later.

"We are with Sam! We are eating beignets! Your brother has NEVER looked better!"

Along with the text came a photo of Sam eating his beignets, and he hadn't ever looked better. He'd lost all last reserves of baby fat, and looked, as a result, like Mark Wahlberg with a bit of Bradley Cooper mixed in.

Sam's handsomeness enraged me. I debated how best to handle it. I decided to go up to my roof to work on my tan. I thought a little tanning might relax me.

So I climbed up the stairwell and went up on the roof. There was a small garden of geraniums there, as well as a full view of Manhattan. It was not an awful place to be.

I'd brought a towel up with me, and put it down now on the section of roof near the geraniums. I lay down and looked at the skyline.

I tanned for a while, and *as* I tanned I thought about my brother's newfound angular features.

It was not a sexual thing. It was just that I was angrily obsessed.

An hour passed, at which point an unknown neighbor appeared on the roof. She wore shorts and a tank top. She accented this otherwise standard outfit with knee-high socks and one of those Davy Crockett hats. I do believe it's called a "coonskin hat." She carried a watering can and began watering the geraniums.

I hoped she might introduce herself of her own volition. When she did not, I said, "NICE DAY, TODAY, HUH?"

The unknown neighbor looked up.

"Oh, uh, yeah," she said.

"I AM SARA, BY THE WAY," I said. "I LIVE, WELL, HERE, RIGHT? HA! I LIVE HERE."

"Right. Well, hi," she said. "It's nice to meet you. I'm Annie."

"ANNIE! GREAT! I LOVE THAT NAME! MY BEST FRIEND IN GRADE SCHOOL WAS AN ANNIE! SHE WOUND UP AT PRINCETON! SHE'S FLUENT IN KOREAN NOW, I THINK!"

Annie nodded. She shifted the position of the coonskin. She looked forlornly at the flowers.

"Right. Well, I should go," she said. "Bye."

"OH! OKAY! BYE!" I shouted back. "IT WAS REALLY NICE CHATTING WITH YOU!"

I waved good-bye. Then, though, I started to wonder if perhaps the neighborly thing might not be to accompany Annie and her coonskin on her walk back into the building.

I decided it was, packed up my towel, and followed her back in.

Annie noticed me behind her.

"What are you doing?" she asked.

"Oh! Ha! Hi again!" I answered. "I'm just, you know, all finished with my tanning."

Annie nodded, and continued briskly down the stairs. She went into her apartment: #3R.

Noted, I thought, and continued one floor down to mine.

Once inside, I examined my tan. It looked pretty good. It looked *so* good, in fact, it convinced me it was time to go out.

I considered different destinations. I considered Williamsburg, but then decided I didn't feel like being intimidated by the neighborhood's various hairstyles. I considered Greenpoint, but then I recalled that, for no discernable reason, most of my enemies live there. I considered the Upper West Side, but then felt overwhelmed by the prospect of an hour-long commute.

I decided, finally, to go to Greenwich Village. There's a good gelateria on the corner of Bleecker and Carmine, and I thought it'd be nice to go get a cone, take a stroll, maybe solicit a heckle or two. Perhaps a "Damn, gurl." Perhaps a "Can I get a lick?" I thought, if Sam can eat beignets and lose all last reserves of baby fat, *I* can eat gelato and have my sex appeal affirmed.

I called four different friends to see if anyone wanted to join me. Three of these friends failed to answer their phone. But the fourth picked up. She said, "What? No. I can't. It's two o'clock on Wednesday, Sara. Some of us have jobs."

I committed to going alone.

I arrived at the gelateria forty-five minutes later and ordered a scoop of gelato (hazelnut) on a cone. I walked west on Bleecker, then north on Seventh Avenue. No heckles occurred naturally, so I tried, while walking, to think of Betty Boop. I suppose the thing to say is that I tried to *channel* Betty Boop *while* walking. I worked for a sexy side-to-side sway of the hips, but the dairy in the gelato had done a real number on me, gas-wise, and the hip-sway served only to force it all out. I passed the kind of gas where *so* much air shoots out of you at *such* a pace, you're shocked—once the whole thing's said and done—to find yourself still standing.

It made no noise to the outside world, but the aroma was another thing entirely. There was one lucky couple downwind, who began to grimace and insult me.

"Jesus *Christ*."

"What the *fuck*?"

"Is that garbage or a person?"

"A person, I think. Some asshole fucking farted."

"Jesus."

"So noxious."

"People are selfish."

"And repulsive."

"Honestly. They *are.*"

This couple made me feel bad about myself, and to compensate I attempted one last side-to-side sway of the hips. I hoped that this might throw them off, might convince them I wasn't the culprit. I hoped that they might think, "True, I just smelled rotten broccoli, and true: I'm downwind of that woman's ass right there. But surely *she* could not have done it! Why, just look at how she struts!"

So I strutted. I farted. I strutted some more. Finally, the couple and I parted ways. I cannot confirm whether they ever found me sexy or if, conversely, they ever identified me as the culprit of the noxious broccoli smell. What I can do, though, is tell you that within a moment of their departure, a flamboyant gentleman in Daisy Duke shorts walked toward me from the opposite direction. We caught each other's eye, and he said, "You look CRAY, girl. Tone it down. Less is more."

I can only assume the gentleman meant *my strut* was CRAY, and that it was *my strut* that needed toning down. And, well, if that was the case—if a man in Daisy Dukes felt *I* should tone it down—I can only also assume that the couple had found me not sexy but ridiculous. Or, as the Daisy Duke wearer might say, that the couple had found me "RIDIC."

NEW YORK CITY has a talent for seeming as though it is not a city so much as a giant human with a giant club she swings at you and you alone. It was true that if I went back home I would be greeted with a level of solitude that felt like a physical ailment. However, it was also true that that level of solitude now looked like the superior option to being swatted in the face.

I walked myself back to the subway. It was rush hour by the time I got there and unsurprisingly packed. I did still manage to score myself a seat, however, and that is because I have a knack for spotting empty seats and beating other people to them. I'd squished myself in beside a woman with a kind-looking face; she looked, I don't know, *employable*—very Ann Taylor Loft. I thought she looked nice. I wished I were her. I felt lonely and sad. I felt a fart coming on. Its predecessors of the last hour had been silent, so I took the risk and farted. It was silent, as expected. However, as was also expected, it smelled like rotten broccoli.

The woman beside me went involuntarily wide-eyed.

"That was me," I said. "I'm really sorry."

It was unprecedented candor. But I'd needed it, the words exchanged.

And then: the woman *laughed*. Well, no, she didn't laugh, really. She rather exhaled in a manner to suggest good-natured befuddlement.

"No problem," she said. "I mean, well, it . . . happens. It just . . . *does*."

I put my hand to my heart.

"Thank you," I said.

"You're welcome," she said.

I AM NOT, by nature, a gamblin' woman. When my stock is up, I quit. I go home. I call work.

"Hello?" said the hostess.

"Hello," I said back. "This is Sara Barron calling. I am back from my vacation. I am free to pick up shifts."

16
In Defense of Band-Aid Brand Adhesive

I had been living alone for a total of five years. I had spent the first three of those five in that studio apartment in Bushwick. I had spent the last two of those five in a different studio apartment, also in Bushwick. The new apartment was one block away from the old apartment, and only a little bit bigger. I did not move, then, for any significant improvements in terms of size or neighborhood. I moved because the new apartment had a better toilet than the old one, because I'd reached that stage of life wherein I wanted a toilet that flushed.

I appreciated the improvement, and to ensure I maintained my appreciation—to ensure I did not become embittered by my now longstanding solitude—I made sure to take Eleanor with me. I also hung up *lots* of mirrors. The mirrors made the space seem larger, yes, but the real benefit was that whenever I needed someone besides Eleanor to talk to, I could just look up, and glance around.

"Idiot," I'd say.

"*You* are," I'd say. "*You* are the problem. Not me."

These devices did a good job of treating the solitude that can, as I said, feel like a physical ailment. They also kept a low cap on the amount I spoke to inanimate objects. They were the treats, if you will, to keep me in line.

My approach to living alone in a functional way mirrored that of a woman who diets in a functional way. Every day, she gives herself a little indulgence so as to prevent herself from, say, shoveling cereal into her mouth *while* unsticking the peanut butter jar . . . so that the peanut butter's ready once the cereal is gone.

I may be speaking from experience.

Like a lady on a functional diet, I put a system in place so that I might enjoy the benefits of solo living without falling victim to its hardships. A positive attitude, a nonexistent canine friend. A hand mirror! A hanging mirror! A wall mirror, oh *my*! My methods were smart, to be sure. But they were not failsafe. Substitutes for living with another person are, well, only ever that: substitutes. There are certain jobs only a human can do.

I WAS AT the local coffee shop one weekend afternoon when I spotted a certain gentleman, and after a series of boring events he and I wound up having sex. It was mostly uneventful, except for the fact that during the proceedings, I sprained my neck. We'd had sex and gone to bed, and when I woke up the next morning, I found I couldn't move it.

"Oh no!" I exclaimed.

My companion groaned wordlessly in response.

I rotated the entirety of my torso to face him.

"I think I sprained my neck," I said.

"From the blowjobs?" he asked, but nodding "yes" was not an option. I pitched my torso back and forth.

"Oh, shit!" He laughed. "Wow. That's really funny."

Really funny, indeed. The ensuing week consisted of too many ineffective neck braces and heating pads until finally I made an appointment with an acupuncturist. The acupuncturist's name was James, and James was very handsome. Which didn't affect the efficacy of his acupuncture, of course, but it *did* unlock my flirtatious instincts while James *performed* his acupuncture. When the needles went in, I made sure to groan sexually, rather than in a way that sounded whiny. When the needles came out and I was told to sit up, I made sure to position myself on the acupuncture table in a manner that was more mermaid-on-rock than it was Sara-Barron-on-table. And when a session concluded and it was time to say good-bye, I made sure to tell James how respectful I was of his practice. I'd roll my neck and shoulders erotically to indicate how much better my neck was thanks to him.

"The healing power of acupuncture is so, like, *tangible*," I'd say. "I really respect what you do."

I saw James three times in two weeks and, thankfully, my neck did get better. At the end of the last session, James bowed silently in farewell, and it was something in the perceived subservience of that bow that allowed me to channel my untapped reserves of self-confidence.

"We should go out sometime," I said.

James lifted his head.

"Yes," he said. "We should."

His response was unexpected, but ideal. It was the most wonderful news.

However, I successfully undermined it by putting Band-Aids on my breasts.

The source of the problem was an off-the-shoulder sweater I'd decided to wear on our date. Because I was punching above my weight with James, I'd initially planned to go all-out, clothing-wise, to pair an extravagant frock with high heels. But then I reconsidered after James suggested meeting at Chipotle. I'd texted, "Any thoughts on where to meet?" and he had written back, "How about the 42nd Street Chipotle? They have delicious margaritas."

Well, I wasn't picky. I *would* go on a date at a Chipotle. However, I would also spare myself the indignity of showing up in high heels and an extravagant frock. I'd go instead with my Forever 21 off-the-shoulder sweater.

I planned to do as one does in an off-the-shoulder sweater and wear a strapless bra. But then I tried one on and saw that it created this unattractive shelf effect. So then I decided maybe I should just go braless, and took off the sweater *and* the bra, and then put the sweater *back* on, but this time without the bra. Then, though, I saw that my nipples looked ridiculous. They were all like, *HELLO! WE ARE NIPPLES!* rather than *Ah, bonjour. Nous sommes les . . . nipples*. It was just too much. *They* were just too much, and after extensive consideration, I decided Band-Aids were the workable solution. They'd provide the optimal level of restraint.

So it was that I taped one extra-large Band-Aid horizontally across each nipple.

James needed five margaritas to invite me back to his apartment. I needed zero to accept the offer, but two to forget I had extra-large Band-Aids on my nipples. I knew what I looked like with them on, of course. I had looked in the mirror before I left, and I had noticed how the fleshy color of the Band-Aids blended with my skin tone to create the overall effect of an alien life form. Something slug-like. Undefined. They were gross and alarming, to be sure, but even so, I thought James's response to the Band-Aids

was unnecessarily dramatic. We'd gone back to his bedroom, taken off our shirts, and he had screamed, for God's
sake. I am tempted to write, "He let out a blood-curdling
scream," but to be more specific about it, James screamed
like he'd seen, not Band-Aids on breasts, but rather cock-
roaches on breasts. Truly. It was as though he'd ripped off
my sweater to discover one tampon-sized cockroach per
breast.

"What is it?" I asked.

"Are those . . . Band-Aids?" he asked.

And I looked down. And I remembered.

"Oh, God. Yes. Sorry. It's sort of, like, this thing I do."

"Why?" he asked.

"Because," I answered, "my nipples protrude too much
without them."

We sat for a moment.

Finally, James said, "I'm sorry I screamed."

"That's okay," I said. "*I'm* sorry *I* put Band-Aids on
my breasts."

"That's okay," he said. "You had your reasons."

We sat for another moment.

"So," he said.

"So," I said.

"Do you want to take them off?" he said.

"Oh. Yes. Sorry," I said. "Of course I'll take them off."

And so I did. Or rather, and so I tried to.

At this stage in the story I would like to vouch for
Johnson & Johnson's Band-Aid brand adhesive. As an unpaid sponsor, I would like to tell you that their Band-Aids
wanted *on*. It was almost impossible to remove them, and
when finally I did, my breasts looked red and raw. Bumpy
and truly diseased.

It is a testament to both James and me that we tried to
carry on. We hemmed and hawed, picked and prodded.

We boogied and we woogied. In short, we did all manner of unmentionable things together, but it was like his libido was this perfect, healthy baby, and my breasts were a pillow, and I had used the pillow to kill the baby. So seemingly benign was the weapon, you almost didn't know it was a weapon. But oh, it *was*. And the baby wound up limp and flaccid. Unresponsive. Irrevocably dead.

Finally—hopelessly—I motioned in the direction of James's genitals.

"Is there . . . anything else we could . . . do?" I asked.

And James motioned in the direction of my breasts. He shrugged, in apology. He said, "I'm pretty sure there's not."

There's a subconscious level on which I think I must like feeling ashamed and embarrassed. I've been that way for, well, ever I guess, and it's what made it difficult for me to blame James in the long term. I mean, sure, he had a dramatic, physical response to a small mess of adhesive, but my dominant feeling was that the fault was mostly mine for failing to think things through beforehand. I do not believe in destiny, but I do believe in predictability. I do believe we are more or less likely to wind up in a given situation based on the way we behave. I, for example, was more likely to drink two margaritas, to forget about the Band-Aids, to carelessly remove my shirt. I know these things about myself, and should, then, have put that self-knowledge toward better social planning. But I got wrapped up in a moment, seduced by my own ingenuity. This can happen when you live alone.

A fantasy returned in the wake of my repulsive breasts. For the first time in a long time, I found myself wanting a roommate. Someone to talk to and check in with. Someone to save me from myself. It was a strange thing to have evoked after all that time away from the idea, and it brought to mind a particular park in Bushwick, just around the block from my apartment. I'd go there once in a while to enjoy the sunshine and/or the physiques of the guys on the basketball court, and while it was lovely by virtue of being outside, it was also kind of gross. There was garbage everywhere. There weren't any benches. The grass was a mess. So it wasn't a question of which part was greener. It was a question of whether I felt like sitting in garbage or in mud. Near a baby or a rat.

A nice day in that park was a hard thing to achieve. A nice life in New York is a hard thing to achieve. You're damned if you do get entrenched in the psychosis of your roommate, you're damned if you don't have a roommate, but then your imaginary bulldog fails to explain the pitfalls of the Band-Aids on your breasts. I must remember this when times are tough. I must not mourn what I don't have. I must rejoice in what I do have. I must remember my pedicure station. I must remember that I pass gas when I want to and that doing so provides authentic joy. I must consider there's no better option out there. I must accept it's as good as it gets.

Part IV

Survivor

17

Vicki's Vagina Is Violet

Often I find myself in one of two positions: I am either (a) bemoaning whatever drama presently surrounds me, or (b) lacking drama, enduring the grind, and as a result, beset with a crushing panic as to the purpose of human existence.

I found myself in one such latter phase several years back. I had recently moved into the second of my Bushwick studio apartments. I had been in high spirits because of it.

But then the winds changed.

The tides turned.

Because this friend of mine, Vicki, had gone and scored herself a boyfriend.

I have, as I've said, an unsavory taste for people who

find partners like I find ingrown hairs. For them, it is effortless, and this fact was never truer than in the case of my friend Vicki.

Vicki is warm, bright, and empirically attractive. She is professionally unintimidating. She has a lot of internalized self-loathing, and that internalized self-loathing manifests as a lack of self-esteem. That lack of self-esteem, then, manifests as a willingness to date whomever just so long as they're around.

In the fifteen years that I've known Vicki, she's been single for a total of four months. Four months. In fifteen years. And although I would like to say that I pity her situation, that I think it's sad for her, actually, how she cannot be alone, the truth of the matter is just that I'm jealous. I, Sara Barron, am terribly, wildly jealous, and so it was that my current joy was undercut when Vicki got a shiny, brand-new boyfriend yet again.

Although perhaps I ought not to use the word "shiny." Since, well, there was nothing shiny about Vicki's latest boyfriend. On the contrary, he was old enough to be her dad.

Before going further, I should admit a problem of my own: I am not amenable to May-December situations. I am terribly judgmental, closed off to even the most sympathetic variations on the theme. It's something I'm consciously working on, always. But Vicki made my stabs at self-improvement really hard. Her elderly boyfriend's name was Don, and whenever their relationship came up, Vicki would present it as a demonstration of her own maturity. She would say, "I just needed a grown-up, you know?"

The statement, to me, was the verbal equivalent of nails running down a chalkboard. Vicki said it all the time, and the process of hearing her do so felt like the process of being pushed into a downward emotional spiral. Down and down I'd go, considering her baser motivations.

You like being the hot one.

You need someone less likely to leave you.

An older man's less threatening than someone your own age.

It was the lack of self-awareness that got me, combined with my long-running resentment about the plethora of boyfriends, *combined* with the fact that I myself had no—I mean *no*—romantic options on the table at the time.

These were the circumstances that came together to put me in a chronically bad mood, and it was in the throes of this mood that I went out to dinner with another friend named Deirdre. Deirdre and I waited tables together at the upscale pizzeria where I was working at the time. Deirdre and I enjoyed this particular dinner on what I recall was the Friday before Halloween. The reason I know it was Friday, was that we'd gone to eat at a TGI Fridays (Deirdre had a coupon), and I remember thinking that being at TGI Fridays *on* Friday made the whole thing that much more pathetic.

The reason I know it was before Halloween was that I'd just received an Evite to a Halloween party, cohosted by Vicki and Don.

They'd been together one month. And they were co-hosting parties.

I received the Evite, I called Deirdre to complain about the Evite, and Deirdre, sweetly, offered to take me to dinner.

"My treat!" she'd said. "I've got a coupon to TGI Fridays."

So we went to a TGI Fridays on Friday, and I ordered a total of three different courses of beef. As I ate, I complained. I said, "It's just, like, ridiculous, you know? Vicki'll break up with whatever guy she's been seeing, and she'll be alone for, like, two weeks! TWO WEEKS! I'm not even kidding! And then I'll see her the next time, and she'll be all coy, and say something like, 'Well, I have some news: I met a guy.' And I'll be like, 'Of *course* you met a guy! You *always* meet a guy!' And she'll be like, 'Yes, but this one's really special. He's *so* smart and *so* cute. I feel . . . really lucky.' But then, Deirdre, I meet the guy, and whoever he is, he just seems fine, at best, and at worst he is truly deformed! I swear to God. She dated this one guy whose face evoked Sloth from *The Goonies*. My mom met him once, and she was like, 'Is something wrong with Vicki's boyfriend? I mean, is there something, like, mentally wrong?' Just because his face was so bizarre!"

"So what's your point?"

I sighed. No, actually, it was more like I huffed.

"Well, my point, Deirdre, is that it is annoying to hear someone always going on about how *this* one's so special, and now how *this* one's so special. It's like, no, Vicki, *none* of them are 'so special.' You just tell yourself they are because you cannot be alone."

Deirdre shrugged. "I don't know," she said. "I think it sounds sweet. I think it's nice if someone cares what's on the inside."

"No," I said. "No, no, no, no, *no*. There is a difference between caring what's on the inside, and having self-esteem so low, you'll pick up the Sloth-looking guy on the street because you know for sure he'll worship you, and never leave. These guys, okay, they're not, like, homely but bursting with charisma. These guys are not homely and rich. No. They are homely, and they are *blah*. And I'd forgive it all if she would only just admit it! JUST ADMIT IT! Be like, 'I'm having a rough go at the moment, and I understand this current guy is not forever. But I cannot be alone.' *That* would be okay! But please don't run me through the paces of how special they all are!"

We sat in silence. For, I don't know, a while. My third course of beef was cleared. I ordered something called a

Chocolate Fudge Fixation. I ate my Chocolate Fudge Fixation. I felt gross, and very full.

Deirdre said, "Well, okay. So you're clearly very angry."

I exhaled.

"Not even," I said. "I think it's just, I feel jealous."

You know how sometimes when you're drunk, the truth comes out? That happens to me when I've had too much processed food. I was deflated now, and hitting at the heart of things.

"I haven't had a boyfriend in ages," I continued. "I haven't had so much as the prospect of a boyfriend, and I feel, I don't know, entitled, I guess. I want the universe to shower me with options."

Deirdre nodded. "It's raining men," she said. "Hallelujah, it's raining men."

"Amen," I said. "Yes, exactly. It's time for a downpour, Deirdre. Even someone interesting to think about would be enough."

Well. What I am here to tell you is that in the forty-eight hours that followed, my wish was granted. My poorly articulated, un-careful wish. The spirit of the circumstance mirrored the spirit of the movie *Big*. If, that is, the whole thing was reconceived to star Elizabeth Perkins as the protagonist. *Be careful what you wish for, grown-up lady. You thought you'd found a boyfriend, but it turns out he's thirteen.* If viewed from this angle, we don't have a boy who learns to relish his youth. What we have, actually, is a thirtysomething woman who fails to get herself a boyfriend. We have a thirtysomething woman who adds an atypical notch on her belt.

SATURDAY, 10:00 A.M.: I awoke on this, the morning of Vicki and Don's Halloween party. After a good night's sleep, I decided to attend.

Deidre had been generous in taking me to dinner the

night before, in listening to me complain. She had helped me work out what parts of the conflict fell, not on Vicki's shoulders, but on mine. I had therefore woken up feeling very pay-it-forward. Very, like, *Okay, Deidre was generous and understanding with me, and perhaps I ought to be more generous and understanding with Vicki.* I'd known her a long time, after all, and just because I was bitter about my own single status, well, that didn't mean I had to pre-judge her elderly boyfriend. Furthermore, I had just read this book called *Gilead*—I'd been forced to by this book club I was in—and it had been this moving literary tale about a romance between a sympathetic seventysomething and his equally sympathetic thirtysomething wife. I read it, finished it, and then I thought, Well. *Those* characters were *awfully* likable. And they had, what? Forty years between them? Vicki and Don reach across the abyss of a mere twenty-three. I really should be open-minded. I owe my friend that much.

SATURDAY, 11:00 A.M.: As a reward for my open-mindedness, I decided I would treat myself to brunch at a restaurant down the block from my apartment. It was a spot I dined at, on average, two times a week. I'd arrive with book in hand and sit at the bar, order a glass of wine, followed by a bowl of soup, followed by a cup of hot water. The routine, as a whole, prompted frequent urination, which both (a) provided helpful intermissions to my reading, and (b) helped me, as Solo Diner, to look occupied.

The restaurant's most winning feature was a loin-achingly handsome waiter I shall henceforth call Brian. If you imagine both John Lennon and Justin Timberlake at their most handsome of stages, shaken, stirred, poured into a tall glass of water, you'd wind up with Brian. I knew, as all patrons knew, that Brian was not to be obtained,

merely ogled; that one did well to appreciate him as exqui-
site décor rather than a realistic option.

On this particular Saturday, however, as though in
response to my beef-drunk wish the night before, Brian's
behavior toward me appeared suddenly to shift. He was
notably more chatty and attentive. He asked, "So, how are
you?" He checked in with me on six different occasions to
see how my wine and soup and water were going. He told
me he liked the shirt I had on.

"Really?" I asked. "I think it has this sort of, like, widening effect on my back."

"No," he said. "Your back looks really narrow."

12:00 P.M.: I went to the bathroom to urinate for the final
time, then returned to the bar to pay my bill. When I did,
Brian sauntered over.

"Listen," he said. "You're, like, always around but we
never get the chance to talk. I'm off at three. Would you
like to get a drink? Around three thirty, say?"

I had, prior to this moment, known true and visceral
joy. I had held newborn babes in my arms. I had caught
wind of divorces I'd predicted years before. *I had known
true and visceral joy.* But nothing could compete with this,
the adrenaline rush of someone so attractive asking me to
get a drink.

"YES!" I answered. And then, "I'D LOVE TO!" And
then, "WHY AM I TALKING SO LOUD?"

Brian laughed. "Are you nervous?" he asked.

"I THINK, YES, I AM NERVOUS!" I said. "ALSO, I
THINK I AM THINKING OF WHAT SHIRT TO WEAR!
SOMETHING MORE SLIMMING FOR MY BACK!"

Brian reiterated that my back looked lovely as it was
and suggested a local wine bar. I told him that sounded
great, and that I'd see him at three thirty.

3:30 P.M.: Brian and I met up for drinks, struggled to drum up conversation, settled eventually on a back-and-forth about the perils of waiting tables. We additionally discussed my encyclopedic knowledge of seasons one and two of *30 Rock*.

5:00 P.M.: As the wine flowed, I noticed a marked absence of flirtation. Of any *impending* flirtation. There was not so much as a hint of physical interest from Brian, in me.

5:01 P.M.: I wondered why this was, why he would ask me out for drinks, if not for the impending intercourse. Did he want to be friends? Was he of the homosexual persuasion? Did he want to be friends *because* he was of the homosexual persuasion?

5:30 P.M.: Brian offered to walk me home. I accepted the offer, and wondered if this was perhaps a sign that there would be a good-bye kiss. I wondered if, to Brian's credit, he was simply averse to in-restaurant, hand-on-knee flirting.

5:40 P.M.: We arrived at my front door. Brian did not move in for the good-bye kiss. He did, though, say, "Why don't we head upstairs. We could, um, watch a little *30 Rock*."

5:41 P.M.: I was delighted by the question. I told Brian, "That'd be really fun!"

5:42 P.M.: I considered how quirky I was, having *30 Rock* used on me as part of a seduction.

5:43 P.M.: I invited him upstairs.

6:45 P.M.: After two episodes of *30 Rock*, nothing physical had occurred between Brian and me. More to the point, I got the sense that nothing physical *was going* to occur. Brian had spent the previous hour sitting on the opposite side of the sofa. Sofa-wise, he was as far from me as he could get.

6:46 P.M.: Yet again, I wondered why this was. Why a person would invite himself upstairs if not for the impending intercourse. The potential explanations reemerged, although this time I added the possibility that Brian had genital herpes. I considered that impending intercourse might therefore require an uncomfortable conversation. I wondered if, as a result of all this, Brian liked to take things slow.

8:00 P.M.: Five episodes of *30 Rock,* and still: NOTHING. *Still:* Brian and I had stayed glued to our opposite sides of the sofa.

8:01 P.M.: I added to the list of potential explanations the idea that Brian had been anally raped at some point and, therefore, had only recently arrived at a place of emotional readiness where intercourse was concerned. I wondered whether he had chosen me as the partner for said intercourse because I projected the necessary warmth and vulnerability for him to feel sexually relaxed.

8:05 P.M.: Brian stood up and excused himself to the bathroom.

8:06 P.M.: I used my moment alone to text my friend Deirdre. She'd been a helpful listener the night before, and I wondered if, in this instance, she might do the same again.

"Im w/a hot waiter!!!!" I texted. "Weve been @ my apt 4ever. NOTHING IS HAPPENING. WHY NOT? Does he JUST want 2 watch TV?"

8:07 P.M.: Deirdre wrote back right away.

"OMG," she wrote. "Your RIDIC. OBVI he is shy! He wnts YOU 2 make a move!"

But no, I thought. It cannot be.

Picture, if you will, George Clooney and Tiny Tim seated on a couch. Picture both of them knowing someone must bite the bullet, and make the first move. Would there be a question as to whose confidence was operating at a higher level? And, therefore, upon whose shoulders such responsibility must rest? No. There would not. It would rest upon George. So would it rest upon Brian.

8:09 P.M.: Brian returned from the bathroom.

"Shall we watch one more episode of *30 Rock*?" he asked.

I nodded yes. I said, "I do believe we should."

8:20 P.M.: During this, our final *30 Rock*, Brian became a bit more fidgety than he'd been before. I thought, Oh, okay. Now *here* we finally go. Because the behavior, I thought, indicated that something was finally en route. Maybe the moves to get the desired intercourse going. Maybe just the explanation as to why Brian liked to take things slow. Maybe the fidgeting would reach a fever pitch and he would say, "Listen. I'm sorry. I know I've been weird. And this is, well, a little hard to talk about." And he'd take a deep breath. "See, the thing is, I've been taking these antidepressants. And they're affecting my ability to"—and he would motion toward his penis—"and it's making me nervous about"—and he would point back and forth between us—"with anyone new."

Brian would ask if I understood what he meant, and I would say, "Of course I understand what you mean. And, for what it's worth, I think penetration's overrated."

Then Brian and I would make out for a while, and then I'd skip Vicki and Don's Halloween party so that Brian and I could cuddle. We'd cuddle for an hour at which point Brian would say, "Sara, look at me and listen: I am your boyfriend now."

8:32 P.M.: The *30 Rock* episode finished.

8:33 P.M.: Brian's fidgeting reached, if not a fever pitch, then a higher pitch. I hoped to urge him on.

"So," I said.

"So," he said.

"Soooo," I said.

"Sooooo," he said.

Come *on,* I thought.

"So. *Well,*" he said. "I have this thing I want to ask. Or . . . I don't know. Maybe it's more, like, a thing I want to tell you. And then a thing I want to ask."

"Great," I said. "Go on."

"Well . . ." he said.

"Wellllllll . . ." I said.

"So," he said. "The thing is that I dabble. As a prostitute."

8:33 P.M.: My first response to this information was a crushing wave of disappointment. Something told me that if Brian dabbled as a prostitute, he probably wasn't in my apartment to have sex with me for free.

My second response to this information was an overriding curiosity. For if Brian wasn't here to have sex with me for free, was he, perchance, here to have sex with me for money? Provided that was the case, I was actually more intrigued than I was offended. I was on the verge of asking Brian if he'd accept payment in installments, but he cut me off before I had the chance.

"I've done it a handful of times," he said, "and I would like to do it more."

"Right," I said. "Of course."

"But the thing is, it's hard to drum up business as a dude. It's like, there *is* a market out there, but it's hard to break into, you know?"

I told him that I did not know.

"And I see how you are at the restaurant," he continued. "You're sharp about how you spend money. You read a lot; I know you're smart. And you're a lone wolf too, you know? Not afraid to be alone. And then I started thinking about it, and I was like, 'Oh my god! Right! Yes.' That's *just* what I need in a manager."

"Manager." I repeated the word. "Your pimp."

"Yes," he said. "You're perfect."

"I'm perfect," I repeated. "To pimp."

8:37 P.M.: I considered Brian's assessment. I considered why it was wrong.

1. Pinching pennies isn't demonstrative of being "good" with money, necessarily. In my case, it's demonstrative of being bad with money—that is, I pinch pennies because I am penniless, and I am penniless because I live alone.

2. My literature of choice varies from "easy" to "beach."

3. I'm not *unafraid* to be alone, I've just been *forced* to be alone. These are different things entirely.

8:38 P.M.: I thanked Brian for his offer, but explained that I was less qualified than I may have appeared.

"Well, I totally get it," he said. "I mean, I hope you're, like, flattered I asked."

"Oh, yes," I said. "I am."

"And I hope there aren't any hard feelings," he said.

And I told him there weren't. Since there weren't. I mean, if Tiny Tim discovered George Clooney wasn't interested in him romantically, you wouldn't think, "Oh. Well, Clooney's a dick." No. You'd be like, "Oh. Well, Tiny Tim's retarded for having thought he stood a chance."

8:45 P.M.: Brian said good-bye.

8:48 P.M.: I watched one more episode of *30 Rock*.

9:11 P.M.: I rallied the energy to put on my costume, and go to the Halloween party. I did this with the help of an ice-cold shower. I hoped it would make the remainder of my night seem pleasant by comparison.

9:35 P.M.: I put on a long-sleeve silver unitard and covered what remained of my exposed skin in silver face-paint. I was dressing as the Tin Man, of course. But sexy-like. For the hat part of my costume, I wore a silver funnel upside down.

9:50 P.M.: I left for the party.

10:20 P.M.: I arrived at the party.

10:22 P.M.: I realized I knew no one at the party besides my old friend Vicki and her new boyfriend, Don.

10:24 P.M.: I made my way toward Vicki and Don. Vicki was in sunglasses, a white beret, and leather mini-skirt, and Don was in a three-piece suit and what appeared to be a motorcycle helmet he'd shellacked with whole walnuts. Glued to this walnut-covered helmet were various small horns, the kind you blow on New Year's Eve. They were purple, these horns, and to their bases Don had glued a dozen imitation, plastic diamonds.

10:25 P.M.: I asked them both what they were dressed as.

"Debbie Harry," said Vicki.

"A busted nut," said Don. "It's a tribute to Vicki's vagina."

I had met Don two times prior to this Halloween party. On both occasions he had presented as overtly sexual, by which I mean:

He had not been opposed to carrying on a conversation while vigorously massaging Vicki's upper, inner thigh.

He had not hesitated to ask me how up-to-date I was on his sex life.

"Vicki and I fuck all the time," he'd said. "Has she told you about it? About how good it is?"

As it happened, Vicki *had* told me about how good it was. Vicki enjoyed speaking on the subject of Don's insatiable appetite, of his unparalleled skill set. I never asked any follow-up questions, however, and that is because my attitudes toward the sex I have and the sex I hear about vary drastically: When I have it, I like it to be good. When I hear about it, I like it to be funny. There's no such thing as TMI in my book unless, of course, you care to wax poetic on your partner's magnificence. If he or she is amazing, great, but then leave out the step-by-step description. Just be, like, "Yeah. I mean, the sex is really good," and I'll be, like, "Really? I'm so glad!" And then, from there, we can move on to other more compelling issues.

It is a time-honored and respected truth: that bad sex

makes a good story. And good sex? Well, you've just had good sex. Don't think you have a story.

10:29 P.M.: I excused myself from my conversation with Vicki and Don. This was partly because Don had brought up the issue of vaginal tribute masks. It was also because the Ludacris song "Money Maker" had come on through the speakers and I wanted to dance to it in a liberated style.

10:32 P.M.: I finished dancing in a liberated style to the Ludacris song "Money Maker."

10:33 P.M.: I began dancing in an equally liberated style to the song "Temperature" by Sean Paul.

10:37 P.M.: I finished dancing in a liberated style to the song "Temperature" by Sean Paul and began dancing to the song "SOS" by Rihanna. My style of dancing was less liberated in this instance because I'd started getting tired.

10:41 P.M.: From across the room, I saw Don coming toward me in his walnut helmet.

"Oh. Hi, Don," I said.

"Hi, Sara," he said. "I thought maybe we could finish our conversation from before."

I hadn't realized our conversation from before had not already finished. Don had said, "It's a tribute to Vicki's vagina," and I had said, "Oh. How nice. Time for me to hit the dance floor."

But now it seemed that Don had more to say.

"I would like to tell you more about my mask," he said.

"Okay," I said.

"The walnuts represent a busted nut," he said. "Because my sex life's so amazing."

I paused for moment. I said, "Well, congratulations. On your sex life."

"Thank you," he said. "Do you know about the color?"

"The color?" I asked. "Of . . . your sex life?"

"Ha! No!" Don laughed. "What I mean is, do you know about the color of *Vicki's vagina*?"

"I'm sorry?" I said.

"The color of Vicki's vagina," he repeated. "Do you know more generally about the varying colors of all vaginas?"

One of my central life philosophies is this: If a man appears crazy in private, run. But if a man appears crazy in public, stick it out. Have fun diving further in.

"I don't know about the varying vaginal colors," I said. "Can you tell me more about them?"

"Vaginas vary in color," said Don. "Most are pink, some are blue. But the really special ones? They're . . . violet."

I sighed, and braced for the inevitable.

"And Vicki's?" I prompted.

Don closed his eyes. He took a breath.

"Vicki's vagina is violet," he said. "Hers is . . . perfect. Hers is . . . very rare."

10:45 P.M.: I scanned the room for eye contact with fellow party guests. *Come: bear witness,* said my eyes. But the silver face paint was having a Botox-like effect insofar as it had dried and I could barely move my face.

"Oil can?" I might've asked, but I knew no one there would answer.

10:46 P.M.: "The horns," Don went on, and pointed to the violet horns that he had glued to his walnut helmet, "are violet. And that is in tribute to Vicki's vagina. And the diamonds . . . see the diamonds?" He pointed to the small glass balls glued to the rims of the horns. "They represent Vicki's ejaculation, because now that she and I are making love, Vicki can ejaculate. She ejaculates all the time, and it's always like a waterfall of diamonds. Hence the diamonds."

10:55 P.M.: Don and I sat in awkward silence. Why? Because. On those rare occasions wherein you have nothing nice to say about your friend's violet vagina, you don't say anything at all.

10:56 P.M.: "Well, that's it," Don said finally. "I just thought that you should know."

"Yes, well, thank you," I said. "Thanks for making sure I knew."

10:57 P.M.: Don migrated to the part of the dance floor where Vicki was standing.

10:58 P.M.: Vicki and Don began dancing in a style that is best described as a rhythmless Lambada.

10:59 P.M.: As they danced, I set to work on the why of it all. *Why* had Don cornered me? *Why* did he want me to be the holder of the key, the knower of the information? Or was I simply one of many? Was he simply making the rounds?

"I want *you* to know, now you, now you, now you: *My* girlfriend's vagina is violet. *She* ejaculates diamonds like a waterfall."

I mulled it all over, and it would've stayed a mystery for, like, *ever*, I guess. Except . . . well, no. It would not. Not as long as the needs of male pre-seniors stay *as* predictable as the circumstances of the women they seduce.

I get it that you're virile, I'd have said.
Except I wasn't in a mood to be that nice.

11:15 P.M.: I said my good-byes.

11:16 P.M.: I walked to the subway.

SUNDAY, 12:45 A.M.: I was—still—on the subway. To be more specific about it, I was stuck on a subway platform in midtown Manhattan. This was especially annoying seeing as how it was a mere four miles between my Brooklyn apartment and the Brooklyn Halloween party. The commute in its entirety should've taken less than an hour, but then the trains started acting as though on a personal mission to make me suicidal. One of them went suddenly, inexplicably express, and they'd bypassed my stop in Brooklyn altogether, and I'd wound up in Manhattan.

For the non–New Yorkers among you, this is the commuting equivalent of trying to get from Florida to Virginia and, through no fault of your own, winding up in Spain.

12:50 A.M.: I fell into a blind rage.

12:51 A.M.: I damned the Metropolitan Transportation Authority as well as women with superior vaginas.

12:58 A.M.: I spotted, amid a handful of fellow commuters, renowned New York drag king Murray Hill.

Murray Hill is a minor celebrity and downtown scenester: rotund, mustachioed, frequently outfitted in '70s clothing. Suits, usually. Formal, usually. To cite my previously mentioned attractions to a certain type of dapperbutch lady, it's a look I can quite get into—*quite*—and hoping Murray Hill might desire me as I did him, it seemed wise to abandon the foot-stomping of my aforementioned rage for a seductive sidestep toward him.

One of the side effects of your friend's boyfriend being all like, "Blah, blah, blah. Your friend's ejaculating diamonds, blah, blah," is that your sense of social norms gets distorted. You feel atypically emboldened, atypically moved to grab life by the violet vadge.

12:47 A.M.: "Hello," I said to Murray Hill. "Sorry to bother you, but I'm, like, *such* a fan."

I checked Mr. Hill's face for any sign my night might take an erotic, gender-bent turn, only to realize no, it would not. For this was not Murray Hill. No. Just another obese man whose outfit—'70s-style suit; wire-rim, double-ridge glasses—was not in any way ironic.

12:48 A.M.: I apologized for my mistake.

"No problem," said the man. "I mean, well, the trains take forever this time of night. It's nice to have someone to talk to."

I condone pitying the obese, but *not* ignoring them. So we talked for a while, and this was for the best, I think, as doing so offered unto me a new target for annoyance.

1:15 A.M.: I arrived home, finally.

1:25 A.M.: I turned on the TV.

2:00 A.M.: I turned off the TV.

2:10 A.M.: I went to bed.

11:00 A.M.: I woke up.

11:10 A.M.: I went to the bathroom to wash off my face paint.

11:15 A.M.: I thought a bit about humanity, and solitude.

12:00 P.M.: I wondered if perhaps I ought to leave my apartment.

12:01 P.M.: I decided I should, and walked over to the local coffee shop. I brought with me my "Funny Thoughts and Ideas!" journal. I also brought a bag of beef jerky, and that is because the coffee shop had recently started shellacking their sandwiches with *way* too much mayonnaise. Nowadays when I went there, I made sure to bring my own food.

1:00 P.M.: I had started to get hungry. I was about to eat my jerky.

1:01 P.M.: Then, though, an attractive man sat down at the table beside me.

This posed a very real problem.

I don't know when you last ate jerky in public, but it's an indelicate process to say the least. For starters, there's the grasping at the base of the jerky—the jerky stabilization, if you will—then there's the *eons* it takes to gnaw through the top. Licking whipped cream off a finger, it is not. What it is, at least for me, is the chance to resemble Prehistoric Man with Drumstick.

1:02 P.M.: I figured I would wait to eat the jerky. Eating it now, I thought, would be counterproductive to looking attractive.

1:02 P.M.: I tucked *The Devil Wears Prada* into my backpack, took out my "Funny Thoughts and Ideas!" journal, and started sketching stick figures of the various coffee-shop patrons and employees. My goal in doing so was to look occupied. But—and this was key—*also* available for eye contact with the handsome man beside me.

1:30 P.M.: The handsome man beside me had still not looked my way. I, however, had given it and *given* it in the eye-contact department. I decided this meant that the handsome man had probably seen my obsessive eye contact and clocked me as psychotic. I thought, Hmm. Okay. So he's probably made a choice to look away.

1:32 P.M.: So then what was the point in not eating?

1:33 P.M.: I dove aggressively into my jerky. I waged war on this one piece, bearing down with my teeth until I'd ripped it involuntarily out of my hands, which, in turn, forced my elbow into the table.

"OWWW!" I screamed.

Everyone turned.

"Sorry," I said.

The cashier glared at me from behind the register.

"No outside food allowed," she said. "Just, like, FYI."

"I'm sorry for that too," I said, and, in penance, bought a chicken sandwich with too much mayonnaise.

1:40 P.M.: I exited the coffee shop and headed back to my apartment.

1:45 P.M.: I offered the mayonnaise sandwich to a homeless guy I saw along the way. I made sure to do it when someone attractive walked by.

1:55 P.M.: I arrived back at my apartment.

2:00 P.M.: I ate some more food.

2:45 P.M.: I turned on the TV.

7:00 P.M.: I perused Facebook to see what other folks were up to, and by "other folks," I mean, of course, "current girlfriends of men with whom I'd previously intercoursed."

7:05 P.M.: It was the usual, natch: "Blah, blah, blah. Best job ever." "Blah, blah, blah. Best friends ever." "Blah, blah, blah. Best. Life. EVER."

7:20 P.M.: I thought about the arrogance of a superlative. I thought about how shitty we all are.

7:30 P.M.: I received, somewhat suddenly, a message from a stranger. His name was Dan, and Dan claimed in his message to know someone who knew someone I worked with.
  Dan said he'd like to take me on a date.

7:31 P.M.: I felt flattered and delighted.

7:32 P.M.: I perused Dan's Facebook page.

7:50 P.M.: I concluded he was not too psychotic, and relatively handsome.

7:55 P.M.: I decided we should go on a date.

8:00 P.M.: I wrote to Dan to tell him I was free.

8:05 P.M.: Dan wrote to me to tell me this was great.

"So then what shall we do?" he wrote. "A normal date activity in a crazy location, or *crazy* date activity in a *normal* location?"

8:10 P.M.: I flipped my mind coin. I wrote, "Crazy date activity in a normal location."

8:15 P.M.: "Oh! Great!" Dan wrote. "Then how's about we meet at the Brooklyn side of the Brooklyn Bridge. Could you do Tuesday? I'll bring ski masks. We'll wear them as we walk across."

It was, to remind you, the first day of November. The weather was unseasonably warm.

8:20 P.M.: "Out of curiosity," I wrote, "can you tell me my option for a *normal* activity in a *crazy* location?"

8:21 P.M.: "Dinner," wrote Dan, "in my basement. I know it sounds weird, but it's actually really romantic."

Years ago, I read an article about how if a woman fears being attacked, she's supposed to verbalize the crime the perpetrator is or could be attempting. For example, if you're walking along a dark city street and you see a guy masturbating at you, you're supposed to go, "YOU ARE MASTURBATING AT ME! STOP MASTURBATING AT ME!" You're supposed to directly confront. Doing so is apparently effective in making you seem strong, and therefore like a less-appealing victim.

8:25 P.M.: "Well, Dan, here's the thing," I wrote. "I know you're probably just a nice guy who puts his own spin on the dating scene. Unfortunately, though, you've left the impression that you're also maybe a killer. In which case, Tuesday's out."

8:54 P.M.: I closed my computer.

8:56 P.M.: I turned on the TV.

11:45 P.M.: I turned off the TV.

11:55 P.M.: I climbed into bed.

MONDAY, 4:00 P.M.: I arrived to work for my Monday night shift.

4:15 P.M.: My coworkers and I had a pre-service meeting. We were told to push a product called "fonduta."

4:30 P.M.: The meeting wrapped up.

4:31 P.M.: I made a beeline for Deirdre.

"So *here's* a thing," I said. "Remember how on Friday we were at TGI Fridays, and I was bitching about my friend Vicki? And then when I was *done* bitching about Vicki, I made the point about how there was nothing on my *own* romantic horizon? Do you remember how I said I wanted the universe to shower me with options? Do you remember how I said 'even someone interesting to think about would be enough'?"

Deidre nodded. She chewed a wedge off the fonduta.

"Well!" I said. "In the two days since I've seen you, I met a gigolo who wanted me to be his pimp! I spent time with Vicki's boyfriend, who yammered on about her violet vadge!"

"What?" asked Deirdre.

"I know!" I said. "Then," I continued, "I tried flirting with a drag king who was actually, really a guy. Then I met another guy in a coffee shop who wouldn't look at me, so I was all, like, 'Screw it. I'm eating my jerky,' and still another who asked me to wear a ski mask on a date!"

Deirdre was quiet for a moment. Finally, she said, "Because he thinks you're ugly?"

And I was quiet for a moment.

"What?" I asked.

"The guy who wanted you to wear a ski mask," she repeated. "Is it because he thinks you're ugly?"

"Oh. No," I said. "At least, I don't think so. I think he's just, like, a weird guy who tries to spin his weirdness as inventiveness. You know the type. They're always all like, 'Look at me! Aren't *I* wild? Aren't *I* so amazing?'"

Deirdre nodded. She smiled. She swallowed her last bit of fonduta.

"Then you've got to call him back," she said. "I think you've found yourself a soul mate."

18

This Might Be Controversial

My family's history is a real slap in the face to the American Dream. That is to say, we do not do better than our fathers. We do worse. My great-grandfather was a surgeon, my grandfather, an internist, my mom, a psychotherapist. As for me, I professionally underearn. I'll do whatever, provided I get paid a meager wage, and it was in keeping with this general approach that I tried my hand at teaching writing.

I had already worked retail and waited tables. Teaching I preferred to both previous careers because, although it sounded more prestigious than my other jobs, I could still make an insultingly low wage. And this was important. If I did not earn less than my parents, it would be an insult to their legacy.

I'D SEEN THE job listing in the back of a free weekly paper. Posted by a local writing school, it called for "writers seeking extra cash." Well, I was a writer insofar as I *had* written different things. I decided to apply. What I lacked in qualifying experience, I would make up for in my choice of interview outfit. The day of, I paired a lady's blazer with a spot-on chignon and barreled in with just the right amount of razzmatazz.

The interviewer offered me the job, and yes, I did think him slow on the uptake for doing so. He hired me because, he said, my "aggressive speaking voice" would help keep the students "awake if not fully engaged."

In advance of my class, I prepared a class plan: I'd lecture, review homework, critique homework. I preemptively practiced critiques: "The ending is shit," or "Don't call yourself a writer if you're not paid to write." I'd keep it generic, but inspiring. I'd be lauded as brilliant. I watched *Dead Poets' Society, Dangerous Minds,* and *Stand and Deliver.* Teaching, I realized, was all in the attitude, and as long as I leaned casually against my desk at just the right angle, as long as I walked with brash confidence between my students' desks, I'd maintain unshakable control.

The only chink in my armor was my ability to lecture. I mean, I could offer up a word or two on structure, dialogue, and so on. I could say things like, "A climax is important" or "It's good when people talk." But these words, wise as they are, would not a lecture make. I needed a buffer, and prepared correlating personal anecdotes for my various lecture topics. At the class in which I lectured on character, for example, I'd say, "Characters are important. They should do things. And have opinions," at which point a student would ask, "Could you give an example? A story from your own life, perhaps?"

"Of course," I'd say. "Why don't we talk about my dad? He's a *character*. What kind of character? Well, consider what he *does*. He sobs like a woman. He sobs at novels, news stories, and sitcoms like *The Wonder Years*. When we went to see the movie *Father of the Bride,* my father's crying got so loud, the woman behind us asked my mom to take him out."

The students would reflect. A shining star would raise her hand.

"His sobbing shows us who he is," she'd say.

"Exactly," I'd say. "Write that down. Now: Who has any questions?"

It was cause for concern that I was entirely without answers, but I figured the students could do the job for me, answering one another. One could ask, "How do you create characters who are round and compelling?" and I could say, "Great question, Paul. Maybe . . . Chris! Why don't you take a stab at it?" And when all was said and done, when the course had finished and it was time to say good-bye, the students would start a slow clap followed by a briskly formed receiving line. I'd stand at the door to shake their hands good-bye.

"You're tough," they'd say. "But fair. You're a molder of minds. A blazer of trails."

"Blazer of trails" would be a phrase they got from me, of course, from my lecture on Creative Use of Language.

I got to the point of feeling really excited about the whole thing, but then undermined myself when, at the first class, I made the choice to call myself "professor."

"Hello, students. Welcome," I said. "I am Sara, your writing professor."

A gentleman—a homosexual, I presumed, who paired

all manner of vibrant color awfully well—shot his hand in the air.

"Do you have a doctorate?" he asked.

"I don't," I said.

"And is this an accredited college or university?" he asked.

"It's not," I said.

"Right," he said. "What it is, I believe, is an *un*-accredited school that offers private writing classes for adults. So you really shouldn't call yourself 'professor.' I didn't sign up for a writing class so I could question the judgment of the *instructor*. You see? Now there's an appropriate word."

This was as chummy as it got those first few weeks. The most significant problem was that my students did not embrace my personal anecdotes in quite the way I'd hoped, and this, in turn, meant we scored ourselves a whopping twenty minutes of unstructured class time. I had no idea what to do with it. In my defense, however, I will say that I was gracious enough to let the students decide for themselves.

"What would *you* guys like to do?" I asked. "We could play a game of Telephone. Does that sound good? Or we could do weekly conversations on celebrity news to ensure that we, as writers, stay up to date on what goes on around us? Or . . . oh! I got it! What about a twenty-minute eating break?"

The students chose the twenty-minute eating break. But then we tried it a few times and realized that people eating but not really talking serves only to heighten one's awareness of the sound of other people chewing.

It was circumstance, then, that forced us into another plan of action, a game of our mutual devising.

We called it "This Might Be Controversial."

"This Might Be Controversial" came about in the workshop portion of the class. Every week, two students submitted essays their fellow students would read and then critique using a series of "positive" and "improvement" comments. So you'd hear things like, "It was good how on page four, paragraph ten, you wore that wig to pretend you're Barbra Streisand. But then on page six, paragraph twelve, it was weird when you wrote about how hot you think you are."

"I didn't mean hot like sexy. I meant hot like 'I'm too warm.'"

"Oh, right. Well, that's unclear."

One student, Sven, an enormous, kind-faced Swede, combined a mastery of the English language with a devoted unwillingness to criticize. He'd eschew anything that felt in any way harsh. "On page three, paragraph nineteen, I am very impressed when the character cries, and then washes her feet," he might say. "And for my improvement . . . I am sorry, Instructor. I think in every part, Good for you, Miriam! Writing is hard, but you are trying!"

Miriam was a recent retiree, who, in lieu of an essay, had turned in a eulogy she'd written for her recently deceased mother. Miriam wore only purple clothes, and would've done well to wear a sign that said, HANDLE WITH CARE, WON'T YOU PLEASE? MY GRASP ON REALITY'S NOT GREAT.

So Sven handled her with care. It was sweet, in its way, but the problem was that he handled *everyone* with care.

I tried urging him toward a more honest critique.

"Sven," I said. "Listen, you have to find a way that works for you."

Sven told me he'd try harder, and in the weeks that followed he started prefacing his comments with, "This might be controversial." For Sven, it worked as an effective disclaimer. He'd say, "This might be controversial, but on page six, paragraph twenty-seven, I thought the line with seven adjectives was very silly." Or, "This might be controversial, but on page five, paragraph nine, when you talk about your boyfriend, I thought, Hello. This part is very boring."

"This might be controversial" freed Sven up and, over time, caught on with his classmates. Two more weeks went by and we hit a point where everyone said it. Where everyone couldn't *not* say it.

"This might be controversial, but on page three, paragraph twelve, it was really, like, *bad* how cheesy the dialogue was when your father tells you he has cancer." Or, "This might be controversial, but on page one, paragraph eighty-five, your interpretation of manic-depression as creative genius feels really self-delighted."

One day, Harry, he of the homosexual persuasion and well-coordinated colors, returned from a lengthy visit to the bathroom. Harry spent most of my lectures in the bathroom; however, on *this* return, he seemed atypically chatty.

"I have an idea," he said.

"What is it?" I said.

"How about if from now on when one of us says 'This might be controversial,' we've got to follow through with something *really* controversial. I think that that'd be fun. Add some spice to the class. A little excitement."

"I think spice and excitement sound good," I said.

"Great," he said. "Then I'll go first: This might be controversial, but gay marriage is a bullshit thing to legalize. I loathe the showers and the registries. I loathe the blah fucking *blah* of it all. And, well, I'm sorry, okay? But if *my* time and money saved means fewer rights? Then fuck it. *FUCK IT. Fine* by me."

Harry took a breath.

"Wow," he said. "That felt *so* good."

"It *sounded* good," I said. "You know, like, cathartic."

I was not the only one who thought so. Harry made his feelings known, and it was like something electric was let loose in the room. You could feel, not judgment— not the sense that anyone had been offended—but rather: a desire creeping out. Other students wanting their catharsis.

One more week went by and this unearthed, universal desire shifted the meaning of the phrase. "This might be controversial" changed from a means by which you softened your critique to a means by which you set yourself up for the truly controversial. We were in the fifth week of class when I clocked the marked transition. Someone had said, "This might be controversial, but when I meet an anorexic, I want to punch her in the face," and someone else had said, "This might be controversial, but I saw a thing on the news the other day about a family with ten kids, where one of the kids had drowned in a river. And there the parents were sobbing and yammering on about how there should've been a fence up to prevent river access in the first place, and I was like, 'You still have nine more kids. You fuck with the planet when you fuck like that. And so the planet fucked with you.'" And *then* someone said, "This might be controversial, but I went down on a black man recently, and his pubic hair smelled African to me. Does that make sense?"

There was a pause as the class considered this last one, and that's when I made my observation. I said, "Wow! This Might Be Controversial is spreading among us like wildfire!" And Sven had shouted, "No, Instructor! Not 'spreading among us like wildfire.' That is so cliché! Let us say instead, 'It is spreading among us like . . . flames upon the gasoline-soaked peyos of a Jew!'"

"Oh! I have another," Miriam piped in. "This might be controversial, but Israelis are so *rude*. Whew! I never met a one who is polite!"

This is how it went, with just one rule in place: You couldn't say something you didn't believe.

This proved not to be a problem.

"This might be controversial," started Dave.

Dave was a twenty-five-year-old Caucasian. He had a waist-length set of dreadlocks, wealthy parents, and a virtual allergy to any and all critiques of his own writing. He was of the opinion that any and all edits to his work affected the "integrity" of said work.

"Integrity" was Dave's word, not mine.

Dave continued, "But, well, I don't think bestiality's that gross. I mean, I get it, how it's hot, you know? Just, like, getting off without having to return the favor."

Harry nodded in acceptance. Not agreement, but acceptance.

"Yes, well," he said, "*this* might be controversial, but the number of photos you post to Facebook is directly proportional to how big a dick you are in life. Upwards of once a day, you *are* a dick. There's no two ways about it."

Was this most of us? It was.

We nodded in agreement.

ONE DAY, SVEN arrived to class looking atypically upset.

"What's wrong?" asked Miriam.

"I have something controversial to say," said Sven, "and it is very bad. I am very ashamed by my very private feelings."

"Don't be," said Dave. "I pretty much confessed I want a blowjob from a dog."

Sven nodded. "Yes," he said. "You were very open on that day. Well, okay. Here I go: This might be controversial,

but the politician John Edwards? I do not blame him for
his cheating. His wife is very homely."

"Not 'is,'" said Miriam. "'Was.' Elizabeth Edwards has
died."

"Miriam! Chill!" shouted Dave. "Sven's just being controversial. Don't make him feel bad! He *knows* it's bad!
Just look how sad he looks!"

Sven did indeed look sad. His shoulders were slumped,
his bottom lip protruding.

"I'm sorry, Sven," said Miriam. "I don't mean to be
cruel. We all have our . . . things, I guess. For what it's
worth, *this* might be controversial, but I only go to male
doctors. I have a problem trusting women."

Sven smiled. "You must hate yourself for this," he said.

"I do," she said. "It's very hard."

There were others in the class—a Paul, a Brian, a Lisa, a
Lauren—and each one of them, like Miriam and Sven, had
their own painful realizations. Statements that prompted
not relief so much as the glorious pain of self-loathing:

"This might be controversial, but I wish divorce upon
most of my friends."

"This might be controversial, but you can't be *truly*
raped if you find the guy attractive."

"This might be controversial, but I hated *The Wire*."

"This might be controversial, but I hate *Breaking Bad*."

"This might be controversial, but I think women who
change their names after marriage are morons. I judge
every single one. Not to their faces, of course. To their
faces, I'm all like, 'To each his own. It's all about a woman's right to choose!' But in my heart, I'm all like, 'C'mon,
woman! PLEASE! Just grow a fucking backbone!'"

THE WRITING CLASS was ten weeks long, and as we
inched toward the end, I, too, made hard admissions:

This might be controversial, but I'm attracted to Rick Santorum.

This might be controversial, but I don't like Malcom Gladwell.

This might be controversial, but if you're living on public assistance, you shouldn't be allowed to have a pet.

When we reached our tenth and final week, something unprecedented happened: We didn't play This Might Be Controversial. We'd reached a saturation point the week before. Dan had said, "This might be controversial, but I think a gay man is more likely than a straight man to be a pedophile," and Harry responded, "But that's not controversial, even. I mean, it's wrong. Just . . . wrong. It's objectively untrue."

Things were uncomfortable now in a way they hadn't been since I'd barreled in and called myself professor. Tension replaced camaraderie, and we lost the will to speak on controversial subjects. More to the point, we didn't need to speak on controversial subjects, and the reason was more shocking than all things controversial said thus far:

For the first and only time, my students cared about my lecture.

The final topic was The Business of Writing, and when I announced it, when I said, "Okay, everyone. Let's talk about how to make money," I clocked unprecedented interest. Suddenly, the students scribbled in their notebooks. Suddenly, their hands flew up with questions: Will I get published? How often? How much money will I make?

"Everyone! Calm yourselves! Please!" I shouted back.

If there was something sad in our loss of camaraderie, it was made up for now, in the pride that I felt. For here I was at the end of the experience, achieving what I'd hoped for at the start: My students were excited and engaged.

My students had questions, and I, their teacher, finally had some answers.

"You *might* get published," I said, "but only online. And you won't make any money."

"*Any* money?"

"Well, no: You might make *some* money, but not the kind that does you any good."

The students sat for a moment, considering my knowledge. Considering *my truth*.

"Is that why you pack a homemade tuna sandwich every week?"

"Yes, Lauren! Good!"

"Is that why your clothes are always stained? Because it's too expensive to dry-clean them?"

"Spot on, Paul! *Also* good!"

My students, it seemed, had done a lot of growing in the weeks we'd been together. Maybe not in terms of effective writing methods, but certainly in terms of how to read people and judge character.

"Wow," I said. "You guys have learned so much."

I saw them eyeing one another. Harry shook his head and raised his hand.

"I'm not so sure," he said. "I think that might be controversial."

19

Daddy's Girl Should Wear a Diaper (A Tale in Twenty-Five Parts)

1. INTRODUCTION

I've only ever enjoyed one athletic activity, and that's biking. I like the lack of skill and study required for adequate performance. It's like photography that way: The training you need is immeasurably less than what's required for other artistic endeavors, and it is why, when seeking a creative outlet, grown adults get into photography in lieu of, say, ballet—the nature of it is couched in enough subjectivity to make the study of the craft look less embarrassing. Whereas if a layperson did a pirouette, you could definitively say, "Wow. That looked pathetic"; if he/she started taking photos, things wouldn't be so clear. It'd be another photo of another landscape. And still you'd say, "Wow! That's so gorgeous! You've got such a great eye!"

Biking is to athletics as photography is to creativity. As such, I knew it was the sport for me.

2. GOOD TIMES

I learned to ride a bike when I was six years old. Between the ages of six and thirty I rode many different bikes through many different landscapes. I therefore looked adept when I did so, comfortable with various accessorizing movements like French-rolling my pant leg and/or making a belt of my kryptonite lock.

Biking has been the singular activity throughout my life that has allowed me to look arguably authentically cool.

As with anything, however, there are factors that can undermine this singular authentic coolness. For example:

1. I look *awful* in a helmet. I look, ironically, like I should not be let out of doors.
2. When riding a bike, I awaken what my therapist calls my "active imagination." This, in turn, makes it hard for me to focus on the road.

The former issue poses the bigger threat to my hair, while the latter issue poses the bigger threat to my body and brain. When I should be zoning in, I'm zoning out. When I should be clocking traffic patterns, I'm imagining instead the development of a voice-box replacement surgery to grant me a stronger singing voice. I'll be speeding alongside a yellow cab, but I'll be thinking about how much I'd love to sing—really *sing*—"Don't Rain on My Parade."

Imagining oneself as Barbra Streisand is dangerous behavior for a woman on a bike. Nonetheless, the worst I suffered at the hand of my own distractibility was a lightly bruised ego. I'd been flying down the Queensboro Bridge after having been dumped by a guy who flipped lamb shanks for a living. I'd forgotten I wasn't alone and had started singing Liz Phair's "Extraordinary" aloud to reassure myself about myself:

I am extraordinary / if you'd only get to know me

And then a stranger rode past me. And heard me.

Singing Liz Phair to myself about myself was a raw and private moment, and I would've preferred to keep it that way.

So. That all had been the worst thing. Until the time I rode full-speed into a car.

3. THE RAIN ON MY PARADE

It was late spring of my thirtieth year. I had to commute from my apartment in Bushwick to this book club I was in that took place in Park Slope. We'd read *Wolf Hall* by Hilary Mantel, and I had struggled with it to the point of having no idea what had happened. I had planned to spend the book club meeting alternately going, "Good point. Wow. Right. *Yes,*" and then hiding in the bathroom for five-minute stints at a time.

I put on my helmet and rode to the meeting. I made it halfway there without incident. But then, there was . . . incident. Or rather, *an* incident. I made the mistake of riding the wrong way down a one-way street. I barreled through a stop sign, and there, like a screeching one-ton bullet, was a livery cab. It came to a halt, but not before my body crashed against it with the force, I was later told, of someone hitting the ground after falling off a two-story building.

In the second before the crash, when I knew it would happen but could no longer try to avoid it, I remember thinking, This'll hurt. But in a funny way! I thought it'd be like Lara Flynn Boyle in *Wayne's World,* when she crashes her bike over the hood of that car. It looks violent, yes, but Lara Flynn Boyle is fine. She's fine! She's up and she's primping in no time.

Sadly, the same could not be said for me.

I stayed conscious only so that I might land on my back, on my bike. The pain was too severe to lift my head, so I strained my eye sockets instead. And that's when I noticed my ankle. It was flopped over like a dog's ear. A right angle had formed between my foot and my leg.

Imagine the most breathless you have ever been from exercise. I was that breathless, but from pain. It was so intense, I shot past any of the beginner reactions—grumbling, swearing—past any of the intermediate reactions—yelling, crying—to a place of being so instantly, thoroughly consumed, I was struggling to breathe. Someone called an ambulance to take me to the hospital. While en route, I called my mom. The EMT had found my phone, called the number, and held the phone against my ear. It was in this fashion that my mother and I could review the progression of events. Then it was mostly:

"Mom! Mom! Mom! Mom!"

"I need you to breathe."

"I can't!"

"Yes. You can. Were you wearing a helmet?"

"Yes!"

"And are you bleeding? Are you losing any blood?"

Weirdly, I was not. I had demolished large parts of myself without getting so much as a scratch on me. The fact of this calmed my mother down, but only until she thought to consider whether or not I might be bleeding internally. Then it was all, "Are you bleeding internally? SARA: ARE. YOU. BLEEDING. INTERNALLY?"

My mother asked this repeatedly, and with an increase in volume every time. Eventually, she got so loud that the EMT could hear my mother through the phone. The EMT then took the phone. She told my mother, "We don't know yet. What? Yes. Tests. Yes. Bye."

4. DIAGNOSIS

As it turned out, there was no internal bleeding. There were, however, bruised kidneys, an anterior dislocated shoulder, and a shattered right ankle. The bruised kidneys would heal themselves. The dislocated shoulder would take one surgery to fix. The shattered ankle would take another two.

The first of these two would take place my second day in the hospital, and would involve an orthopedic surgeon attaching to my lower leg a series of large metal poles that pierced through my skin and into my broken bones for the purpose of stabilizing my leg. The surgeon would then wait for the swelling to go down. When finally it did, I'd have the second operation. It would take place one week after the first, and would involve two foot-long incisions made along either side of my right calf: from just above my ankle, to just below my knee. They, the incisions, would facilitate the installation of four five-inch titanium plates, and twenty-four half-inch titanium screws.

5. SNAP, BITCH. CRACKLE POP.

After arriving at the hospital, someone or other shot me up with a large quantity of morphine. The pain did not abate, however, and this is really saying something when you consider my aforementioned susceptibility to all manner of alcohol and drugs. A large quantity of morphine should have left me unconscious until it was fun to be conscious again. But my pain was too assertive for all that. A saucy RuPaul, she was. All like, "*Snap,* bitch. Mama's here . . . to *stay.*"

I would like to tell you that I stared her down or argued even the littlest bit, but I did not. I just looked at her, helpless.

You're too much, I thought.

Death is preferable.

I mean it.

Let me die.

I was both worried and surprised by this instinct to capitulate. By the marked absence of a fighting spirit. I was so quickly willing to check out forever, if it meant no more pain for now, and the fact of this bodes poorly, I think, for my apocalypse survival. Fantasies of natural childbirth went straight out the window, and speaking of windows, I had this vision of myself hanging off a ledge, and thought, I just *know* that I'd let go. My arm would cramp up, I'd be like, "Nope. I can't take it," and that would be that.

I shared this revelation with my friend Maggie. She was the first person who came to meet me at the hospital. After several hours and the eventual implementation of a more effective drug cocktail, I lay more calmly in a gurney. Maggie sat beside me in a folding chair.

"Let me tell you something dark," I said. "When I was *in* it, I wanted to die."

Maggie, in response, made the point that my wanting to die might be the byproduct of my knowing that I *wouldn't* die; a sort of perverse luxury, if you will, that came part and parcel with knowing instinctively I'd live.

"In other words, maybe try not to be scared of the feeling. Maybe try to be, I don't know, appreciative, I guess, for having experienced a dark emotion from a safe, if painful, place."

"The word 'appreciate' is hard for me right now."

"I know. Of course, I know. What I mean to say is just that it's a little less dark to have wanted to die if, in point of fact, you wanted to die *because* you knew you wouldn't."

6. SKEDGE

Maggie had arrived at the hospital a mere twenty minutes after I'd arrived; I'd called her from the ambulance after

I'd called my mom. She had come to stay with me until my parents could come to stay with me themselves. She stayed through the night, into the next morning. Then she left for work.

My parents, for their part, booked the next available flight from Chicago to New York.

Maggie and my parents doing as they did required generosity and effort. I knew this, and appreciated it.

Nonetheless, I'd been left with a ten-hour gap between visits. Over the course of those ten hours, I'd have to occupy myself.

7. HOME, STERILE HOME

I did so in my newly assigned hospital bedroom. The pain was more manageable by this stage, but still too intense to be ignored. So I didn't sleep, really. I watched the nurses come and go. I practiced the art of self-pity, and regret. I watched a lot of TV. A television set hung above my new little hospital bed, and thank God, too, since without it I would surely have figured out a way to drown myself in the toilet in the bedroom. I watched *The Golden Girls, Legally Blonde, Legally Blonde 2, Law & Order, In Her Shoes, The Silence of the Lambs,* and, for the first time, a horse race. I learned to use a bedpan.

The use of the bedpan was especially upsetting. I'd always loved the idea of a bedpan, but what I learned from the reality of a bedpan is that they're not nearly as decadent as you might think. They require quite a bit of abdominal strength, and that's to say nothing of the angle guesswork involved. Talk about a small margin for error! If you aim right, you're good. If you aim wrong, though, you're soaked in your own urine, forced to wait for whatever length of time for a nurse to clean you up.

I met my roommate, Terri. Terri I took to be a heroin or methadone addict, and our medical situations were different insofar as, well, Terri was on heroin or methadone. Also, Terri could sit up, stand, and walk, whereas I could not lift my sternum without the help of a motorized bed.

Terri put her surefootedness to good use by wandering over to hug me. There had been a dividing curtain between us, and she threw it back the first time she heard me roll in.

"Oh. Hi," I said.

"You okay?" she said.

"Not really," I said.

"Well, you *gone* be, girl. Someday soon, you *gone* be A-okay."

Then she waddled over, stroked my hair, and hugged me.

It was a caring and sensitive action. However, my ability to appreciate it was curtailed by the fact that Terri smelled of shit-strewn barn, and looked—she *always* looked—like she was on the verge of throwing up.

As for appearance/aroma combinations, this one is never my favorite.

8. THIS PART IS VERY JEWISH

I had pictured myself in a hospital before I wound up in a hospital. Involved in the fantasy were floral bouquets and sympathy cards detailing how much I meant to the hundred different people who had sent them. I'd pictured a chenille blanket at the foot of my bed so that visitors could come and sit comfortably beside me. They would sit and ask questions, while I, generous of spirit and heart, doled out the wisdom afforded to me by my illness.

The piece I'd failed to account for, however, was the physical pain. Mine had stabilized at a more manageable level, as I said, but every inch of it—every second—was still mortifyingly oppressive. What came with it was a profound sense of isolation. What went with it was my appetite. Pain and stress are known as effective appetite suppressants, and so perhaps the loss should not have been surprising. To me, though, it was. Because I *am* my appetite. I eat like clockwork: once an hour, every hour, provided I am not asleep. And so to not eat at all? To not foresee a time when I would want to eat again? The whole thing seemed as strange as the precarious way my foot had dangled from my ankle. As strange, but not as traumatic. For as any daughter of any Jewish mother will tell you: There is always a destructive modicum of joy involved in weight loss.

So it was that I asked one of the nurses for a hand mirror. I looked in it twice a day to see if my collarbone looked more pronounced.

9. THIS PART IS *SUPER* JEWISH

The first day in the hospital I met my surgeon, Dr. Dean. The first thing I noticed about Dr. Dean was that Dr. Dean was very handsome. He had hair that looked plucked from a Ken doll, and his shoulders were so, like, erotically broad I'd have licked my way across them if given the chance.

Dr. Dean was the director of the hospital's orthopedics department, and this meant that wherever he went—whenever he went there—a gaggle of medical residents trailed along behind. These medical residents were also very handsome. I hadn't known I had a thing for doctors, but now I realized this was only because I'd never seen a slew of handsome ones together. The cumulative effect suggested I'd died and gone to Vegas heaven, to a place where the showgirls were not showgirls at all, but rather Harvard-educated, scrubs-clad show-*boys*.

Except, of course, they weren't. They were not Vegas show-boys, and I was not in Vegas heaven. I was in a hospital, and I had a question for my surgeon.

"Will I walk again?" I asked.

"Of course," he said.

"Oh, good," I said.

"But not like before," he said.

"Then how?" I said.

"With marked limitation," he said, "to your ankle's range of movement."

"I don't know what that means," I said.

"It means 'with pain and discomfort,'" he said.

"Forever?" I said. "Or just, like, for a while."

"Forever," he said. "Or until there are advances in the field."

"*Will* there be . . . advances . . . in the field?" I asked.

"It's hard to say," he said.

There was a moment of silence between us.

"Well. Okay," he said. "I'll see you on my evening rounds."

And after that he left. His residents trailed behind him.

It was a depressing prognosis, and because Dr. Dean was an orthopedic surgeon—a style of individual who's chosen of his own volition the most violent of surgical fields—it was delivered unto me with the sort of emotional sensitivity you'd associate with a waiter telling you he's sorry but the kitchen's out of steak.

Not that I'm complaining.

An orthopedic surgeon needs a bedside manner like a fish needs a bicycle. If you're dead in the eyes and robotic of voice but you keep a steady hand while sawing human flesh, that's fine by me, and it only gets more fine when you're central casting handsome.

To distract from my prognosis, I decided to obsess on this, the fact of the central casting handsome. It seemed strange that every orthopedic surgeon and/or surgeon-in-training would be in possession of such a particular quality.

I decided to ask the nurse about it the next time she rolled through. I said, "I'm sorry to bother you, but may I ask a question about the doctors?"

The nurse gave a knowing nod. "They're all really hot, am I right?" she said.

"Yes!" I said. "But *why*?"

The nurse went on to explain that, by her estimation, the orthopedic surgical field drew the "hot jocks."

"They're the guys who played sports in high school," she explained. "The ones who played sports but are also pretty smart, and who decided to go to medical school. They're into sports, they're jocky, so they pick a surgical field that'll let them work with athletes."

"Right," I said. "I see."

"Also," she said. "They have to be physically strong. They're getting in there, breaking bones, resetting bones, amputating limbs, and so on. Wander past an operating room when they're doing orthopedic surgeries, you hear electric saws. You hear"—and then she made that noise people make, that signifies either (a) an electric saw, or (b) a car going fast—"and you think, Oh. Right. They're just carpenters. *Of the flesh*. They're just *sawing* things. Like your ankle. I mean, like, *literally*: They saw *through* the flesh, and *through* the bone, and . . ."

"Right," I said. "Thank you. I think now I understand."

10. THE STUPIDS STEP IN

After ten hours alone, my parents arrived. They entered the hospital room I shared with Terri to find me looking slightly thinner, I'd like to think, but otherwise not great. I couldn't move much. I had various IVs. My leg, for the moment, was wrapped in miles of gauze and had been suspended at a seventy-degree angle from my body. It wasn't an ideal setup, but it wasn't cancer either. Nonetheless,

when my dad saw me for the first time he released a traumatized gasp, which he then followed up with the sputters
of willfully restrained hysterics.

So my mother shuffled him back out. They huddled
right outside my doorway.

"Joe, take a breath. And do your crying here, okay?
This—right here—is *your* little spot. Ask a nurse for a
chair if you need one."

My mother came back in.

"Hello," she said. "*I* think you look well."

"By 'well' do you mean 'thin'?"

"Maybe a bit. What I meant, though, is you've had a
bad twenty-four hours, but you seem, you know, coherent.
Aware."

To prove her point, I asked, "Is Dad okay?"

"Oh, yes," she said. "He's fine. He just . . . went out. To
get himself . . . a coffee."

My dad's spot for crying was a mere ten feet from where
I lay in my hospital bed. So although I couldn't see him, I
could hear him: Sniffling. Breathing. Gasping.

"Dad, I can hear you," I called.

"JOE, SHE CAN HEAR YOU," my mother called.

My father took this as his cue to come back in. He did
so with his hand cupped over his mouth to show he was
working to restrain himself. He sat in a chair at the foot
of the bed.

I heard Terri rustle behind her curtain. She whisked it
back and looked around.

"Hello," she said. "This you momma and you daddy?"

"Hi, Terri. Yes. These are my parents, Lynn and Joe."

"Hello," they said.

"Hello," Terri said. She pointed a finger at my dad.
"You too sad," she said. "But you don't gotta be too sad.
You seem rich, and okay."

My dad sniffed, and wiped his eyes.

"Thank you," he said.

"You welcome," Terri said, and then waddled past my mother and me, and over to my dad. She hugged my dad, and *as* she hugged my dad, he stared at us, wide-eyed, from over Terri's shoulder.

"She seems nice," my mother whispered.

"She is," I whispered back. "But the smell."

"Yes. Wow," she said. "The smell."

We stayed silent for a moment.

"What is it, anyway? Vomit?"

"No," I said. "She *looks* like she's *going* to vomit. But the smell itself is actually more like manure."

My mother sniffed the air.

"Right," she said. "Now I can smell that you're right."

11. MY MOTHER, THE WIND

The days rolled on. I'd spend them in surgery, or recovering from surgery. My father would sit in the chair at the foot of the bed, bleary-eyed mostly, but more composed than he'd been when he arrived. My mother, for her part, would stand at my bedside and perform what she referred to as "my Reiki." In recent months, she'd been studying Qigong at her local senior center, and was now of the opinion that the skills she learned in seniors' Qigong were Reiki-translatable.

"I'm going to recite the script from my Qigong class," she told me, "but I'll do it with my hands near your face. It's very calming. Okay. I am doing it now: I am wind."

I'd close my eyes. Not because I was supposed to, but because I was troubled by the sight of my mother moving her hands above me like some Ouija-packing schoolgirl.

Although I like poking fun at the seriousness with which my mother approached her Reiki, the fact of the matter was that she managed the impossible task of maintaining focus while in a hospital bedroom. Terri was always watching *The Price Is Right* and screaming her own bids at the television screen. A nurse was always coming or going with a shot, a pill, or a fresh bedpan. My dad was always puttering around, drinking coffee, sniffling. And through it all—and provided it was Reiki time—my mother focused in.

The only thing that broke her was when Terri started smoking.

12. AND THE WIND TAKES A STAND

By hospital standards, it had been a day like any other. I had watched TV and my mom had done her Reiki. As per usual, she'd referred to herself as the wind.

"I am a broom of wind," she'd said. "The broom of wind moves through you, through us all."

The broom of wind did move through us all, but only for a minute. It stopped moving through us all when Terri found a cigarette.

Terri lit the cigarette and started smoking.

My mother opened one eye, then the other.

"Is someone . . . smoking?" she asked.

Terri was huddled near the window surreptitiously puffing away. The weird thing, though—or, rather, *one* of the weird things—was that she had not opened the window. She had placed herself near the window, but she had not opened the window. In an instant, the whole room smelled of smoke.

A situation like this is tailor-made to explode my mother's brain. Her temper, and her brain. My mother is put off by any and all lit cigarettes, even the more reasonable ones—those smoked out of doors and/or on the property of those doing the smoking. Even in those situations, my mother will perform a cough and say some combination of the words "son," "deadly," "asthma," and "selfish."

I am therefore happy to report that when confronted with Terri's legitimate smoking violation, my mother's head did not explode. I am happy to report that she behaved—at first—like a completely normal human.

"Terri," she said, "would you please put out your cigarette?"

Terri smiled, but said nothing.

So my mother tried again.

"Terri," she said, "we're in a hospital room. Would you please put out your cigarette?"

This time Terri glanced up and feigned surprise.

"Oh. Yes," she said. "Yes, yes, yes, yes, *yes*." But then instead of putting out her cigarette, she shuffled into our shared bathroom and slammed the door behind her. From what I could smell—from what we all could smell—she then continued smoking.

My father and I stared at the bathroom door, our mouths agape. Not at the in-hospital smoking, so much as the sight of my mother being flagrantly ignored. It's not a thing that happens to her often, and that is because it is not worth enduring her response. My mother reacts to being ignored like you or I might react to an unanticipated butt plug: There is shock, and a sense of having been rudely abused.

Terri ignored my mother and stole away into the bathroom, and my mother, in response, ran shouting out of the hospital bedroom.

She literally ran. And she was literally shouting.

"I NEED HELP! **HELP!** I NEED A NURSE WHO IS A MOTHER WHO WILL UNDERSTAND! SOMEONE'S *SMOKING* IN MY DAUGHTER'S ROOM! **SOMEONE HELP ME SAVE MY DAUGHTER!**"

I looked at my father.

"This is embarrassing," I said.

But my father just shrugged.

"Say what you will," he said. "Your mother gets things done."

13. HOW DO YOU TALK TO AN ANGEL?

My father wasn't lying. My mother gets things done.

It was only a matter of minutes before she returned arm-in-arm with what appeared to be a Hispanic catalogue model.

"Hello," said the man. "I am Angel."

My mother was wide-eyed with delight, with a face that said, *Oh, don't mind me. I just went for one of my rage jaunts, and came back with a MALE MODEL on my arm.*

"Hello," I said.

"Hello," my dad said.

"Angel," my mom said. "Here is *mi hija,* Sarita. Sarita is *so* sick in the leg, and she must breathe good air for to be *fuerta* again. The *mujer* who do the smoking, she in *el baño* now."

Angel nodded in response, then knocked on the bathroom door. When Terri didn't answer, Angel reached into his pocket for what appeared to be a master key. He unlocked the door himself and went inside.

He closed the door behind him.

"Well," said my mom, and let out a satisfied sigh. "So about him?"

"Who is he?" I said.

"*What* is he?" my dad said.

"A physical therapist," my mom said. "I ran into him in the hallway, and he said, '*Mami,* you've got to calm down.' And he was just so cute! I thought, Okay! For you, I *will* calm down!"

Minutes later, Angel emerged from the bathroom with a subdued, nonsmoking Terri.

"Ms. Terri, she is finished smoking now," he said. "She will not smoke again."

And he was right: She didn't. Terri never smoked again.

Angel had that sort of control over people, and that, I was learning, was a gift he owed to the combined effect of his handsomeness and warmth. The orthopedic surgeons had their own aforementioned brand of detached, robotic sex appeal. But Angel was different. Angel was *as* empirically attractive, but with the added bonus of being sensitive and socially adept. Dr. Dean would make his rounds every day at 4:00 p.m., and every day Angel would swing by almost immediately after. The process of seeing one and then the other felt always like wrapping oneself in a heated Puerto Rican flag after a dip in frigid Aryan waters.

14. *LOS HUEVOS*

Every patient in the orthopedics department was assigned a physical therapist following his or her surgeries. There were dozens of therapists employed by the hospital, and the process of pairing them with the individual patient wasn't a choice of the patient's so much as it was the luck of the draw within the hospital system.

The luck of any draw leaves my mother feeling less in control than she desires. As such, my mother used her connections to the Midwestern branch of the Underground Network of Jewish Hypochondriacs to reach her way through the East Coast branch of the Underground Network of Jewish Hypochondriacs. And, lo: She learned that her friend Marci Goldfarb knew Julie Glick, who knew Carol Feinstein, whose sister-in-law, Deborah Kagan, was on the hospital's board of trustees.

Deborah Kagan made a call on my behalf and requested

that I work with Angel. For this I was—and still remain—very, truly grateful. Working with Angel was the singular part of my hospital reality that in any way mirrored my hospital fantasy. Here was a kind and handsome man who'd visit every day for the primary purpose of lavishing me with attention. We'd do a series of ankle mobility exercises and chat about a wide range of subjects up to and including my mother's love of Central and South American cultures.

There was one afternoon in particular when she, my mother, brought up the continents' approach to swimwear.

"I have traveled extensively throughout *mucho* of Central and South America," she began, "and so do I know that the men of the south prefer the tiny swimsuit. Here, though, they do not."

Angel and I nodded. My mother motioned toward my father.

"For example, Joe, my husband, does not prefer the tiny swimsuit."

"It is true," my father said. "I do not prefer the tiny swimsuit."

"But Angel," said my mother, "do *you* prefer the tiny swimsuit?"

Angel nodded. "*Sí.* Yes," he said. "I do. I wear many tiny swimsuits. Many 'Speedos,' they are called. For me, though, I say 'Speedoritos,' because to wear them nicely, I no can eat Doritos!"

We all laughed.

"Oh, Angel. You're so funny!" I said.

"He really is!" my dad said.

"Angel," my mom said. "Did you say '*many* Speedos'?"

"*Sí.* Yes," he said.

"How many?" she said.

"Very *mucho* many," he said. "Maybe eight? Maybe nine? Maybe ten?"

"But why so *mucho* many?" she said.

"For to use them in the competitions."

"The . . . competitions?"

"*Sí*, yes. My Mr. Puerto Rico competitions. In 2001, I did win."

"You did . . . win?"

"*Sí*. Yes. I did win."

"I'm sorry, Angel. To be clear: You're saying . . . you *won* the Mr. Puerto Rico competition?"

"*Sí*. Yes. In 2001 I did win the Mr. Puerto Rico competition. So then I go on to the Mr. Model Millennium competition. But then, when I am there, I did not do so good. Because, you know, I'm *muy peludo* . . ."

"Very hairy."

"*Sí*. Yes. I'm very hairy. So when I am there, I am in my Speedorito, and another man in the competition come by and say, 'Ay yay yay! Your back is wild. You want for me to shave?' And I say, 'Okay, brother. *Gracias*.' And then he shave my back."

"You let him shave your back?"

"*Sí*, yes. I let him shave my back. But then *when* he shave my back, he shave it to look like *los huevos*."

"*Los huevos?* Some . . . eggs?"

"*Sí*, yes. Some eggs."

"But why, Angel, *why*?"

"For to look like—*como se dice*—'escroto'?"

A pause.

"Your scrotum!"

"*Sí!* Yes! My scrotum! This man use my hairs to make a scrotum on my back!"

We all laughed at the expense of the scrotum on the back, of the ruined male pageant. We told Angel how funny he was.

"*Muchas gracias*," said Angel. "But now we back to business. Sarita, ankle circle going left. Thirty seconds *por favor*."

15. THE GOOD-BYE GIRL

I spent nearly three weeks in the hospital. Over the course of those three weeks, there were three surgeries, four visits from Maggie, seven sessions with Angel, eleven hugs from Terri, twelve Reiki sessions with my mother, twenty inspections at the hand of Dr. Dean, two hundred and fifty hours of television, and a single rock-hardiest of rock-hard bowel movements ever made in the history of man. I'd lost a total of fifteen pounds, and looked (if I may say) lithe upon my hospital departure. My midriff was flatter than my A-cup chest; my collarbone, balletic. I would say I had never looked better, but the lack of attention to hair, makeup, and clothing one confronts in a hospital meant that this was not technically true.

There had been many unpleasant aspects to my hospital stay, and one of them was being forced to look so disgustingly unkempt amid the ongoing parade of male hotness. I had bigger fish to fry, of course, but all I mean is that those bigger fish did not feed upon the smaller ones. I hoped to use my hospital departure as an opportunity to show off my new figure and potential for attractiveness to Angel and Dr. Dean, and therefore asked my father to make an extra trip to and from my Bushwick apartment to collect what I referred to as my "Good-bye Outfit." This is the one I'd change into from my hospital gown. I chose a racer-back tank top and a pair of Daisy Duke shorts. Additionally, I asked for contact lenses, my makeup bag, and a hairpiece I'd worn three Halloweens prior to facilitate a fuller up-do. I had my father sit at the foot of my hospital bed holding a hand mirror in front of my face for an hour and a half while I put on the makeup, the hairpiece, and the contact lenses. Having completed my preparations, I awaited the oohs and aahs, the Sara-we-had-no-idea!s. But then when the moment finally came neither Angel nor Dr.

Dean showed up. There was only a nurse and an orderly. The nurse helped me into the wheelchair, then handed a set of crutches to my father for my own future use, for when I transitioned out of my wheelchair.

The orderly reached for a pack of baby wipes on the tray beside my bed.

"These yours?" he asked.

"Oh, yeah," I said.

"Well, here," he said, and put them in my lap.

And that was pretty much that. My father gave the crutches to my mother. Then he pushed me out the door.

16. SHE HAS TO SUPPORT THE FAMILY

I had been told that I would spend two weeks in the wheelchair until I was ready for crutches. I had been told that once I got up on the crutches, I would stay there for an additional four months.

This is not an ideal prognosis for anyone, but I do believe it's especially grim for someone in New York City who lives in a walk-up apartment, who commutes via subway every day. There are people out there who do it, of course, and with a certain grace. You see them around, navigating public transport and busy city streets, and most of these folks, due either to physical competence or a positive attitude, project an air that says, "I'm fine."

In my wheelchair, however, I did nothing of the sort. I moved like I was in a broken bumper car, and on crutches, I was even worse. I used them for the first time to get myself out my wheelchair and into the cab that would ferry me back home. But I was so clearly *so* clumsy, the cabbie intervened.

"I am no psychic," he said, "but I think you gonna break another leg."

There is a tradition in my family of discounting positive

predictions, instincts, and feelings whilst clinging to their negative equivalents. If someone says, "Don't worry. Things'll work out," we think, "Yes, well, that's what *you* think, because *you* are ill-prepared." Conversely, if someone sees tragedy looming, she is perceived as wise and insightful.

The cabbie told me I was poised to break another leg, and we, the Barrons, figured he was right. We riffled through various solutions to the problem until we hit upon one that would work: For as long as I was on crutches, my dad would stay on with me in New York.

My brother, Sam, had predicted this exact turn of events. Toward the end of my hospital stay, my parents had gone to buy me a Kiehl's astringent. I'd called Sam while they were out, and he'd asked how I was doing.

"Miserable," I'd said. "Although I *am* pretty skinny."

"Skinny like you look sick?" he'd asked, "Or skinny like you look good?"

"I think it's skinny like I look good," I'd said. "Or, you know, *could* look good. With makeup and a better outfit."

"Well, great then, right?"

"You'd think so, but the nurse made me try to stand up the other day, and after two weeks lying down, my body was like, 'No, thanks. We're not doing this. We're fainting now,' and then I fainted into the arms of my physical therapist. Which wasn't so bad—he's really handsome—but the point is just that if I am literally too weak to stand, then my current weight is not sustainable. I won't have the strength to use the crutches."

"They want *you* to use . . . *crutches*?"

"I know, right? I will be that person. I'll survive a car crash, and then just trip on the street one day and crack my skull and die."

"No. You won't," he'd said.

"I won't?" I'd said.

"You won't," he'd said. "Dad'll wind up staying with you, don't you think? He'll just . . . I don't know, like, follow you around. He'll catch you if you fall. Which sounds cheesy."

"It does."

"But I mean it in a literal sense."

It turned out Sam was right. My dad decided he'd stay with me in New York, to catch me if I fell. And I mean this in a literal sense.

My father had retired six months prior to my accident, and had so far spent his abundant free time watching TV and reading historical biographies. To sacrifice these leisure activities to a career of live-in nursing was not an ideal situation, but he didn't have a choice. Because my mother couldn't do it. She was still gainfully employed as a suburban psychotherapist, and while Sam and I had both grown into solvent-*ish* adults, she nonetheless continued to pay for every dollar of our medical coverage. And, of course, the day-to-day life of her husband and herself. What this meant, then, in practical terms was that my father's "golden years" had thus far been underscored by the following soundtrack:

"Well, have fun with your book, then. I'm off to support the family."

Or: "How many hours of TV have you watched so far today? What's that? Sorry. I don't have time to listen. I'm off to support the family."

Or: "Since *I'll* be supporting the family all day, I'd like *you* to clean the basement. Throw out everything that's yours. Save everything that's mine."

It was therefore unsurprising that as we hammered out a plan for my at-home care, my mom said, "Well, since *I've* been supporting the family, I think your dad should be the one to stay. Since *I* support the family."

Placing the burden on my dad made the most logistical

sense, but it also felt like the smarter investment in my future. Had my mother stayed instead—had she been made
a slave to a bedpan, a sponge bath, to another person's
schedule—I do believe she would've mentioned it every
day, for the rest of her life.

Every day.

For the *rest* of her *life*.

My mother returned to Chicago the day after I was
discharged from the hospital. She hugged my dad and me
good-bye.

"Good luck," she said. "You two will be fine. And if
you're not—if you need me—just try me at work. I'll be
busy supporting the family."

17. LOOK WHO NEEDS HER BACK WASHED NOW

When you, age thirty, and your father, age sixty-five, are
forced to stare at each other from across the studio apartment that is now your shared accommodation, the first
word to jump to mind is "privacy."

How will you have it, or get it?

The thought occurred to me, and I do believe it occurred to my father as well. But we had to forgo the luxury of that concern, and fast. Because *somebody* needed a
sponge bath. I had neither bathed nor showered while in
the hospital, and the crushing urge to feel soap-and-water
lather on my skin far outweighed any thought of how odd
it might be to have my father bathe me.

I had been forbidden from getting my leg wet, so we
worked out a bathing-suit contingent plan to cope. Every
evening, I would slip into a modest one-piece suit. As I did,
my dad would fill a bucket with soap and water, which he
would then set down on the floor of my bedroom/kitchen/
den. Alongside the bucket, he'd place a large pile of bath
towels. Having positioned both the bucket and the towels,

my dad would go stand in the corner with his back toward the room. He would stand there and begin to read a book, at which point I would cast my crutches to one side and hop to it. Literally. I would hop on my good leg to the bucket and the towels. I would sponge bathe all private and reachable parts of myself while my dad continued reading.

I would call to him when I was done.

"Dad! Back!" I'd call, at which point he would set down his book and come to wash my back.

You'd think I'd enjoy all this being tended to, but I did not. I *could* not, you see, for I had already spent years of my life dreaming up my ideal sponge bath scenario: I am on a sun-lounger beside the water in the southern coast of France. Jean-Paul, my manservant, brings me half a glass of champagne and a tub of guacamole. He feeds me the guacamole out of his hand, then rinses his hand in the sea.

A sponge appears at this point, and Jean-Paul lathers it with Aveda body scrub and uses it to wash me.

Throughout the experience, I remain horizontally positioned on the lounger.

At the very least, I should have felt lucky to have my dad there to take care of me. But as his aging body crouched behind my own, as he washed my back with some year-old sponge from Walgreen's, I mostly just thought, This is bullshit. Where's Jean-Paul?

High expectations are a bitch.

18. DADDY'S GIRL SHOULD WEAR A DIAPER

I am someone who takes a comparatively small amount of pride in self-sufficiency. The skill sits low on my priority list, and still: Even *I* feel mildly compelled to be able to clean my own body. Not to *clean* my own body. To *be able to* clean my own body. A lady likes an option. I felt depressed having that taken away, and I only got more depressed when, along with my knack for self-cleaning, I lost my knack for the efficient disposal of my very own urine.

It was late one weekday night, and my dad and I were both in our usual bedtime positions: he, on an air mattress, me, in my bed. I have always been one for a nighttime pee, and so on this night in particular, I did as I have always done and got up to go to the bathroom. I grabbed my crutches and was galumphing along when one thing or another went wrong, and because it was dark and I could barely see, I slipped and fell and landed on my dad. The process was terribly un-erotic, but also pretty lucky. For if I had crashed anywhere else in the apartment, it would have been on tile flooring. This would not have been the worst thing, but as I was now a delicate flower in possession of a delicate frame, it was a process worth avoiding.

The episode served as a warning shot, and the warning shot called for a commode.

From that point on, instead of going to the bathroom in the middle of the night, I would use a wide-mouth vase. I would keep it at my bedside.

Pissing in a vase might sound degrading, but I don't actually think that it is. It's like a remote control, is all: a welcome convenience to eradicate small-distance walking. As far as I was concerned, the problem was not that I pissed in a vase, but rather that I had to *dispose* of my piss in a vase.

Imagine that you are on crutches, and that if and when you walk, your hands are never free. Add to that scenario a vase full of urine that needs to be transported from your bedroom to your toilet.

Imagine trying to hold that vase while hopping.

Transporting a piss-vase like a normal person was not

an option, even in an apartment as small as my own. It was ambitious for me to think I could, but nonetheless I wanted to. Craving a semblance of competence, I sent my father out for kneepads.

"Why do you need kneepads?" he asked.

"No reason," I answered.

So my dad went and bought me kneepads, and these, the kneepads, enabled me to get down on the floor and "walk." I would "walk" on my knees, and to my toilet while precariously carrying the vase.

My father did not bear witness to this routine the first few times I tried it; he'd gone to the local coffee shop to buy himself a coffee and croissant. Eventually, though, he bore witness. And when he bore witness, he cried.

"Calm down," I said. "It's not that bad."

"It *is*!" he cried. "You look *deranged*!"

"I don't *feel* deranged," I said. "I just feel"—and I considered how I felt—"competent, I guess."

My dad shook his head. He reached for the vase.

"Please. Let me take it," he said.

I obliged my father's request, thereby giving him something to do while robbing myself of the same. To keep busy I tried feeling sorry for myself. I did this exceptionally well and to further the cause focused on the most depressing thing that I could think of: that I would not be walking normally again. When that line of thinking got old, I moved along to the second most depressing thing that I could think of: that I'd become a daddy's girl.

A daddy's girl.

It's a term that gets tossed around too much, and always in a tone to suggest it's somehow *not* a mark of shame for both the daddy and the girl. It's said always with a self-delighted subtext:

Isn't it so sweet? How I'm so close with my daddy?

And the thing is, it's not. Not when you infantilize yourself. Not when you're desperate for credit.

I'd thought this way, always, and although the sanest part of me understood that I was not *this* variety of daddy's girl, I liked feeling sorry for myself; and pretending like I was, well, it helped nudge that whole process along. After all, my dad and I were living together full-time. He was bathing me, cooking my meals, tending to the transport of my makeshift commode. It might not have been sitting in my father's lap or father-daughter cocktail hour, but I nonetheless felt like a hypocrite if I tossed the phrase around. Judging other daddy's girls—and other girls, *and* most men *and* various children—is one of my most treasured pastimes. It enlivens me to the furthest reaches of my ability to be enlivened. With the skill set chipped away, I felt terribly bored and depressed.

19. THE PUERTO RICAN SOCIAL CLUB

Neither my boredom nor depression were helped by the fact that I almost never left the house. Mine was a fourth-floor walk up, and the fact of that combined with the overall process of maneuvering through a city made it too much of a hassle. Besides, I didn't have much reason to leave the house anyway, seeing as how most of my friends were mostly unavailable to socialize. The fact of this surprised me. My social requirements seemed fair enough to me. I asked only that:

1. The friend in question met me at my local coffee shop.
2. The friend in question spoke exclusively about me, Sara, and The Thing That I Had Gone Through.

The bulk of my out-of-home activity centered around Angel, whom I saw three times a week for my ongoing physical therapy. The appointments were a highlight at first, but then they got annoying. Because Angel got a girlfriend. His doing so set up an awful dynamic wherein my physical therapy was forced to overlap with his honeymoon stage, wherein *I* was forced to overlap the already unpleasant process of an ankle mobility exercise with the even worse process of listening to Angel talk about another woman.

"Sarita, you cannot *believe* her kindness."

"Sarita, *my* woman is *so* more beautiful than *all* the other womans."

"Sarita, for to know someone so *mucho* special? You cannot know the joy."

I couldn't know the joy. I didn't know the joy. I myself was wildly, flagrantly single at the time, and I did not appreciate the way in which Angel's new relationship interrupted my suspension of disbelief. Naturally, I knew Angel was out of my league, but at least when he wasn't going on about some real, actual woman, I could trick myself into thinking otherwise.

Seeing as how you have to join them if you cannot fight them, I decided to ignore my impulse to fake snore whenever Angel mentioned his girlfriend, and instead I feigned interest. By this I mean that whenever Angel and I were together, I asked him questions about his girlfriend as a means to the end of stalking her online.

1. "What is her name again, Angel? Great. And her last name as well?"
2. "And is she on Facebook?"
3. "And does she hail, perchance, from Trenton, New Jersey?"

I went on in this vein until I learned everything I wanted to know: That Angel's girlfriend was a midlevel hairstylist with an adequate face and a fitness-model figure. That she maintained an active presence on both Facebook and her salon website. That she liked posting photos of haircuts she'd done, which she'd then intersperse with posts thanking Jesus for her talent, for the chance to "take advantage of this one life by doing what I love."

These bits of information made my current situation easier to bear.

20. THE FOUR QUESTIONS

After three months and three weeks on crutches, it was time, once again, to try walking on my own. I could not do so casually, however. I could not simply cast them aside in my apartment, then see how the ol' ankle coped with a victory march. The process of walking independently would have to be approved by Dr. Dean.

My mother called the night before the visit.

"Are you preparing?" she asked.

"Preparing?" I asked back.

"Preparing questions," she answered. "For Dr. Dean. You should do that, you know. Prior to the actual appointment. You'll get intimidated once you're in there, overwhelmed by the prospect of walking again."

"So?" I said.

"So," she said, "plan your questions in advance. Here's what I want you to ask: '1. Will the range of motion return? 2. Will the swelling go down? 3. Where can I expect to be one year from now? 4. (And this is important.) What can *I* do to make *myself* better?'"

I did as instructed. I wrote down these four questions and took them with me the following day.

Upon arrival, I was relegated to Dr. Dean's usual minimal eye contact and monotone speech.

"Hello," he said, staring at my ankle.

"Hello," I said, staring at his wider-than-a-mile chest.

"Okay," he said.

"Okay," I said.

"Let's walk," he said.

"Just like that?" I said.

"Yep," he said. "Just like that. Just go ahead and walk."

I was thrilled at the chance, but disappointed by the lack of fanfare. I would've liked . . . I don't know, applause, maybe, from some of the surrounding staff. Instead, I took my first steps to resounding silence, and this granted unto me the charming opportunity to focus solely, silently, on what it felt like, now, to walk.

21. WHAT IT FELT LIKE, NOW, TO WALK

My ankle was flexible like a piece of damp timber is flexible: There's *some* give, but barely. So it was that walking felt not at all like walking, but rather like carting an albatross around. A spiky, grinding pain set in.

"This feels . . . bad," I said.

"That's to be expected," Dr. Dean responded.

Dr. Dean and I stared at each other. Or perhaps it was more like I was staring *at* Dr. Dean because I wanted a more reassuring answer, whereas Dr. Dean was staring *through* me because that was just sort of his deal.

Finally, my father broke the silence.

"Sara," he said. "You had questions you wanted to ask."

"Oh, uh, yeah," I said, and reached into my pocket for my list.

I read with the robotic stiffness of an unseasoned actor.

"Will the range of motion return? Will the swelling go down? Where can I expect to be one year from now?"

I left out the bit about asking what *I* could do to make *myself* better, and that is because an eminent surgeon and I aren't going to have similar definitions of the word "work," now, are we? The difference in our thinking would be the difference between a ten-minute stroll for the prize of a decent New York bagel versus a ten-mile run for the prize of bruised nipples. And anyway, even if I could channel that sort of dedication, why would I want to put it toward my ankle? I'd have one less thing to complain about if I did. One less thing to make me feel special and unique.

Dr. Dean answered my questions concisely.

"A little. Not really. That all depends on you."

"That all depends on you" sounded, to me, like the answer to the question I had purposely left out. The overall point here was that shouldering responsibility for my own recovery would rob me of hours in the day I preferred to devote to self-pity.

I therefore made the choice to let the questions lie. All I said in response was, "Um, okay. Well, thanks. Am I done?"

And Dr. Dean had nodded.

"Yep," he'd said. "You're done. Just check out with my nurse before you leave."

22. US PEOPLES RESPONSIBLE FOR US PEOPLES

The orthopedics department was located on the third floor of the hospital. The physical therapy department was located seven floors above it, on the tenth. I had been told to schedule a physical therapy appointment with Angel as a follow-up to my orthopedics appointment with Dr. Dean. Which is to say, I had been told to schedule an appointment with Angel as an immediate follow-up to being taken off my crutches.

My father joined me at both of these appointments, and when we arrived to the second he made the unnecessary and (if I may say) moronic decision to mention my least favorite part of the first.

"Angel," he said, "Sara's surgeon made an important point today, I think."

"*Bueno,*" said Angel. "Tell me, please, then. Let me know."

"Well," said my dad, "the surgeon said that now that she's off crutches, the recovery is largely up to her."

"*Bueno* point-o, *yes,*" said Angel. "Very *bueno*. I was discussing with my girlfriend the other day, how important it is for us peoples to be responsible for us peoples."

"For ourselves, you mean?"

"*Sí,* yes. For ourselves. My girlfriend, she is wise. She understand very much, and anyway, Sarita, yes: You must work for to make the ankle strong and good. *You* must push *youself.*"

"Pushing myself isn't my thing, really."

"But this is okeydokey. Angel make it *be* your thing."

To his credit, Angel tried. He really did. Our physical therapy sessions took on a new, markedly more tortuous quality. On crutches, they had involved gentle stretching and presses. Off crutches, they involved crippling pain on a treadmill. They involved an excruciating game of hop-scotch designed to engage the ailing limbs of deformed adults. They involved a little piece of hell on earth built around a seat belt and a folding chair. They involved a butter knife, which Angel would use for the delightful and specific job of "loosening the skin" of my "very big scars."

The physical therapy facility had been lined on all sides with floor-to-ceiling mirrors, and it was thanks to these mirrors that I knew how I looked as I did my various exercises. It was thanks to these mirrors that I knew I looked like some contestant off *The Biggest Loser.* I'm talking, like, one of the ones for whom gratitude is trumped by anger.

Too much hurt too much. And that—by my estimation—is how you know it's time to walk away.

23. THE SAD BATON

Speaking of walking, now that *I* was walking, it was time for my dad to go home. Following our double-bill appointments, he booked himself a flight back to Chicago.

Four months together. Every hour. Every day. But then he books a flight. And then he has to go.

My mom tells this story about how when she and my dad dropped me off to go to college, he, my dad, requested a window seat for the return flight so he could slump against the window and sob. His little girl was gone to the Big Bad Apple, gone to do as young girls do once they arrive: fail at creative enterprise, sleep with the occasional homosexual.

I thought I might get a similar bit of fanfare at this good-bye. However, at *this* good-bye, my dad wasn't leaving behind a daughter becoming a woman, but rather a woman who'd been peeing in a vase. There wasn't reason for him to cry so much as there was opportunity for him to wash his hands of the final urinary splash. So it was that for the first time in his life, my father, Joseph Barron, didn't cry. Perhaps I should've been impressed, but instead I just felt sad myself and did the crying for him. It was like I'd been handed some supremely sad baton. *Here, sweetie. Take it. Since now you're all alone.*

24. PAPA, CAN YOU HEAR ME?

It's weird how quickly one adjusts to company, in general, and servitude, in particular. I'd hoped my father's absence would be compensated for by the fact that I was walking again, but then it turned out the whole walking thing wasn't nearly as much fun as I thought it would be. I tried drumming up new activities to occupy myself, but I'm never great with that sort of thing, and instead wound up stuck with what I'm good at: TV watching. Bagel buying.

Rigorous rounds of self-pity. The TV and bagels were, as ever, really delicious and fun. But the rounds of self-pity were less so. I couldn't enjoy them as much without my dad around to hear them, and so I started calling home. Complaining over the telephone was the only viable alternative to complaining in person. So I'd call my parents in the morning, to complain to them into their afternoon. Or I'd call them in the afternoon, to complain to them into their evening. The routine worked well enough, but only until they got hip to my game, only until they learned to avoid the calls until they absolutely had to answer.

"Sweetheart! Hi! Sorry we missed your call."

"You missed *five* calls."

"Did we? Gosh. Well, I'm sorry about that. We were out for a walk. The weather's lovely at the moment."

"Out for a walk, eh? Sounds great. We should all be so lucky."

The truth of the matter is that I dislike taking walks and always have. However, it is important when seeking attention to instill guilt in whomever you can.

25. THE END

When I visit home now, I like involving my family in bits and pieces of my ongoing physical therapy. I've been prescribed a half hour's worth of ankle exercise that I'm supposed to do every day. I'm *supposed* to do it every day, but I *don't* do it every day. And that is because I don't like to do it if other people aren't around. If other people *are* around, well, then it's much more fun. *Then* I'll make a show of it. I'll ask someone to massage my scars or to push back on my foot to increase the mobility in the ankle.

But other people mostly aren't around. In which case, I mostly do not do them.

The byproduct of this ongoing neglect has been an

ankle like a baby: feeble and incompetent. It hurts a lot. I limp a lot. I know there are worse problems out there, and I know that a good thing to do, probably, would be to think about those problems, to remember how lucky I am.

But that is not my way.

I am not designed to push myself nor to focus on the positive. This is maybe self-indulgent. Or it is maybe realistic. It is maybe life examined, then stripped of self-denial, of the inauthentic lesson learned. It is maybe both. It is hard to tell. What is not, though—what is painfully clear—is how much I like to wallow. And this, to be sure, is a different thing from being *left* to wallow. That I do not care for. I like to know I'm being overheard.

Acknowledgments

It takes a village to raise a child. More to the point, it takes a village to assist me in the wonderful and tortuous project of writing a book. Thanks are due to each of the following people:

My agent, Elisabeth Weed, whose guidance and overall loveliness have made of me a published author.

Everyone at Three Rivers Press for their patience and support, most especially my editor, Alexis Washam, who is sharp and thorough beyond description.

Each and every one of my students. They've worked together over the years to give me a reason to leave my apartment. Not only that, they've used their questions and insights to force me into my own improved understanding of this ridiculous business of writing.

My friend and early reader, Diana Spechler, who is profoundly intelligent when it comes to people and to writing, and who has made me (as a person and a writer) a little better than before.

My friend Michelle Newman, upon whose couch I've edited a portion of this manuscript, and who says—without fail, and *every* time I see her—"Tell me about the book. I know you think it's boring, but *I* don't think it's boring."

My friend Maggie McBrien, without whom I'd be short on material. I'd also be terribly lonely.

My friend Joseph Zvejnieks, from whom I've stolen more than one story because, well, no one else's are as funny. This is true about the man, and it is true about his stories.

My brother, Sam Barron, who does me the favor of allowing me to write about him. He does this despite the fact that I convey 1/100th of his massive brain and overall charisma.

My father, Joseph Barron, who—at the age of sixty-five and across the span of four months—had to care for me as though I were a toddler. It was during those months that I began the process of writing this book. Without him there—without the sense that I was not alone—I would not have had the energy to do so.

My mother, Lynn Barron, who in real life would never speak about another person as though that person were an enema. To her I owe every part of me that is—for however brief a moment—in any way funny or kind.

My husband, Geoff Lloyd, whose talent inspires, whose nimble mind and unparalleled sense of humor serve as my beacons in the night: What a gift to trust your taste. What a gift to have at my disposal a brain as big as yours. This book, Geoff, is for you.

ABOUT THE AUTHOR

Sara Barron is the author of *People Are Unappealing, Even Me*. She hosts the Moth in New York City, and her work has appeared in *Vanity Fair* and on NPR, NBC, and *This American Life*.

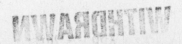

ALSO BY

SARA BARRON

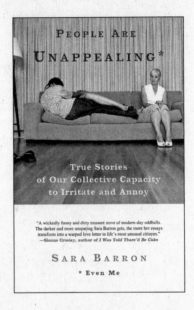

PEOPLE ARE UNAPPEALING*
*EVEN ME

The strange, funny, and sometimes filthy stories of Sara Barron's twisted suburban upbringing and deranged attempt at taking the Big Apple by storm—first as an actor (then a waiter), then a dancer (then a waiter), then a comic (then a waiter). It's there that she meets the ex-boyfriend turned street clown. The silk pajama–clad poet. The OCD Xanax addict who refuses to have sex wearing any fewer than three condoms. Barron has a knack for attracting the unattractive. *People Are Unappealing* is her wickedly funny look at the dark side of humanity.

THREE RIVERS PRESS • NEW YORK
AVAILABLE WHEREVER BOOKS ARE SOLD